There and Back

Second Edition

There and Back

Robben Island 1964 - 1979

EDDIE DANIELS

First published 1998 in South Africa by Mayibuye Books, University
of the Western Cape, Private Bag X17, Bellville 7535, South Africa.
© Eddie Daniels
ISBN 0-620-26786-0

Cover design, layout and typesetting by **jon berndt Design**

PRINTED AND BOUND IN THE REPUBLIC OF SOUTH AFRICA BY THE RUSTICA PRESS,
NDABENI, WESTERN CAPE

D8441

CONTENTS

	Page
Foreword by Nelson Mandela	7
Acknowledgements	9
Illustrations	176 - 182

Part 1

Chapter
1. Childhood in District Six: 1928 - 1950   15
2. Sport and the mountain: 1940 - 1950   29
3. Work and Apartheid: 1940 - 1964   42
4. The Trawlers: 1954   53
5. The Whalers: 1954 - 1955   65
6. Diamonds in the desert: 1955 - 1959   76
7. Peaceful change - a fading hope: 1959 - 1990   89
8. The Liberal Party of South Africa and the Emergency:1960 - 1964   93
9. The African Resistance Movement: 1961 - 1964   105

Part 2

Chapter
10. Arrest and Detention: 1964   117
11. State Witness: 1964   133
12. To the Island: 1964 - 1979   143
13. Work, study, visits: 1964 - 1979   155
14. News, the garden, the earthquake: 1964 - 1979   162
15. Warders; release hopes: 1964 - 1979   168

Part 3

Chapter
16. Politics and improvements: Section B: 1964 - 1979   185
17. Five who helped us to survive: 1964 - 1979   193
18. Escapes that never were, 1: 1964 - 1976   203

19. Escapes that never were, 2:
    The Mandela rescue plan: 1976 - 1981   211

Part 4

Chapter
20. Discharged and banned: 1979 - 1983   221
21. Romance!: 1980 ...   226
22. Support and opposition: 1955 onwards   231
23. Teaching: the Schools' uprising: 1976 - 1985   237
24. Nelson Mandela's release; the Sisulu's visit: 1990   243
25. From violence to peace - the new South Africa: 1990 - 1994   249

Letters   253
Epilogue   255

Foreword

Edward Daniels' book on the Robben Island experience is another welcome addition to the growing volume of works on this important aspect of the struggle for justice, non-racialism, and democracy in South Africa.

We had the pleasure of working closely with Comrade Eddie throughout his fifteen-year stay on the Island. We recall his loyalty and courage; his sense of humour, and justice as well as total commitment to the struggle of the prisoners for the eradication of injustice and for the betterment of their conditions.

Literally hundreds of political prisoners passed through Robben Island during its three decades as a political prison. Apart from their common experience, each prisoner will have had experiences unique to himself, and will therefore add further dimensions to our recollections. Taken together, they will undoubtedly make valuable and much-needed contributions to the history of Robben Island.

Nelson Mandela

President of the Republic of South Africa

This poem by W.E. Henley, was taught to me by Nelson Mandela in Robben Island prison. May it inspire others as it inspired me.

INVICTUS

Out of the night that covers me,
Black as the pit from pole to pole,
I thank whatever gods there may be
For my unconquerable soul.

In the fell clutch of circumstance
I have not winced nor cried aloud.
Under the bludgeonings of chance
My head is bloody, but unbowed.

Beyond this place of wrath and tears
Looms but the Horror of the shade,
And yet the menace of the years
Finds, and shall find, me unafraid.

It matters not how strait the gait,
How charged with punishments the scroll,
I am master of my fate:
I am the captain of my soul.

Acknowledgements

Acknowledgements

I am indebted to many who showed great loyalty and goodwill to me throughout my incarceration and after, as well as those who assisted me to find my feet after being released from prison.

Foremost among those are my brother Norman, who also kept my family together over time; my mother, a brave lady if ever there was one; and the other members of my family . My sincere thanks go to the International Defence and Aid Fund which financed the cost of my trial; Barney Zackon and Advocate Gibson who defended me; Dot Cleminshaw, and her late husband Harry-friends indeed, who took up the cudgels on my behalf from the first day I was detained and were there, with Peter Brown, when I was released from prison 15 years later; Randolph and Gillian Vigne, Ann Karson (née Tobias) and Sheila Clare (née Robertson), all of whom went into exile and who looked after my interests abroad.

I am also indebted to many members of the Liberal Party of South Africa, among them (now all deceased): Alan Paton, Joe Daniels (no relation), Moira Henderson, Brian Bishop, Cromwell Nodidile, Tom Walters, Joan Bloch and Joe Nkatlo. Back to the living: Peter Brown and his wife, Phoebe, Bill (Sir Raymond) Hoffenberg and his wife, Margaret, Alan Baldwin and his sister Edna, Di Bishop, Mrs Hendrickes, Maggie Johnson, Jean Ridge, Ralph Aitchison and his wife, Bunty, Eulalie Stott, Bill West and his wife, Evelyn, Hamington Majija, Neil Ross, and many others; those who organised, of whom the prime initiators were Randolph Vigne, Dot Cleminshaw and Hugh Lewin, and those who contributed to the 'Eddie Daniels Fund' both in South Africa and in England.

I am indebted as well to the Western Province Council of Churches, which gave me a study bursary of R1000, as well as the Institute of Race Relations, which gave me a study bursary of R500. These bursaries helped me to obtain my teacher's diploma.

Then there were those who helped me build my lovely home in Hout Bay: architect Alex Robertson, brother of Sheila Clare who was also detained by the security police, drew the plans for the house; Raymond Clarke, a friend from primary school days, donated 60 000 bricks from his brick factory and Gerald Hendricks, a quantity surveyor, gave his time unstintingly to supervise the building of my home.

I am also indebted to the Honourable Justice Jan Steyn who gave me a job, when I sorely needed one, at the Urban Foundation, (shortly after I was discharged from prison and while still under house arrest) where I found good friends, Steven Dietrich, Hilmi Daniels and David Daniels .

Mr A J Snyders of Garlandale High furnished me with a teaching post when a number of principals from other schools to whom I had applied for a post, looked the other way. There is also the Legal Resources Centre, represented by Steve Kahanovitch, who assisted me when I laid a charge against the unknown persons who were abusing and threatening me over the telephone, as well as Malvern Meyer who also proved to be a good friend in later life.

Then, there is my lovely wife, Eleanor, whom I married twice, once when the Mixed Marriage Act was still in force and again when the portion of the act that applied to our marriage was repealed. Eleanor helped me build our home and my life.

There are many, many others, some I know and others I do not, who have assisted me in ways known and unbeknown to me. To all of you, a deep and heartfelt 'Thank You'.

Last, but by no means least, I would like to thank Randolph Vigne, Simon Pamphilon and Barry Feinberg for helping me to prepare my story for publication.

I have received permission from Adrian Leftwich to include in
* **There & Back** the letter that he had written to me shortly after my release from prison.
* The **Epilogue** is a fulfilment of a promise that I had made to **Irene Mkwayi** – now deceased.
* I am indebted to **Mayibuye Books** for publishing the original **There & Back**.

The great day dawned peacefully. It had been preceded by terrible violence. But the violence and the schemes of evil men failed to destroy the miracle of 27 April 1994: the day that heralded the first non-racial election in South Africa's history. This day epitomised the fulfilment of our hopes and dreams, the election of a democratic government by all South Africans of voting age. This achievement was made possible by the millions of unsung heroes and heroines of past generations who struggled bravely and doggedly against overwhelming odds towards, what many felt to be, an impossible goal. It is because of the great sacrifices of the past that we, the democratic forces of today, have attained victory.

The Struggle, which took place over generations and which culminated in victory over those who advocated racialism and injustice as personified by the National Party government with its apartheid philosophy, slowly but inevitably drew me into its vortex.

I derived the title of my book, There and Back, from an incident that occurred during my teenage years, when a few friends and I returned home from a party in the early hours of the morning. Because Lanky (David Williams), was more under the weather than the rest of us, we felt we should take him home first.

We had to tug and pull Lanky, who was a big chap, up a large number of steps leading to his front door in Upper Cambridge Street, Walmer Estate. After getting him to the top of the steps, we propped him up against the door, knocked loudly, and then fled to avoid the wrath of his parents. But we hid nearby, to make sure Lanky got in all right.

We heard the door opening and Mr Williams angrily saying, 'Do you know the time? Where do you come from now?' And Lanky nonchalantly replied: 'Theeerrre and back.'

PART
1

Chapter 1

Childhood in District Six: 1928 - 1950

I sprung from the loins of wonderful parents: my father was white (English-born) and my mother a South African of 'mixed blood'. I am therefore a South African of 'mixed blood' known racially as 'Coloured'. My ancestry can be traced to slaves as well as Europeans, both of whom have enriched me with genes inherited from those far-flung forebears. I take exception to being referred to as 'Coloured' as I see myself as a South African. If I must be referred to in terms of colour then I prefer the term 'black'.

I was born on 25 October 1928, in the heart of District Six in Ayre Street. Ayre Street was one street up from Hanover Street, the main street of District Six and just a few metres away from the famous (or notorious) Seven Steps. District Six became well known in the 1960s when, though almost 100 percent black, it was declared a white group area. Around 60 000 people had to vacate their homes which nestled in the hollow formed by the slopes of Devil's Peak, Table Mountain, Lion's Head and Signal Hill. Until then, the mountains were within easy reach for walks and climbs, and the beach a short distance away. They were available, and free. The residents were mostly respectable, law-abiding, God-fearing people, but poor.

On summer evenings, before the people were forced out of their homes by the state's bulldozers, the residents of D6 would stroll down Hanover Street, pass Castle Bridge, where Dolly's chemist was situated, and along Darling Street. They would window-shop in Adderley Street and the surrounding streets where most of the big department stores, with their large and brightly-lit windows, were situated. On Saturday mornings everybody would dress up in their best clothes to go and do their shopping, pay their accounts, or just take the air.

Hanover Street itself was long and just wide enough to allow two buses to pass abreast. On a Saturday morning the street was alive and colourful. A large section of the street was lined on both sides with shops selling anything 'from a needle to an anchor'. There were greengrocers and butcheries. There were also sweet shops, cafes, hotels with bottle stores and bars, a fish market and the Star Bioscope. Hawkers, either pulling their heavily laden carts or parked against the curb, would shout their wares. Throngs of people dressed in their weekend best would dodge each other among the carts, while weaving cars and buses added their hooters to the bedlam.

But then there was the 'skollie' menace, the scourge of the poor and the weak. There was the 'Black Cat' gang, the 'Seven Steps' gang and later, when we moved to Lavender Hill, about two kilometres from Ayre Street, I was to encounter many others. Friday night was the most frightening. Almost everyone had to pass a gang to reach home. The gangsters would hang out on the pavements, gambling, singing or arguing or just sizing up the passers-by. Their victims would be robbed, often stabbed, and regularly kicked to a pulp. When one safely passed a gang, you breathed a sigh of relief. But there were more to pass before reaching home. You said a silent prayer as you saw them waiting there. You braced yourself. You passed through. You survived. But, what about the next time, and the next gang? For a child to survive to adulthood in a township he or she had to be lucky indeed.

We were a poor family and lived on the ground floor of a house with a big balcony. This balcony cast a permanent shadow, denying us any sunshine in our home. I was the youngest of six children. Eileen was the eldest, followed by Ryland, Norman, Gerald, Laura and myself.

I gave my older brothers a hard time. I remember one occasion when my brothers and friends were playing cricket in the street, and, because they would not allow me to play with them, I staged a sit-down protest in the middle of the 'pitch'. I was dragged away kicking and screaming.

One of the big events of my childhood was the weekly delivery of coal to the boilerhouse, which was across the road from our front door. The boilerhouse supplied hot water to the wash-house, situated round the corner in Hanover Street. The other boys and I would sit around watching the bags of coal being offloaded from the cart and carried into the boilerhouse. The labourers would sometimes accidentally (and at other times deliberately) let a lump or two of coal fall out of the bag and on to the street, and a mad scramble would ensue. One day a larger than usual lump rolled off and under the cart. Like a flash, I dived under the cart, grabbed this lump of coal, hugged it to my chest, and sprinted for home with the other boys in hot pursuit. I made it to the house and proudly displayed my prize to my mother, who was very pleased with my effort.

We moved to Lavender Hill when I was about seven. Our house, number 18, was a happy home. It was a semi-detached with large windows which allowed the sunshine to stream in. We also had two taps (compared to the one in our home in Ayre Street), with one in the kitchen and the other in the yard.

My father, a parking attendant on the Grand Parade, died shortly after we moved to Lavender Hill, and my mother had to fend for us. My two eldest brothers, Ryland and Norman, had to leave school to go and work. My mother got a job at Stuttaford's Department Store, polishing the showcases and counters and cleaning the floors. I would watch out for her coming home from work, walking up Lavender Hill, which was a bit of a climb. When I saw her I would abandon whatever I was doing and run down to meet and hug her and help her with her parcels. Then she would still have to prepare supper for her family. She was a tremendous mother indeed.

Three years later she married Christy Jutzen, a widower. He proved to be a good husband to my mother and a wonderful father to her children. He had two children from his previous marriage, Helen and David. Helen died just before he married my mother. I remember Helen, who was a sweet young lady, coming to my assistance on one occasion. I had come from the shop and my arms were loaded with firewood, precariously balanced. A stick on top of the bundle rolled off and fell on to the street. Helen immediately left her friends with whom she was chatting and graciously came to help me, a little boy of ten. She picked up the stick and with a lovely smile placed the stick back on top of the bundle. I remember that incident with pleasure.

I went to Sydney Street school, a three-storey building with classrooms and cloakrooms on the first two floors and a hall and storeroom on the third. It also had a small playground. Opposite one side of the school was a blacksmith's shop. On many a winter's morning we would creep into the blacksmith shop and stand next to the inside wall, basking in the heat of the furnace and watching the red-hot sparks spiral up to the ceiling, as the blacksmith transformed a piece of metal into a horseshoe. His assistant would pump the bellows and the fire would glow with fresh intensity, turning the metal in the furnace into glowing pieces of iron. When the horseshoes were ready for fitting, the blacksmith would turn his back to the horse, bend down, put his hands between his legs, and grab the horse's hind leg. He would pull the horse's leg up between his own, place the hoof on the thick leather apron that covered his thigh and start to cut away a portion of the hoof with a sharp knife. Then he would fit the horseshoe and drive in several nails. We always cringed when the nails were hammered in, because we expected the horse to experience pain.

If the blacksmith was working on the front hooves he would actually have to get under the horse, facing its hindquarters with his back to its belly, so that he could pull the hoof up between his legs.

We marvelled at this world, and a few of us dreamt of becoming blacksmiths with big, bulging muscles.

At school my cousin Arthur and I were barred from the playground for being too rough. As a result, during breaks we had to have our lunch outside in the street. We would often, during these breaks, run down to the nearby beach or stand on the railway bridge and let the smoke from the steam engine engulf us as it passed beneath.

One day Maurice, who was in the same class as Arthur and myself and who became my best friend in later life, decided to join us during a break, although he was not supposed to be outside during school hours without permission. We went down to

Lower Main Road, which was a busy road, and decided to play a game which involved hanging onto the backs of moving lorries. We would all wait at a point where the trucks slowed down to take a bend, run in behind them, look for handholds, grab, then hang on for dear life. We would jump clear before the lorries hit the straight and picked up speed.

At times one of us would jump too late and miss a handhold, and then those who had succeeded in catching on would drop off so we could regroup.

On this occasion all three of us caught the same lorry. This lorry, however, accelerated around the bend, and we had to hang on for dear life. When it hit the straight we had no alternative but to grit our teeth and hang on. Eventually we reached the round-about at the bottom of Salt River Road, about four kilometres from where we first caught the lorry, and it reduced speed enough for us to jump clear. We then had to make our way back to school on foot, because the lorries going in the opposite direction were travelling too fast to risk jumping them. When we eventually reached the school Arthur and I made some excuse for being late and were let off, but Maurice had no excuse as he was not allowed out the grounds in the first place.

Arthur and I watched from upstairs through a banister as Maurice received six of the best from the school principal, Miss Ravenscroft. We had a hearty laugh at his expense.

During the Second World War, which started when I was in Standard Five, the school practised air-raid drill. The whole school, 600 children, had to walk crocodile fashion some three kilometres along Chapel Street to Trafalgar Park, where public air-raid shelters had been built. I thought to myself, that, as there was absolutely no cover along the length of Chapel Street, if a real air raid did take place we would be slaughtered long before we reached the shelters.

I was put in charge of the fire-fighting squad at school. We were taught during drill to walk on floorboards that had nails hammered down their centres, as this indicated that they were above beams and were the ones least likely to collapse in a fire.

We were fascinated by war books. After school we would

often go to town and search the shops for books that showed Spitfires screaming down on German planes with all guns blazing; or German submarines being blown out of the water. These books were very exciting and at school we would swap them. I would also get regular hidings for coming home so late from school. My mother would ask me, 'Where do you come from now? It is past 5 o'clock!'

'I went to collect war books, Mommy,' I would reply, showing her my treasures.

'War books! War books! I'll give you war books!' Then I would get a good couple of smacks with a strap on my behind.

At the end of school days I had the option of going home via Hanover Street, which was the shortest route, or via Chapel Street, which was a roundabout route. A number of my friends walked the Chapel Street route and at times I used to accompany them. My main reason for this was that one of them, Stanley Jacobs, used to ride to school on his bicycle. I was bicycle mad, and while Stanley walked and chatted with the other guys on the way home, I got to push his bicycle for him. Sometimes I would stand on the pedal and propel myself along with my other foot. My biggest thrill occurred one day when, while I was pushing myself along, the bicycle began to fall over. I instinctively turned the front wheel and recovered my balance. I suddenly realised that I could ride a bicycle.

Sometimes, when I went home by way of Hanover Street, I would stop at a shop that sold toys, among other things. I would stand in front of the window and point out, to whoever was with me, the toys that I liked. The proprietor of the shop would often come outside, stand next to me and surreptitiously give me a painful pinch through my short trousers. When I moved away from him he would sidle up to me and give me another of those painful pinches until I left the window.

Hindsight tells me I was smudging his windows with my hands and fingers, but he seemed to enjoy hurting me, because he always grinned as if it was a big joke.

One day Georgie Williams and I were walking home from school along Hanover Street, and I picked up a vegetable, either a potato or turnip. As we came alongside this shop I took the vegetable and let fly at a high stack of buckets inside it. The stack began to fall and I grabbed Georgie's arm and ran. As we were running we passed a greengrocer's shop, and I bumped a big wicker basket of green beans on a shelf outside the shop. Georgie, who was close behind me, tried to catch the basket as it fell, but I shouted to him to let it go.

The proprietor of the toyshop chased us for some distance, but fortunately he did not have much stamina. When I looked back I saw him speaking to a policeman and pointing in our direction. Georgie and I turned into a side street and split up, each of us making his way home in a very roundabout manner. For the rest of the year and more I would go home along Chapel Street, even though it was the longer way home.

We were surrounded by gangs in Lavender Hill. The Shepherd Street Gang was the oldest, but a new group had come to the fore. The Globe Gang, which got its name from the furniture shop in Hanover Street where the members used to congregate, started off as a vigilante group protecting residents from attacks by gangsters, but it eventually became one of the most vicious and powerful gangs in the area.

There would be regular battles between the Globe, Jesters and Killer gangs. If any member of one gang was found in the territory of another and caught, he would be badly beaten or killed.

One Saturday evening when I was in my early twenties, Willie Petersen, Louis Lotter and I were returning from cricket after a drink at the Altona Hotel. We were passing the entrance of the Trafalgar Swimming Baths when a gangster called Chingy approached us and started being abusive. Willie swung his togbag at him and he retreated. We persuaded Willie not to go after him. Shortly afterwards we parted ways.

I was just short of Lavender Hill when I was attacked by about five or six gangsters, including Chingy. I was hit over the head from behind with an empty paraffin tin. We fought from Hanover Street into Lavender Hill. I was hit on my head with a belt. I kicked Chingy full in the face, then managed to break loose and run. Even though I lived in Lavender Hill I had the presence of mind not to head for my house. Instead I dashed through a lane that ran from Lavender Hill through to Summer Hill. In the process I tripped over a dustbin and went sprawling, damaging my practically new cricket club blazer. I made my way up Summer Hill, down Upper Ashley Street and back into Lavender Hill.

I had managed to lose the gangsters, but I had also lost the bag containing my cricket togs as well as those of my brother, Gerald. (Gerald and I played for the same club, St Luke's. He had left cricket early that day and had asked me to bring his togs home).

I told Gerald what had happened, and that I knew it was members of the Junior Globe Gang who had attacked me. We armed ourselves with a hammer and a large spanner and set off for the gang's headquarters.

Meanwhile, at home, my mother asked my sister, Laura, to tell me my supper was ready. Laura had overheard me speaking to Gerald and told my mother, 'Eddie and Gerald have gone to fight with the gangsters.'

My mother abandoned everything in the kitchen and went charging down Lavender Hill and into Hanover Street. She caught up with us and urged us to return home, which we did.

That should have been the end of it, but I had a feeling there was more trouble to come.

I was supposed to go out that evening, but instead I stayed at home. I was sitting in a chair in the lounge, keeping an eye on the front gate, when a large crowd gathered in the road. I realised from the distinctive caps they were wearing that these were members of both the Junior Globe and Globe gangs.

As the gate clicked open I shouted to Gerald, 'Here they come!' I rushed to the kitchen and grabbed a hammer from under the stove. By the time I got back to the lounge door my mother was already there. So were Gerald, Laura and Linda, my sister-in-law, whose two babies, Noreen and Eddie, were sleeping in the bedroom. As I brought up the rear I heard my mother say in a very determined voice, 'Where do you think you are going?'

Between the front door and the lounge door was a one-metre square hallway. This hallway, the outside porch, the path to the gate and beyond was crowded with gangsters brandishing chains, bayonets and an assortment of other weapons.

My mother, short in stature but big in heart, had her out-stretched arms firmly placed against each side of the lounge doorframe. She had stopped this whole lot of terrible gangsters in their tracks. Chingy was bleeding and crying and drunk from the dagga (marijuana) he had been smoking. He was leaning over my mother's outstretched arm, holding his face up for inspection.

'Kyk hoe hy vir my geskop.' ('Look how he kicked me'), he said over and over again.

My mother replied, 'You people interfered with my son first.'

Because Gerald and I looked alike the thugs were not sure who the offender was. One of them held up my tog-bag and asked whose it was. I said it was mine.

'O, jy is die een wat ons wil hê' ('Oh, you are the one we want'), said Chingy.

I was thinking of going out the back door, running down the lane, then coming up Lavender Hill behind the gangsters and confronting them in the street. This way I could at least save my family and our house from being smashed up. But I was held back by the fear that anything could be happening in the time it took me to get around and behind them.

Suddenly Laura, who was pregnant, fainted.

One of the gangsters said, 'Ek sê , daai vroumens is siek; kom ons waai.' ('I say, that woman is sick; come let's go.')

Chingy, still bleeding and crying, extended his hand towards me and said, 'All right, daar's my vyf.' ('All right, there's my five.')

I shook his hand and the gang left. What a relief! Those two gangs combined were ruthless. Just two doors further up this same crowd had kicked down Jackie Smith's front door and smashed up his home for his daring to stand up to them. They showed scant respect for anyone who obstructed them. My moth-er's extremely brave stand had saved her family and home.

When I next saw Willie he told me the same group had also been at his girlfriend's home. Chingy was armed with a rapier but, fortunately, Willie's girlfriend managed to convince the thugs they were at the wrong house. I suppose Chingy was so high on dagga he was not sure what was going on.

At my mother's funeral many years later, both my brother Norman and I referred to the incident of the Globe gang and paid tribute to her for being such a wonderful mother.

The threat of violence was an ever-present one in my neighbourhood. During an end-of-year party at Bally's Shoe Factory, where I worked, I went to the toilet and found two men violently pulling and pushing a woman around, presumably with the intention of raping her. I intervened and they turned on me. As the woman disappeared I fought them. They both ran out of the toilet. I grabbed an empty liquor bottle lying in the toilet, and while the one ran upstairs, I chased the other down the stairs (our party was being held on the third floor of a multi-storey building) and out into Ravenscraig Road.

He shouted at me to wait there, and that he would be back shortly. I shouted after him to bring his gang, and that I'd be around.

When I returned to the third floor I walked straight into the guy who had run upstairs. He had about six cronies with him. I fought with them but was soon overpowered. People intervened and saved me from further punishment. A short while later I was on the landing when a number of members of the Gympie and Freda Street gangs, led by the thug who I had chased outside, came upstairs at a gallop. I remember a chap, who I was only slightly familiar with, standing at the top of the stairs with an empty liquor bottle in his hand, challenging the gangsters to take him on. He looked like Horatio guarding the bridge. He made a brave figure, but did not guard the stairs for long, for very soon they were at me. They pushed me into the same toilet in which the woman had been dragged. The last thing I remembered before losing consciousness was three dull thuds as somebody jumped or stamped on my face.

When I came around I was being half carried, half dragged up Pine Road by a friend of mine, Andy Millar. I recovered and cleaned up as best I could at Andy's home. The fighting must have started about 10:00 in the morning. It was about 5:00 in the afternoon when I made my way home, and told my parents what had happened.

My father wanted to lay a charge with the police but the factory was closed for the Christmas holidays. After three weeks the matter no longer seemed so pressing. When we returned to work the thug who had led the two gangs in their attack on me, and who was also employed at Bally's Shoe Factory, came to apologise to me and we let bygones be bygones.

After the Globe gang incident my mother decided we should move to a safer area. The night before we moved, to 8 Hilyard Street, Woodstock, I narrowly managed to avoid being ambushed by gang members. And in an earlier incident, my brother Ryland's home was smashed up when he tried to help his neighbour who was being attacked by gangsters.

What a change Woodstock was! How lovely it was to live there, to be able to come home in the small hours of the morning and walk with confidence through the streets to one's home. It was bliss. It was a far cry from District Six where I was afraid to go out because of the risks one ran on returning home.

But the gangs were not the only social evil with which we had to contend. Even more pervasive and inhuman was the racial inequality. From an early age, I noticed that white was associated with superiority and black with inferiority. It was the white man who drove a motor car and who was prosperous. He owned the large businesses and the houses in which we lived. He was everywhere in authority: he was the doctor, the policeman, the magistrate, the judge, the parliamentarian. He was the clerk in the post office, the inspector, the conductor or the driver on the buses and trains. He was the religious minister, the teacher, the principal or the inspector at the school. He was in charge at the dispensary and at the hospital.

On the other hand it was the blacks who were arrested, who were drunk in the streets, who made up the street gangs that preyed on the weak and the poor. They were also the many, decent, honest and hard-working citizens of District Six who performed jobs that carried no authority.

There were exceptions to the above: blacks like Dr Gow, a

minister of the African Methodist Episcopal Church and later a Bishop; Dr Abdurahman, a medical doctor and chairman of the African Political Organisation (a major campaigning force for the blacks before and during the Second World War); Cissie Gool, his daughter, who was a city councillor; and Mr Charles Calvert, who held the highest military position-Sergeant Major-in the Cape Corps (a black soldier regiment), and who had been awarded the DCM (Distinguished Conduct Medal) in the First World War; but they were few and far between.

When one is born into such an environment one initially accepts the status quo. Then little incidents occur which make one start to question it.

One of the things that would upset me most was to see how policemen abused their authority. A typical example: a police van pulls up outside a black-owned store. A policeman gets out, strolls into the store, waves a casual greeting to the shopkeeper, and lifts the counter-flap that separates the customers' area from the goods. He helps himself to a few large slabs of chocolate and a packet or two of cigarettes, then leaves without paying.

I used to think to myself that if a poor man came into this shop and was a halfpenny short for a loaf of bread, he would be chased out like a scavenging dog. But here the shopkeeper would just stand back and accept the fact that the forces of law and order were blatantly robbing him.

I had no idea at the time about licences and trading after-hours. I knew one shopkeeper in Hanover Street who would demand payment from the police, and I admired him for standing up to them. One day I noticed that his shop was permanently closed-perhaps it had something to do with his defiance.

One day Gerald and I were on our way to Sunday school when we passed four men playing cards on the pavement, watched by a few spectators. Suddenly two policemen pounced, and everyone scattered. But the policemen caught one of the card-players. Instead of just subduing and arresting him they proceeded to practise some kind of judo or karate tricks on him. He shouted that he surrendered but that was not good enough for them. They choked him, twisted his arms, and threw him to the ground while he was screaming for mercy. By this time a crowd had gathered, and was becoming increasingly agitated by the brutality of the arrest. Someone threw a full bottle of hair-oil at the policemen, and it hit one of them on his foot. The policemen realised that they had overdone the arrest and proceeded to handcuff the prisoner. They set off on foot for the police station, which was some distance away. However the onlookers, who usually had great respect for the law and no objection to a fair arrest, were now incensed. They followed the policemen and their prisoner, shouting abuse. A little further on an elderly man went up to one of the policeman and tried to hit him with a half-brick. The policeman held him easily at arm's length, drew his revolver (they had recently been issued with guns) and placed the muzzle against the old man's temple. The old man was defiant, and shouted, 'Skiet! Skiet!' ('Shoot! Shoot!'). They stared at each other a while, then the policeman gave the old man a shove that sent him flying. A young man, I assumed it was his son, led the old man away from the scene.

The crowd was now becoming a mob, and a number of people, including Gerald and me, started to throw stones at the policemen. They both drew their guns and we scattered. We regrouped and the stones flew through the air once more. The policemen turned and fired at us. There was blind panic. Those in front could not get out of the line of fire because of the houses lining the street on both sides. Some tried to get over the walls of the houses, while others turned and ran. However they collided with people behind them, who felt relatively safer and had not moved with the same alacrity.

When we eventually sorted ourselves out and regrouped, we found nobody had been injured. We came to the conclusion that the policemen had fired blanks at us, and set off after them again. The next time they shot at us we took cursory avoidance action, just as a precaution, and jeered at them, 'Steier klappertjies! Steier klappertjies!' ('Halfpenny crackers! Halfpenny crackers!')

A police van appeared but left hurriedly under a barrage of stones. At the corner of Tennant and Hanover Streets the crowd attacked the two policemen. Gerald and I left at this stage because we were being knocked about by adults rushing hither and thither.

I later heard - I do not know if it was true - that the policemen were beaten up, with one being shoved into a street drain, and that the prisoner was freed.

Another image enters my mind. I was passing the intersection of Lavender Hill and Hanover Street when I saw an elderly man, who, judging from his dress was desperately poor, being accosted by about eight thugs. They opened a paper bag the old man had with him and took out little parcels containing tea, sugar and bits of food. The old man asked the thugs to give them back, but they just laughed at him. They passed the parcels to each other behind their backs, then in turn held their empty hands out to the old man and claimed they had nothing of his.

Then a policeman came along on a bicycle. The old man stepped into the road, stopped the policeman and told him he had been robbed. The policeman looked at the grinning thugs and at the poor old man, and, deciding discretion was the better part of valour, said to him, 'Wie is dronk, ek of jy?' ('Who is drunk, me or you?')

The thugs and some fawning spectators laughed at the policeman's response, and the old man, his head and shoulders drooping with despair, turned and shuffled away in his tattered clothes and broken shoes.

As the policeman cycled off the thugs put the old man's bits and pieces on a little ledge jutting out from the corner-shop, then they walked away, laughing.

Chapter 2

Sport and the mountain: 1940 - 1950

I was keen on sport but was only an average participant. I initially played soccer for Hotspurs, then when that club closed I joined Hillside Rangers. I also played cricket for St Luke's.

Hillside Rangers was so called because the founding members lived on the slopes of Signal Hill. I was elected club secretary after being with them for a couple of seasons, and held the post until I left to go to sea on the fishing trawlers in 1954. I was also elected captain of the first team after a few seasons with the club. We usually ended second or third last on the log, but we enjoyed our soccer. When I resigned from the club to go to sea I was presented with a watch in appreciation for services rendered.

My grandparents lived in Newlands, a lovely and peaceful area. Everyone there was rugby mad and almost everyone, myself included, supported the Villagers rugby team. I used to watch my brother Gerald poring over the newspaper, reading about the exploits of his rugby heroes and relating how well they played at the Newlands rugby grounds, which I had never been to.

One day my Uncle Polly and Gerald decided to give me a treat and took me along with them to this famous rugby ground. When we got inside I was astonished by the large crowd and the excitement in the air. I asked Gerald why our section was cut off from the field and the rest of the stands, while those in the other stands had free access to the fields and could move around freely between stands. He pointed out that this was the Malay stand, and was the only area that blacks were allowed to occupy. The only black person allowed on the white side was the man who looked after the players' kits.

I was disgusted by the fact that people paid to be hemmed in as they were. To add insult to injury, not only did we have to stand in a long queue exposed to the elements to get into the grounds, but also the toilet facilities left much to be desired.

At the age of eleven I decided I would never again go back to the Newlands rugby stadium, and I never have. I have the same attitude to the Newlands cricket ground, although the segregation there was not so strictly enforced. Even though the apartheid humiliation has fallen away at these two venues and my resentment towards our national rugby and cricket teams has softened, because of those early memories I have no desire at all to go and watch rugby or cricket matches at those grounds.

Table Mountain was right on our back doorstep, and my friends and I would often run up the mountain or tackle one of its many climbs. I spent many happy moments up there. One day Maurice and I were doing a climb, called Gully, when we got lost and found ourselves in unfamiliar territory. We continued climbing and the ascent became narrower and steeper. At one stage a large rock blocked our path. We had only one haversack between us, which I was carrying at the time. I slipped it off, passed it to Maurice then climbed up over the rock. Then I stretched out my foot so Maurice could slip the strap of the haversack over it and I could drag it up. As Maurice was taking the haversack off his back he cried out, 'Eddie, my arm!'

I knew Maurice had a bad shoulder that would spring out of joint at the most unexpected moments. His face was like a parchment. The bag was hanging from his other shoulder and I was afraid he was going to lose his balance.

I shouted to him, 'Hang on, Jug!' (his nickname), and quickly slid down the rock to him. I was now between Maurice and the rock, and on the other side of Maurice was nothing but a long way down. The ledge on which we were standing was very narrow, literally standing room only. I took the haversack from him, wedged it between my legs, and held Maurice against me. I had to twist his arm to get the shoulder back into joint. I heard the click as the ball of the arm clicked back into its socket. Maurice closed his eyes and I was afraid he was going to faint. Again I held him against me and shouted his name. He snapped out of it and recovered quite quickly. We were in such an awkward position I could not turn around to get over the rock again, so Maurice had to climb up and over me. Afterwards he often referred to the time he did 'face climbing'. It was my face he climbed that day. I put on the haversack, climbed the rock and followed Maurice up. I was worried his arm would pop out again but he climbed well, and we eventually reached the top of the mountain.

I would often climb the mountain on my own. One day after climbing Kloof Corner I met a student from the University of Cape Town. He had just abseiled down Arrow Face, which was directly below the upper cable station, and asked if I would like to climb the face. I jumped at the opportunity. He led the climb and I followed on the rope. It was the first time I had climbed using a rope and also the first time that I had climbed such a steep and exposed rock face.

Afterwards I told all and sundry about my climb, including a friend of mine, Jimmy Griffiths. Jimmy wanted me to do the climb with him. I tried to dissuade him by pointing out that we did not have a rope, that I had only climbed that rock face once, that someone else had led the climb and, finally, that the face was very exposed. Jimmy would not hear any of it, and promised to bring along a rope. I reluctantly agreed.

On the morning of the climb Jimmy produced a few long strips of sash cord, and I contributed some strips of wire that could be used as karabiners. We climbed up the mountain to the foot of Arrow Face. It looked awesome.

I looked at Jimmy, hoping he would change his mind. No such luck, he was as keen as ever, so I roped up and started to climb. The pitch of the first part was relatively easy, compared to the rest of the face that became more difficult the higher one ascended. I reached a comfortable point some way up, roped myself to the face and called on Jimmy to start climbing. He soon joined me, and we sat down and surveyed the panoramic view of Cape Town and the harbour at our feet and the sea stretching away to the horizon. It felt good sitting up there, feeling so free, listening to the silence and breathing in the invigorating and unpolluted air. It was tranquil. It was magic just being there.

After drinking in the beauty of our surroundings. I started to climb once more. The going became tougher. Following on the rope was one thing, leading up the face was quite another. I came to a portion on the face where a small loose rock obstructed my passage. I called down to Jimmy, explaining the problem and that I was going to dislodge the rock so he must take cover. He was against the idea, but I told him I had no alternative. I heard the rock falling down the face and I hoped Jimmy would be clear of it. When I called down to him he indicated he was all right, and we made it safely the rest of the way.

When we reached the top, two tourists who had come up on the cable car came over to speak to us. One of them noticed the rope Jimmy was carrying and said, 'Your rope is not very thick.'

I replied, 'We are not very heavy.'

Once a year the Mountain Club of South Africa would have a memorial service on Table Mountain in memory of members who had died in combat during various wars. A group of us climbed the mountain one Saturday night before a service that was to be held at Maclear's Beacon.

The next morning, while we were making our way to the memorial service, one of our group, Sophia, walked into a thornbush branch and scratched her eye. She was in pain. I told the others they should carry on and that I would take Sophia down the mountain. Peggy Marola, another of our group, offered to accompany Sophia and me down the mountain.

I first took Sophia to the Mountain Club hut at Kasteels Poort, where somebody put a bandage across her eye to protect it from further damage. I then started to lead her down the mountain. It was an ordeal. Sophia was a big person and, being partially blinded, she frequently lost her balance or missed her footing. I could not always hold her up and sometimes we would both fall over. Peggy assisted where she could, but she was slender and light, and the result was that all three of us would fall over. We also had to stop often to enable Sophia to catch her breath and recover from the bumps. After about six hours, on a path that under normal circumstances would have taken an hour at the most, we at last reached the Pipe Track, a fairly level path. Sophia was in bad shape from the pain and the exhausting descent, and I too was quite tired.

As we made our way slowly along the Pipe Track, a girl burst out of the bushes near Blinkwater Ravine. She was panic-stricken, had scratches on her face, arms and legs, her wrist seemed to be bent at an awkward angle and her clothes were all dishevelled. I thought she might have been assaulted or raped. She rushed towards me and said, 'Please, please help me.'

I asked what was wrong, and she said her boyfriend had fallen. She had rushed down, often falling and rolling herself, to get help. I told her there was nothing much I could do on my own but I would try. She pointed out the place where she thought he had fallen, and I asked Peggy to take the two injured girls to Kloof Nek and phone for an ambulance.

Meanwhile I went looking for help. Fortunately, it was around 5:00 in the afternoon and people were leaving the mountain for home. I approached a group of mountaineers and explained what had happened. They immediately removed their haversacks and placed them in a small hollow at the side of the path, told their wives and girlfriends to carry on home, and started to organise a rescue party. As other mountaineers appeared on the path they joined the rescue team without any hesitation, and my respect for the members of the Mountain Club grew in leaps and bounds.

Four of us ran to the filtration plant, a good distance away, to fetch a stretcher, then ran all the way back with it. In the meantime scouts had been sent ahead to try and find the person who had fallen. Night was setting in when we climbed up the mountain with the stretcher. Whistles were blown to guide us to where the injured person was lying. Somebody called out, 'He's lying above Porcupine Buttress.'

It was pitch dark when we reached a ledge below the injured climber, and passed the stretcher up to those who were already there. A number of us huddled on the ledge shivering with cold. A call for more assistants came down from the upper ledge. I volunteered, but was turned down because I was wearing 'tackies' (gym shoes) and the rock face separating us from the top section was steep and slippery.

We waited and shivered. Somebody shared out a few cigarettes. We heard occasional calls from above, for somebody to fetch more torches, or morphine. Immediately a volunteer would set off. I thought to myself that to go down in this utter darkness and find one's way up again was really something.

At last the call came from the top ledge, 'Stand by below, we're lowering the stretcher.'

I looked up to see a large oblong object, silhouetted against the black sky, being pushed out horizontally. After about half the length of the stretcher was pushed out, the front end was gradually lowered until the stretcher was lying vertically against the rock face.

The stretcher itself was big and heavy, even more so with the injured climber securely strapped to it. As it came within reach we took hold of the front end and guided it down until it rested on the lower ledge. We stood clear of the rock face to make room for those now descending from the upper ledge.

The lower ledge was quite narrow, with plenty of gaps overgrown with brush. These gaps were treacherous, as one would assume there was solid ground beneath the brush and suddenly find oneself crashing down through it. We therefore had to move very cautiously. Each bearer was attached to the stretcher with a leather strap. If anyone slipped he would be supported by the other seven stretcher-bearers, as well as those hanging on to an anchor rope attached to the back of the stretcher, until he could regain his balance. In some places the ledge was so narrow the rescuers had to lie on their backs and pass the stretcher over themselves.

Eventually the ledge widened, but the going was still very difficult. At times we had to lower the stretcher down a rock face which we could not bypass. Some of us would wait with the stretcher, while others would make their way to the bottom of the rock face and wait for those above to lower the stretcher. As we slowly made our way down the mountain scouts went ahead to find the easiest route. We had one rescuer with a lantern who walked mostly backwards, guiding us along.

At the bottom of one rock face we encountered a mass of thorn bushes. We hesitated because most of us were wearing shorts. The person who was in front of the stretcher at that time (we had been taking turns), and who was wearing shorts said, 'To hell with these bushes, think of the injured chap.'

Then he led the crash through the thorn bushes. I subsequently read in the newspaper that one of the rescuers had to be treated for blood poisoning, and I assumed it was that chap.

After a lot of fits and starts, we at last reached relatively level ground and were able to proceed much faster.

We passed through more thorn bushes and at one point a branch hooked on to somebody's jersey and snapped back, hitting the person behind him in the eye. Fortunately, we were near the Pipe Track where the injured rescuer received medical attention. At the bottom some ladies plied us with very welcome coffee and sandwiches.

We had a short rest and regrouped. We still had to carry the stretcher to the filtration plant where an ambulance was waiting for us (this took place around 1950, long before helicopters, which now play such an important role, were used in rescues). I collected my haversack from the clearing on the side of the Pipe Track where I had left it eight hours earlier. I was very, very tired. The ambulance was at the filtration plant as well as the press and a lot of lights. I just carried on walking towards the Kloof Nek bus terminus, from where I managed to get a lift home.

The members of the Mountain Club of South Africa were outstanding. They volunteered with alacrity for the most arduous of tasks. Their cool courage and professional handling of rescues was impressive.

I enjoyed many happy moments on the mountain, as well as other hair-raising ones. The nights up there could be heavenly. Sleeping under the stars, hearing the murmur of the breeze passing through the trees, or simply listening to the silence, was beautiful and so peaceful. Looking out across the city and seeing the myriad lights far, far below, one was elevated both physically and spiritually.

One evening Maurice and I slept in a cave on the face of the mountain so we could see the sun rise the next morning. We had, as Maurice put it, a 'bedside' view. While still lying in our blankets we saw the sun appear on the horizon. It gently kissed the sea and spread its influence wider and wider until its rays started to reach out to us. The scene was transformed from a night-time one of sparkling lights, twinkling stars and a soft full moon to a trillion sparkling diamonds in a blue sea and a huge, golden orb which rapidly grew in intensity, bestowing light and life to the world below us.

On reflection, the mountain gave me more than aesthetic and outdoor pleasure. It taught me resourcefulness and self-reliance, and it gave me a break from the growing menace of apartheid that would have been hard to acquire in a life spent solely in the streets and segregated sports fields of a big city.

On Robben Island, in about 1974, we were put to collecting seaweed to be made into fertiliser. As we slowly made our way along the shoreline, I came around a point and suddenly, there was Table Mountain. I was overwhelmed with nostalgia as a flood of memories of the happy and carefree times that I had spent on that mountain washed over me. In my mind's eye I measured the distance to that mountain. When I had first come to jail it was fifteen years away, now it was five. With a bit of luck, I thought, I'd be climbing it again.

Jummy and I both owned bicycles, and in 1951 we decided to cycle from Cape Town to Port Elizabeth. My sister-in-law, Linda, had family in Port Elizabeth, and they had invited us to join them for the Christmas holidays. When Maurice heard about our plans he wanted to join us. He scrimped, saved and borrowed, and bought himself a bicycle for £2/5/-.

We worked out our plans carefully, prepared the necessary spares, clothes and blankets, and studied the relevant maps. We decided to go along the Worcester, Robertson, Ashton, Montagu and Barrydale route (now called routes 60 and 62) and return along the Garden Route (N2).

The top route was untarred, terrible and corrugated. Every time a car passed us we were enveloped in red dust from the road. At Worcester we spread out our maps on the stoep of a shop. It looked very impressive and the onlookers were agog. They asked where we were going, and we told them. One person advised us not to go that way. He said he had just travelled the route on his motorbike and found that water was scarce. However, we decided to carry on.

We had planned to cycle from 6:00 a.m. to 6:00 p.m. each day. But, because we were so loaded down we had a lot of unpacking to do in the evenings and repacking in the mornings. This meant that, as we travelled, we started out later in the mornings and stopped earlier in the afternoons.

We slept on the side of the road and would, at times, go to nearby farmhouses to buy milk. At every town we came to we would buy postcards of the town and send them home.

We reached the top of Kogmans Kloof Pass quite late one afternoon. We had no food and had to hurry to the nearest village before the shops closed for the evening. Because I had a 'racing' bike it was suggested I should go ahead of the others.

As I raced down the pass I came to a sharp bend and gently applied brakes, but nothing happened. My brakes had failed. I tried again, but still did not slow down. In desperation I stood on one pedal and dragged my other foot along the ground, to no avail. I was hurtling towards the edge of the cliff. I could not even jump clear at this point, as my outward momentum had carried me to the edge of the road and I would have gone over anyway.

I desperately tried the brake once more, and this time they held. The bicycle squealed to a halt.

I dismounted and checked the brakes. The mounting had come loose and was resting on the rear wheel. My last desperate application of the brakes had caused them to hook between the spokes.

I dropped the bicycle right there on the edge of the cliff and staggered across the road, utterly shaken. I sat down with my back to the mountain and tried to recover from the huge fright I had received. A while later Jummy and Maurice came along. I told them what had happened and asked them to repair my bicycle, as I felt quite helpless at that moment.

While they were working on my bicycle I heard Maurice say to Jummy, in a stage whisper, 'Wouldn't it have been funny if Eddie had gone over the side, and we were not aware of it, and just cycled on.'

This sick joke made me even more depressed, and I thought to myself, 'Maurice, I owe you one; a big one!'

Our biggest ordeal was the Huisrivier Pass. Jummie got ill shortly before we reached the pass, and, although he tried his best, he simply could not ride up it nor even push his heavily-laden bike.

The pass was so steep we all had to push our bicycles to the summit. While Jummie walked, I would take my bicycle a good distance up the pass, leave it there, then go back to fetch Jummie's. In the meantime Maurice would push his bicycle beyond the point where I had left mine, then come back down to mine, collect Jummie's, and take it up to his.

We continued in such a fashion to the top of this heartbreak pass. At one stage a railway lorry came struggling up behind us. I flagged it down, and asked the driver if he would take Jummie and his bicycle to Oudtshoorn. He said he could take only the bicycle, so we carried on.

Eventually we reached Calitzdorp, where we took Jummie to a doctor. The doctor diagnosed diarrhoea and advised Jummie to discontinue cycling. However we decided we would press on to Oudtshoorn, and work out what to do after that.

When we reached Oudtshoorn we tossed a coin. Tails we would take the train to Port Elizabeth, heads we would go to Mossel Bay. It came down heads.

We camped for three days on the side of a river in Mossel Bay, after which Jummie was fully recovered. We then set off home along the Garden Route.

This was much easier than our outwards journey had been, because the Garden Route was tarred almost its entire length. What got to me, though, were the telephone poles. As we cycled along we would see these poles rising in the distance, heralding the start of yet another hill. We would speed down one hill to gain as much momentum as possible for the next, before being forced to dismount and start pushing again. We would get over the crest of that hill and, sure enough, there we would see the poles rising in the distance.

After many hills a large lorry came along. One of us must have stuck out a thumb, because the driver stopped and told us to climb aboard. He was going to Cape Town. We were too ashamed to catch a lift all the way to Cape Town when we were supposed to be on a bicycle trip, so we asked the driver to drop us at Faure.

We shared the back of the lorry with two workers. In an attempt to be friendly, and as a gesture of appreciation, I offered them a drink from one of two half-jacks of brandy we had with us. One drank almost half the contents of the bottle then passed it on to his friend, who did the same. To show there were no hard feelings we drank the little that remained, but we did not produce the other bottle.

We were dropped off at Faure, from where we cycled home. On reaching home we received a warm welcome. During the trip we had suffered three punctures, a failed set of brakes, and Jummie's illness. When I look at a map to see the distance we travelled, a large part of it over untarred roads, then I think we did not do too badly.

There are two families-the Hillman and the Marola families-to whom I have to pay tribute.

The Hillmans were, and are, a beautiful family. They lived at 21 Prospect Avenue in District Six. From their stoep, one had a glorious view of Cape Town harbour and the sea to the right, the city straight ahead, and Table Mountain in all its majesty to the left. When District Six was declared a 'white area' and the Hillmans forced to leave, they not only lost their happy home but also a priceless view.

We all went to the Sydney Street School, where Maurice Hillman and I became the best of friends. Maurice had four love-ly sisters, Ethel, Adelaide, Norah and René and two brothers, Dickie and Neville. Mrs Hillman, a widower, was a gracious lady indeed. As we grew up and started to attend parties I was part-nered with Ethel. René, the youngest sister, did not have a part-ner at that time, so she usually accompanied Ethel and myself. The three of us would also often climb Table Mountain. What happy times we had together!

It was accepted by everyone that Ethel and I were 'going

steady', but it was actually just a practical arrangement. I went along with it because Ethel was a lovely young lady and I was happy and comfortable in the company of both Ethel and René. But one day, out of the blue, I realised I was in love with René. It put me in a cold sweat.

I told Ethel at the earliest opportunity, and she was very disappointed. However Ethel was such a fine person that she made arrangements for me to speak to René privately.

René did not respond warmly to my declaration of love, partly, I feel, out of loyalty to Ethel. They were very close. We have, however, remained friends over time.

Neville, as we shall see, joined me in the African Resistance Movement.

The Marola family lived at 16 Ormskirk Street, Woodstock. Like the Hillman family, they were also forced out of their home, in which they had lived for several decades, by the Group Areas Act. When we were teenagers, a group of friends and myself would go regularly to the Marolas' home on Friday and Saturday nights. This lovely family was made up of Mr and Mrs Marola; their sons, Jummy (Angelo), Eric and Utah; and their daughters, Valerie, Teresa and Peggy. Occasionally we would have a party at their home but always, and I mean always, we would have happy 'sing-alongs' with Jummy on guitar, joined occasionally by Mr Marola.

A sad memory comes to mind. One Christmas or New Year's Eve a group of us, full of anticipation, were on our way to a function. Valerie, who suffered from tuberculosis, was in the party. As we were walking along the main road a bus pulled up at a stop nearby. We all made a mad rush for the bus, and Valerie collapsed. We carried her home. She was such a lovely person, and her collapse devastated us.

Over the years the demands of life have caused us to drift apart, and we see one another only occasionally, at functions or funerals, but I still fondly remember the Marola family and the times we spent together.

One of these times was a trip to the famous Cango Caves in Oudtshoorn, in 1950.

We hired a lorry to take 22 of us to the caves. I remember Lanky (David Williams), who was forced to stay behind because he had just struck a job, waving goodbye to us with tears in his eyes, while Michael Petersen, also with tears in his eyes, waved back.

When we arrived at the Cango Caves we were confronted with a mass of apartheid boards, instructing where whites could go and where blacks could go, and at what times each group could enter the caves. Some of us objected to the instructions and refused to go into the caves. The rest of the party felt they had paid a lot of money to come on the trip and did not want to forego the opportunity. My brother Norman, Gerald Morkel, two others and I went back to the lorry while the rest of the party went into the caves.

Many of my memories are pleasant to recall, but-as at the Cango Caves-there was no escaping the presence of apartheid laws and regulations. For most people they were insulting and humiliating. For a few, like me, they were also a challenge to be responded to.

Chapter 3

Work and Apartheid: 1940 - 1964

In 1948, just three years after the allies had defeated Nazi Germany and its racial policies in a world war costing millions of lives, the National Party came to power in South Africa and entrenched racial segregation in its policy of apartheid.

The nationalist government ruled for more than four decades, and in the process brought the country to the verge of bankruptcy and destroyed the lives of millions of its citizens.

While still at school I worked every Sunday morning for a Mr Katz. He went door-to-door during the week selling goods on account, and I would help to collect money on Sundays. I received five shillings for working from 8:00 a.m. to 1:00 p.m.

I enjoyed the job because most of the people I met were very nice. My round covered Newlands and Kirstenbosch. It was lovely walking the tree-lined, leaf-shrouded streets in those pleasant surroundings. The people in Protea Village, Kirstenbosch, were like an extended family. Two names come to mind: Mrs Poggenpoel and the Stuart family. Mrs Poggenpoel was a lovely lady with an infectious sense of humour who lived in the heart of the village. To get to the Stuarts' home, I had to cross a small stream by a flat bridge. I was always warmly welcomed by the Stuart family. Mr Stuart had some huge pigs that he loved to show off.

The village was peaceful and tranquil, but the residents were black. Some years later the community was destroyed by the cruel Group Areas Act. I do not know what happened to Mr Stuart, but I guess that wherever he was forced to move to it was unlikely he was able to continue rearing prize pigs.

I also worked, in the afternoons after school, for the Graphic Press in Dorp Street, Cape Town. I would earn between five shillings and seven shillings and six-pence depending on the number of hours I worked. I would do the gold dusting and the interleaving of papers. I lost my job after an inspector visited the printing works. I think the proprietor was warned against employing under-age employees.

One or two years after the start of the Second World War I went down to the Cape Town docks to sign on with one of the merchant ships in the harbour. When I arrived at the docks I discovered one could not enter without a permit.

There was a queue of trawlermen at the dock gates, and I went up to one of them and told him I wanted to join the merchant navy, but did not have a permit to get into the docks. He made me stand in front of him in the queue, and said when I got to the guard-box I should just duck down and carry on.

The guard-box had a small counter on which those entering the dock gates had to place their permits. The man in front of me in the queue also helped. As he approached the guard-box he spread his elbows wide and I pushed up close behind him and ducked down below the level of the counter. The man behind also closed in, so the guard could not see there was a gap in the queue. The man in front handed over his permit-a little silver disk-for inspection, retrieved it and walked on. I huddled after him, and was in.

I made my way to where the cargo ships were berthed and approached various captains, but they all turned me down. Somebody told me to go and see Captain White, who, seemingly, was in charge of the recruitment for the merchant ships. While looking for his office I met Percy Watson. Percy was our neighbour and my brother's friend. Because he was fair of complexion he had 'crossed the line' and joined the 'white' South African Navy.

Percy could not afford to be seen with the likes of me. He gave me a wave and walked on.

Eventually I found Captain White's office and I told him I wished to join the merchant navy. He replied, 'Come back in a couple of years' time, sonny.'

When I attained my Standard Six certificate my mother, who was very proud of my achievement, said, 'My boy, now you can take up a trade.' My Uncle Peter, who lived in Simon's Town, had indicated he would try to get me apprenticed as an electrician, but nothing came of that.

My first job after leaving school was as a delivery boy, with Cape Milliners in Buitenkant Street. I remember once going to the railway goods yard at the bottom of Adderley Street, to dispatch a consignment of hats. I approached a man at a kiosk, and informed him in English that I wanted two boxes delivered to Beaufort West. The man said to me, 'Ons praat nie daardie taal hier nie.' ('We do not speak that language here.') I replied 'Ek praat nie daardie taal nie.' ('I do not speak that language').

I had refused to speak Afrikaans from a long time previously, associating the language with the police, brutality and bullying. Later, I would refer to it as the language of the oppressor. The man in the kiosk refused to serve me, and I had to ask a stranger who was standing nearby to send the boxes for me.

(Years later, on the Island, I related this incident to Nelson Mandela. He told me, 'Danny I am studying Afrikaans now, because I want to be in a position that when I speak to any official or member of the government I will be able to converse with them in their language and not have to rely on an interpreter.' He suggested I should do the same, and I did, without reservation.)

While working for Cape Milliners I attended night school, but had to withdraw after the third quarter because my mother could not afford the fees.

From there I 'graduated' to working for Old Mutual as a messenger boy. At times I would have to go down to the basement of the Old Mutual building, where huge numbers of files were kept, and I would see men sleeping there. I was told these were office cleaners, who started work in the early hours of the morning, had a break during the day, then continued again when the offices closed. It was considered a promotion if a messenger became a cleaner. After seeing these 'old' men sleeping during the day and working long hours, I lost my appetite for the job and resigned.

I was 15 when I landed a job at Bally's Shoe Factory, although I had told the manager I was 16. Dorothy Lesar, a neighbour in Lavender Hill, had recommended me for the position. I worked at this factory for nine years. The third floor was divided into two departments, the finishing department, where I worked, and the packing department. The machine I operated was near one end of the finishing department, close to the beginning of the packing department, and from where I could see everything that happened in the latter.

In about 1949, apartheid was starting to take hold of South African society and all the managers at this factory were white. For some unknown reason, though, the manager of the packing department disappeared and was replaced by one of the more senior black employees. I thought this was a terrific breakthrough. Unfortunately, his fellow workers felt they did not have to show him the same respect they had shown their previous manager, and they gave him little co-operation. After several frustrating weeks he resigned and was replaced by a white manager. I was disgusted with the packing workers and told them so.

Another incident involved Stanley Lesar, brother of the person who had recommended me for my job. He was promoted from being an 'edge presser', a job which involved smoothing the leather edge of the shoe, to 'edge trimmer', which involved operating the trimming machine. He was thrilled about the promotion. However, after a few weeks the manager called him aside and told him he had made a mistake in promoting him. The machine was reserved for 'whites only'. Stanley was both heartbroken and humiliated.

As I grew up I came up against sharper apartheid. All the beauty spots were reserved for whites, including the beaches, the parks, the swimming pools and holiday resorts. Empty 'whites only' buses roared past long queues of blacks standing at bus stops in the cold and wet, anxious to get home from work before night set in. At the hospitals the white sections were spacious and comfortable while the black sections were overcrowded and uncomfortable. At the post office the whites were served with courtesy and alacrity and the blacks in an offhand way or with contempt. Job reservation saw incompetent whites placed in positions of authority, where they bullied and humiliated blacks.

The manufacturing of all the apartheid signs that stated who could go where was an industry in itself. But then expense was no criterion when it came to enforcing apartheid. The apartheid board industry got a further boost when it was discovered that boards which used the word 'European' instead of 'white' caused confusion among white tourists from the United States of America, Canada, and Australia, among others, who joined the 'non-Europeans' in their inferior situations. Thousands of boards with the words 'European' and 'non-European' were scrapped and replaced with ones reading 'white' and 'non-white'.

All of these and more reinforced my contempt for apartheid and my active opposition to it. The insulting manner in which many whites addressed blacks was disgusting. A young white policeman might call over an elderly black, accompanied perhaps by his wife and child, and say, 'Kaffir, waar is jou dompas?' ('Kaffir, where's your passbook?')

After checking the passbook the policeman would toss it on the ground, make some threatening remark and walk away. The black man, now thoroughly humiliated in front of his wife and child, had to bend down, pick up his precious 'dompas' and move on.

I supported all anti-government activities, including prayer meetings, protest meetings and marches. In 1952, Maurice and I attended the Torch Commando protest meeting and march in Cape Town. This huge demonstration, which started with organisation in each of the provinces, was against the removal of 'Coloured' people from the common voters' roll.

English-speaking South Africans feared that if the government could remove this constitutionally-entrenched provision, they would also be able to scrap English as one of the official languages and even declare the country a republic.

I had persuaded Maurice to ask his mother if we could wear his father's First World War medals, and she grudgingly agreed. (On the way back from the march we were almost robbed of the medals by thugs but we managed to save them, otherwise we would have had to bear the wrath of Mrs Hillman.)

'Sailor' Malan, one of the heroes of the Battle of Britain, was the main speaker on the platform. He equated the nationalist government with the Nazis and called on people to oppose their cruel and undemocratic rule. The march itself was well organised and impressive. Each marcher was handed a metre-long stick with a shallow tin attached to the top. Piles of tar were placed at strategic points. Each marcher collected some tar in the tin and the tar was set alight. We gathered into ranks and marched through the city with our blazing torches held high.

When Maurice and I reached what we thought was the end of the march, we left for home. The next day we read in the papers that some marchers had continued to parliament and been badly assaulted by the police. The government accused the Torch Commando of being infiltrated and led by Communists and threatened to ban some of its members.

The Torch Commando's failure to open its ranks to all races-like the 'colour-bar' United Party-severely restricted the role it could play in fighting apartheid, and it quietly faded away.

In those days I still hoped that peaceable political change could be brought about. In the early 1960s an evangelist of the Methodist Church, Reverend Alan Walker, came from Australia to South Africa to spread the Christian message. I attended both his services at the Goodwood show-ground in Cape Town. He was tremendous. The first service took place on a Wednesday. The stands were packed. He told us a story that brought tears to the eyes of many of us.

It seemed there was a boy who had quarrelled with his father. Then, because of the quarrel, he left home. Years later the boy, now a young man, had to undertake a journey by train. The railway line ran past his parents' home. He wrote to his mother saying that he would be passing the house at a certain day and time. If, on passing the house, he saw a white towel on the hedge that ran round the house, he would know he had been forgiven. He would then get off at the next railway station and come home. If there were no towel on the hedge he would know that he had not been forgiven and would continue his journey.

As the train neared the house the young man became increasingly anxious. He told his story to a fellow passenger, who consoled him but also began to peer anxiously out the window. As the train rounded a bend the house came into view, and the young man gave a cry of joy as his fellow passenger hugged him. For there, instead of a single white towel draped over the hedge, were white towels, white sheets and white cloths draped over the hedge, the lawn, the walls and the roof of the house.

Just writing down this tale brings a tear to my eye once again.

The following Sunday evening I was back at the show-grounds, once again being enthralled by Rev Walker. Towards the close of the service he called on all of those who wished to give their hearts to God to come forward. I went, but I had an ulterior motive. I wanted to talk to Rev Walker and tell him about the great evils of apartheid. I wanted to urge him to call on all Christians throughout the country to march to the towns, sit down in the streets, block the railways and bring the country to a standstill.

I told a steward who took charge of me that I wanted to speak to Rev Walker when he came to address us in the room below the stands. The steward said it would be impossible for me to do so. He wanted me to sign certain documents, but I refused. I'm afraid I gave that steward a bit of a hard time.

Eventually Rev Walker made his appearance. We all stood up. Rev Walker then said a prayer. As soon as he had finished praying I put up my hand, but he turned towards the door with his head bowed, and walked out. I continued, long after the others had left, to tell my steward about the evils of apartheid. An official whose duty it was to lock up kept walking past our table and hinting that we should also go, and eventually we did. I then discovered that I had missed my last bus and the steward gave me a lift home. I had certainly given him a hard time and I had still not signed any papers. I hope he has forgiven me.

Soon afterwards, on a Sunday morning, I saw a notice at my church stating that a follow-up to Rev Walker's evangelical mission would be held in the Goodwood Methodist Church. The theme of the meeting, which was for delegates only, was 'Where do we go from here?'

Though I was not a delegate, I wanted to attend this meeting. The church in the early 1960s had reacted very poorly to the evils of apartheid. With the exception of a few individuals such as Rev

Michael Scott, Father Trevor Huddleston, and bishops de Blank, Winter and David Russell, no churchmen had confronted the government about its un-Christian policy. (This weak approach eventually changed with the advent of Archbishop Tutu, Dr Alan Boesak, Rev Peter Storey, Rev Beyers Naude and others.)

I went along to the 'delegates only' meeting, and entered the church without anyone challenging my credentials. I chose a seat at the edge of the aisle between the pulpit and the communion rail. Rev Theo Kotze, who had shown his opposition to apartheid-he later became Director of the Christian Institute and was also banned by the South African Government-was in the pulpit. It was an all-male gathering.

I waited for the meeting to begin. A hymn was sung. Then somebody sitting next to me said a prayer. Then more hymns and prayers followed. Rev Kotze gave a sermon and with the last hymn number on the board I realised that this gathering was not a meeting but simply an all-male church service. I put up my hand, looking at Rev Kotze. He looked at me then at two men standing at the communion rail. One of the men asked me what I wanted, perhaps thinking I was in some distress. I said I wanted to address the gathering, and everybody waited expectantly.

I then criticised the church. I said I had not lost faith in Christianity but in the church. 'Reverend, you said we must go from here to be good fathers, good husbands and good sons. The question is not where do we go from here, but where does the church go from here? You can't expect the individual to lead the church. The church must lead the individual.'

I pointed to the person sitting next to me: 'This person said that the Christian Church is going from strength to strength in South Africa. That is not true. People are turning away from the church because of its weak stance against apartheid.'

At the time I was chairperson of the Windermere Branch of the Liberal Party of South Africa, which had a large African membership. The government had declared the Western Cape a 'Coloured labour preferential area', resulting in Africans being forced out of the region to the apartheid-created 'homelands'. Families were being torn apart: if a husband belonged to one tribe and his wife to another, then they had to go their respective homelands.

I told the Goodwood gathering about these forced removals. 'Not far from here there are African marriages being broken up by the government. 'What God has put together let no man put asunder.' What is the church doing about it?'

I then sat down. There was dead silence. Then a faint ripple of applause came from the back of the church. Rev Kotze responded, asking, among other things, 'Do you believe that God is in your heart?'

I said, 'Yes, I do.'

Then he said, 'You must believe,' or words to that effect, and we ended the discussion there.

As I left the church my arm was forcefully grabbed. A man asked me if I was one who had made the speech, and I said I was.

'You should be under 90 days,' he said. (The government had recently passed a law empowering the security police to arrest anyone and detain him or her, without charge, for a 90-day period. At any stage of this period the detainee could be re-arrested and detained for a further 90 days. This type of detention could continue indefinitely).

I jerked my arm free and told my adversary it was people like him who claimed to be Christian who were actually supporting an un-Christian government. He backed off, and the small crowd that had gathered around us dispersed.

I went into church hall next door, where refreshments had been laid out for the delegates, and helped myself to a cup of tea and a slice of cake. Various groups were chatting in the hall, and I went to join one of them. As I walked toward a group, however, it simply dissolved. At first I thought it was coincidence, but when I tried to join another group it too dissolved.

I returned to the counter, put down my cup of tea and slice of cake and walked out the hall. As I was leaving an embarrassing incident occurred: I could not remember where I had parked. I passed the church three times looking for my car. People began to laugh at me. I shrugged off their laughter and eventually found my car.

I wondered how many of those people agreed with me, in their hearts, but said nothing out of fear of the consequences, of losing their jobs, of the security police, or even of what Africans would do if apartheid were abolished. How much easier it was to ignore my words and even to ridicule me when they had the chance.

White religious ministers in the 1950s and 1960s, if they were not stationed in the townships, knew very little of what was happening there. One day I received a membership card from my church, the Roodebloem Road Methodist Church in Woodstock, stating that I belonged to the 'European Circuit of the Methodist Church of South Africa'. I was furious. I telephoned my minister, Rev McCrystal, and told him I wanted to leave the church, as I felt there was no such thing as a white Christian nor a black Christian, there were only Christians.

Rev McCrystal asked to see me after church the following Sunday. He persuaded me not to leave, but rather to fight for change from within the church. I told him about the pass laws, influx control and the terrible suffering of the Africans. He seemed unaware of any of these things, and wanted to know if I could substantiate what I was saying. I went to the Civil Rights League and the Institute of Race Relations and bought five shillings worth of literature dealing with the matters we had discussed. I took the literature to his home one evening. He was not at home so I propped the parcel against his front door and left.

While I was in prison, Rev McCrystal wrote to me from Namibia (then South West Africa) to where he had been transferred. His letter bore the letterhead 'Methodist Church of South West Africa European Circuit'. I spoke about this to another minister, Rev Bosch, who was visiting the Island. I told him no matter how much good work the Methodist Church might do, the apartheid practices within the church would undermine all its good works. I also wrote to Rev McCrystal about that offending letterhead. I do not know whether he received that letter but I still have a copy of it.

(I must point out that Rev McCrystal, as the family's church minister was very good to my mother when my father died. He also came to see me when I was in detention as well as when I was on Robben Island.)

The Methodist Church no longer refers to its 'European Circuit' and even the Dutch Reformed Church eventually combined with what it then called its 'Sendingkerk' (mission church) for blacks. All too few of the ministers of these churches played any part in opposing apartheid, though we must honour those, many of whom were not in prominent positions, who did.

Chapter 4

The trawlers: 1954

I had long held an ambition, stirred by stories I had read, to go whaling. While working at the shoe factory I had twice gone down to the Netherlands Whaling Company in town, but both times I had been told that previous experience at sea was an essential qualification for joining the fleet.

Then, one Tuesday, I was given a three-day suspension for smoking at the shoe factory. We were not allowed to smoke during working hours, although many of us sneaked a quick one when we went to the toilet. On this particular occasion the foreman caught me and, wanting to make an example of someone, took me to the general manager.

For the next three days I haunted the Prince Alfred Basin, from where the trawlers would put to sea and to where they would return to offload their catch. I thought that if I managed to sign on with the trawlers I would get the sea experience that would enable me to join the whaling fleet. Maurice joined me with the same aim in mind. We made many enquiries for berths but without success. We walked round the docks for hours at a time, watching the trawlers go out to sea while others entered the harbour.

Eventually it was Friday afternoon, and the last fishing trawler going out that week, the Richard Bennett, was preparing to cast off. Maurice and I sat dejectedly on the quay, our hopes for a berth dashed, when a man came down the gangplank and approached me. He said one of the crew had failed to turn up and did I want to take his place for just the one trip. I asked if there was also a position for Maurice. He said no, the skipper had told him that he must approach only me. I accepted the job immediately, and asked Maurice to inform my family that I had gone to sea. In my excitement in getting on board I twisted my ankle, but carried on. I waved to Maurice as the Richard Bennett put out to sea.

That first trip was a ten-day one, with sailing time to and from the fishing grounds being two or more days, depending on weather conditions.

I was a bit sea-sick at first, but by the time we reached the fishing grounds my nausea had disappeared. My fellow crewmen were rough and ready, but friendly. I had heard stories of the thuggish behaviour of trawlermen but in my experience this was not so. They were hardy all right, but decent. They too had families to support and jobs to look after.

I was a spare hand, the lowest rung on a ship except for apprentice, and there were no apprentices on the Richard Bennett. There were three spare hands, and we were called on to do all the dirty and menial work. If one were not sharp enough one would get slapped with a fish-head.

Working on the fishing trawlers was the hardest job I had done. A standard joke among the crew was that they worked for 26 hours a day, with two hours overtime. And fishing off the west coast of Namibia (then still called South West Africa) was the hardest part of a hard job.

When we arrived off the Namibian coast we immediately threw the trawl, or net, over the side. We trawled for four hours at a time, then hoisted the net aboard and emptied its contents, and put it over the side again. During the day we trawled for stockfish (hake) and kingklip, and during the night for sole.

When the trawl was put over the side the ship would steam ahead so that the trawl would spread out behind it, but when it was being retrieved the ship's engines would be cut or allowed to idle, depending on weather conditions. There were two reasons for this: it was much easier getting the trawl on board when the ship was stationary, and if the ship's propeller was turning it could become entangled with the trawl.

Trawling started when the bo'sun (who was in charge of the deck) started up the winch. The roar and clatter of the winch while it was warming up was a signal for everyone to stand by.

At all times of the day and night that winch would thunder remorselessly away, causing the whole ship to vibrate and forcing us out of our slumber and staggering onto the deck. Everyone would take up their positions: the bo'sun and the deck hands would be pushing the trawl overboard; I would be guiding the rope to the winch to make sure there were no kinks in it; the skipper would be on the bridge making sure that every thing was operating smoothly.

The mouth of the trawl had two large heavy timber 'doors', each somewhat taller and wider than an ordinary house door. These doors kept the trawl below the surface and its mouth open. They had metal-covered edges to add extra weight and to protect them from being damaged on underwater obstacles such as rocks or submerged wrecks.

In front of the trawl were two thick and strong nylon or manila ropes for paying the trawl out or retrieving it. They also helped to keep the mouth of the trawl open.

The skipper used an echo-sounder to monitor the depth of the sea beneath the ship and avoid the trawl being snagged by underwater obstructions. He would be informed by radio of where the fish were running. If the fishing was poor the skipper would order 'Up trawl!' and we would race off to another area.

I have vivid recollections of our first successful haul:

After four hours of trawling the winch was placed in neutral and started up. When everyone was in position it was put into gear. At first, as the winch took up the slack, there was little to do. Another spare hand and I guided the ropes to each side. As the ropes started to take the weight of the trawl they stiffened and became taut, with drops of water shooting out from them, and we no longer had to guide them onto the winch.

The excitement mounted and there was tension in the air as all eyes were glued to the spot where we thought the trawl would appear. The winch laboured under the strain and the whole ship vibrated as it started to take the full weight of the trawl. The ship started to lean towards starboard, the side on which the trawl had been launched. Everyone silently asked himself the question 'What is the sea offering up?'

The anticipation was painful. This was the first trawl of the trip and everybody was hoping for a good catch. (Later we would look forward to a smaller catch so we could get some rest.) Then a cry of delight went up in unison from the crew, 'Thar she blows!'

The trawl came out of the deep with such force that the winch ropes slackened.

The huge black mass gradually settled back into the sea, bobbing vigorously with the swells and the turbulence it had caused when it so forcefully broke the surface. Water and foam cascaded off the sides, and concentric circles of waves and foam rushed away from the trawl before gradually dissipating into the comforting bosom of the ocean.

Suddenly the air was filled with screeching. Seagulls had arrived, hundreds of them, making a cacophony in anticipation of a feast, as they dived and wheeled over the trawl.

Everyone was smiling from ear to ear. The way the trawl had burst up meant it was packed. If it had gently broken the surface that would have indicated a poor catch. (And if it did not appear at all it would indicate a catch of maasbanker. As the saying went: 'maasbankers don't float'.)

But the massive top of the trawl indicated that the gods of the ocean had been kind. As the trawl was drawn nearer one could see the silver sheen of thousands of trapped fish. Those that had space to move were desperately trying to get out and return to the comfortable depths from which they had been plucked. The seagulls became bolder and swooped down on the fish, without much success.

The ship had righted itself as the trawl came to rest against the side. It was a huge catch. The trawl was like a huge floating mattress stretching the entire length of the ship. Now one could see the different shades of silver, as well as red, pink grey and a variety of other colours. The winch was unable to lift the whole catch. It had to be divided into three lifts. A rope was manoeuvred across the body of the trawl and pulled tight, cutting off one third. Again the winch took the strain. Slowly the demarcated section was raised from the sea.

As it was raised clear of the side rail and swung on board, it hovered over the foredeck like a big black Christmas pudding filled with gifts.

The bo'sun and the deck hands all helped to guide the trawl. It was lowered close to the deck so that when the fish came out they would not spread far and wide but be confined to a limited area. The bo'sun, wearing oilskins, bent down and moved under the trawl, which was still pouring water, grabbed the rope at the end and gave it a hard yank.

Hey presto! The end of the trawl opened and a shimmering, silver harvest of fish slithered out and onto the deck. It spread out as the now easier-running winch raised the trawl.

The bo'sun once again applied his knot to the end of the trawl and it was taken over the side so that the next third of the catch could be cordoned off.

As soon as the fish had hit the deck, the spare hands and half the crew jumped in to start sorting them, while the other half raised the next part of the trawl.

The majority of fish caught were hake, some very large. There was also a lot of kingklip, some angelfish, ribbonfish and a variety of other creatures.

We worked at full speed, thigh deep in fish. We would grab a fish by its gills, tail or even around its body (if it was not too big) and hurl it to the section of the stock pond reserved for that particular type. No fish went gently. They squirmed, bit, and pierced one's hands with their fins. The kingklip had a nasty habit of bracing itself and pushing a sharp bone out of each of its gills if one carelessly grabbed it there. Some kind soul had sold me a pair of sea boots that leaked like a sieve, but at least they protected my feet and lower legs from the sharp teeth, fins and spikes of the fish.

One also had to station oneself in such a position as to avoid being hit by 'flying' fish being hurled by someone else. I quickly became so good at flinging the fish I did not even have to check they were landing in the right place in the stock pond. I just remained bent, with arms flailing away. It was backbreaking work. To obtain relief someone would point upwards and say, 'Look, there's an aeroplane!' We would all look up, pretending to fall for it, and quickly stretch our backs.

We were still knee-deep in the first lot of fish when the second came slithering towards us, and we were once again enveloped, almost overwhelmed, by this fresh load.

The skipper called a halt to the raising of the last third of the catch, to enable all hands to work away at the mass of fish on the deck.

Night was falling when the skipper, becoming impatient, ordered that the last third be brought aboard. We had been on deck since 11:00 a.m. One could stagger to the galley for a gulp of hot tea or coffee, or stand at the side of the rail and relieve oneself into the sea, but these breaks were sparse.

As the winch laboured to bring up the last batch, the bright deck lights attached to the wheel house were pointed towards the foredeck and switched on.

We were once again engulfed in fish, this time almost waist-deep. I was glad that the last batch of fish was on deck, because now the end was in sight and we did not have to worry about another load still to be brought aboard. Then, to my horror, we were ordered away from what we were doing and told to throw the trawl over the side once more. We were now fishing for sole. Moving from the clinging mass of fish was strenuous because we had been standing in the same spot for hours. It was like pulling oneself through a swamp.

Throwing the trawl over the side this time round was not as easy as the first time, when the deck was dry and the wind was light. With a wet, rolling deck under our feet and a stiff breeze blowing, conditions on the now slowly-steaming ship became hazardous. I had to be careful not to get tangled in the rope I was playing out from the winch. (On a later trip, when the rope was slack I put my foot into a loop. As the winch took up the slack I had to throw myself backward in a desperate somersault to get free.)

In four hours' time the trawl would be hauled aboard. In my heart of hearts I was praying for a small catch. My hands were cut and painful. I could hardly close them. But the pace did not slacken and any loafer got a fish against his head. One 'old hand' told me that if I urinated into my hands it would heal the cuts and ease the pain. I did as I was advised and it did help. Later, when the fish had been cleared and we had a relaxing moment, the other crewmembers insisted on shaking hands with me. Every handshake brought me to my knees with pain, but it was done in good spirit and I accepted it as such.

When the time came for the trawl to be raised again, the wind had grown stronger, the night was cold, we were wet from our previous exertions and from the spray of the swells that were breaking against the side of the ship, and we felt miserable.

We stood by in the darkness, unable to see whether the trawl had burst out or surfaced gently. I was paying in the slack to the winch when the rope started to stiffen and then become taut as it took the full weight of the trawl. But we could hear that the strain on the winch was not as heavy as the earlier trawl. I said a silent 'Thank you'.

The wind had increased in velocity. Swells were breasting the side-rail, soaking us afresh each time. One had to grab at anything, including other seamen, to keep one's balance. One of the crewmen, an 'old sea dog', was missing. We found him standing in the chain-locker trying to catch some sleep.

The poor haul gave us the chance to clear the decks. This meant all the fish had to be beheaded, gutted, thoroughly washed and packed into baskets. The deck hands could relax now, but we spare hands had to continue. The baskets were lowered, using the winch, through a hatch to the fish room below the fore-deck. This was the mate's department but again it was the spare hands who did the work. We had to use picks and shovels to smash the hard ice in the holds, and pile it to one side while the fish were being placed in layers; first a layer of ice, then a layer of fish, then a layer of ice. This was a crucial task because if the fish were not iced properly and the inspectors found a single rotten one, the whole catch could be condemned.

The spare hands also had to work in the offal room in which all the skates, sharks and other miscellaneous creatures of the deep were cast.

On our homeward journey the spare hands would also have to get the ship shipshape, by scrubbing the deck and polishing the brass (a job I hated). There was a lot of brass on the ship. It was a tough job.

After ten days at sea I went home with my 'fry'. (Each crewmember was allowed ten pounds of fish as a bonus. On later voyages I would take home extra fish and share it with my friends and neighbours. And once, fishing on the west coast, we caught a large alligator shark and boiled its liver. I received two bottles of oil from this liver, which I took home to my sister Laura who was suffering from asthma. I think it may have helped, because today her asthma is not as chronic as it was.)

My family was overjoyed to see me, as they had not known how long I would be away.

When I went to Bally's Shoe Factory to tell the foreman I was resigning, he took me to the general manager who tried to persuade me to carry on with my job at the factory. But I was adamant. They accepted my decision and told me to call in later for my pay and other benefits such as my holiday pay.

After 48 hours ashore I returned to the Richard Bennett, hoping for another berth. Lady Luck smiled on me: the crew was a man short and I got first preference. This 'being a man short' continued for the next five trips in a row. This frequent exposure to the hard life helped me adjust to it quickly.

After my sixth trip I was informed that the crew of the Richard Bennett were all present, and I was without a job. Fortunately, the skipper put in a good word for me with the skipper of a ship sailing the Cape Columbine route, and this got me work on the trawlers for the next six months.

Being on the trawlers was not all hard work. The environment was clean and beautiful. It was a pleasure feeling the stiff breeze in one's face. The air was fresh and clean and the continuing changing moods of the sea made life interesting. Sailing to and from the fishing grounds was relaxing. On days when there were no fish and the day was pleasant we would relax on deck. On cold or stormy days we would relax in the fo'c's'le (forecastle), playing cards or reading books.

It was enjoyable standing watch at night. On the Cape Columbine route we did not fish at night because there were no sole to catch. The nights were relaxing. I would stand on watch looking into the darkness, unconsciously adjusting my balance as the ship rolled, admiring the stars, the wide open spaces. Life was thrilling, the accommodation fair, and the food good. Whatever the cook made, he chose fresh from the sea. The tea or coffeepot was always on the stove. When we were on watch we had sandwiches to help while the night away.

We slept in bunks placed around the fo'c's'le in twos, one above the other. A small table in the centre served as our dining table. On the Richard Bennett, the oldest trawler in Irvin and Johnson's fishing fleet, I sailed before the mast, meaning that the crew's quarters were in the bow of the ship.

It was an eventful and interesting life. We once caught a trawl full of sponges, of all kinds, shapes and sizes. We dumped the lot. On another occasion the trawl had just poured its silver harvest on to the deck and we rushed in to clear the mass of fish, then beat a hasty retreat as it erupted. A huge bull seal emerged and made his way down the deck till he got to a low portion of the rail and did a clumsy flip-flop back into the sea.

One evening on the west coast the bo'sun, who had taken a liking to me, asked me-which was as good as an instruction-to join him on the bridge during his watch. I enjoyed being on watch so I did not mind. (Standing on the bridge I would sometimes focus the binoculars on the Namibian coast, looking at the town of Oranjemund. I had no idea that one day I would work on the diamond mines there, or that there I would meet my wife to be.)

Because we were fishing for sole we trawled close to the seabed. When we pulled the trawl aboard all we had caught was a pile of stinking mud. The bo'sun was fed up because the skipper was fed up and so everybody else became fed up too. We tried again. Again we caught a trawl of stinking mud. In addition, the trawl had ripped on some rocks, which meant we had to spend the rest of the night repairing it. The bo'sun felt I was a jinx (all the world loves a scapegoat) and did not ask me to join him on his watch the following evening. That night he again caught a bag of mud. I was glad, because it seem to prove he was his own jinx.

Another time, we were homeward bound at full speed when we were engulfed in heavy fog. We did not slow down, but gave long blasts on our foghorn to announce our presence to other ships. We heard another foghorn, but the heavy fog distorted and muffled the sound, and we could not tell where it was coming from or how close the other ship was.

Two deckhands were instructed to stand watch at the bow. If they saw any dark shape in the mist they were to signal the bridge. The fog was so thick it was difficult to see the two deck-hands.

Suddenly, and still strenuously sounding our foghorns, both the other trawler and we emerged into bright sunlight. I looked back at the thick bank of fog we had just left, and the bright sunshine we were in now, and it seemed incredible that two such vastly different types of weather could be separated by such a straight boundary. One moment we could hardly see our hands in front of our faces and the next we could see all the way to Cape Town, with its backdrop of Table Mountain.

I loved the days when the sea was roaring and a gale was howling. I marvelled at, and was fascinated by, the tremendous power of the sea, as well as its serenity when it was tranquil. Returning from the fishing grounds on one occasion we ran head-on into a tremendous storm. The spare hands had been woken up in the early hours of the morning and told that three 44-gallon drums of fish liver had come loose and were rolling around on the deck. It was almost daybreak when we stumbled out of the fo'c's'le to salvage the drums. They had earlier been lashed to a handrail that ran along the side of the wheelhouse below the bridge. When we got outside we realised the ship was ploughing into the teeth of a gale. Huge waves of green water were crashing over the bow, racing down the length of the ship, and then pouring over the stern.

The three drums were moving about in a narrow walkway leading from the foredeck to the stern. As waves crashed over the foredeck, the drums would bob up to just below the ship's rail, then settle down again as the water drained out of the scuppers. The waves were hitting with such force that the whole ship would shudder, and the engines would race as the stern lifted out of the sea.

While trying to get to the drums we would watch, fascinated, each time the ship raced down a swell and this mighty green wall topped by a white crest towered over us. Seemingly alive, the movement of water within the swell itself seemed to urge the wall to still greater heights above the bow of the ship. There would be a momentary pause before this force crashed down on the foredeck. Each time we would turn, sprint down the walkway and shelter behind the galley as the water rushed past.

At times it seemed the ship would not make the crest of the wave. With its engines groaning under the strain, and our hearts in our mouths, it seemed as if the ship would tumble backwards. And then part of the wave would break over the bow while the rest glided away beneath. Again we would go racing down a wall of green water, like a skier down a snow- covered slope, while the ship's engines screamed in anticipation of the next strenuous climb.

As the water on deck subsided we would rush forward and try to manoeuvre those three large, heavy and cumbersome drums into position. But, before we could even put the rope around a drum, we would have to abandon it as the next mighty wave threatened us.

We then hit on the idea of manoeuvring the drums into position while the deck was still full of water, and the drums were floating.

We waited for the full force of a wave to pass us, then plunged into the swirling water on the deck, manhandled a drum into position, managed another, then abandoned them as yet another wall of water came surging towards us.

Because the situation was so dangerous one of us acted as lookout while the other two tried their best to lash the drums in position. But it was impossible. No sooner had we positioned two drums than the lookout would shout 'Run!'

We decided that under these conditions we would, at best, be able to tie down only two of the drums. We made sure that no-one on the bridge was watching us, waited for the next wave to rush past, plunged into the still-surging water, and gave one of the floating drums the old 'heave ho' over the stern.

We had a fleeting glimpse of the drum, before it disappeared in the swirling water, being washed away at great speed. It was a sobering moment. We realised that if one of us had gone over he would not have stood a chance.

At our next attempt we managed to lash the two remaining drums securely to the rail. We reported to the skipper that one had been washed overboard. He accepted our explanation, glad, probably, that he had not lost his commission on all three.

For all the hard work and exhilaration of life on the trawlers, it was simply a preparation for the real thing: the whalers. And that, possibly, was preparation for the hard life on the Island and the companionship that was to follow.

Chapter 5

The whalers: 1954 - 1955

December 1954: the recruitment office of the Netherlands Whaling Company had opened for the current whaling season. After eight hard but happy months on the trawlers I had sea experience and could now apply for a job on the whalers.

I did not want to risk failing the medical examination, and, as two of my upper teeth were bad, I went to a dentist, a Dr Kleyne at Castle Bridge, Hanover Street, and asked him to extract all my teeth. He refused, saying he would take out only the teeth in my upper jaw. Today, 39 years later, I still have all of my teeth in my lower jaw.

When I reported to the hall where the medical examination was to be held there were a large number of men already there. The examination was straightforward at first, but then we came to a part that I dreaded: providing a urine sample. I always found it difficult to do this while others looked on, impatient for me to finish so they could have their turn. (Years later, on Robben Island, Raymond Mhlaba and I were at the doctor and the doctor asked him for a urine sample. Raymond took a glass phial and, without batting an eyelid, turned his back to us and filled it. I admired him for that.) That day at the medical examination I took a phial, found a quiet corner and, after a bit of huffing and puffing, managed to pee. I passed the medical with flying colours, and got the job.

On 15 December 1954, the Willem Barendsz, factory ship of the Netherlands Whaling Fleet, was to depart for the Antarctic at 10:00 a.m. She was carrying supplies for the catchers and would process the whales they caught during the three-month season. She would leave the Antarctic before the long nights and wild storms set in.

My father came along to see me off, but the departure of the ship was delayed so he left. My brother Norman came along with some members of the Hillman family but they too had to leave before we sailed. When we finally left, at about 3:00 p.m., there was no one to whom I could wave.

The sun shone brightly on a beautiful summer's day. The band played all the sentimental numbers, such as 'Wish me luck as you wave me good-bye', and 'We'll meet again'. Colourful streamers were strung from ship to quay and from quay to ship. The mood was happy and excited, the quay crowded with well-wishers. Everyone on the ship waved to someone on the quay and shouted last-minute messages. The ship's whistle gave three shrill blasts. The mooring ropes were removed and thrown to the quay. One rope fell into the water and was pulled on to the quay. Was that an omen? The murmuring engines increased in volume, and the ship moved away from the quay. Louder shouts came from those on the quay and from those on the ship. I felt left out because I had no one to wave to. I was once again on my own. I started to wave but I knew no one was responding.

We cleared the harbour. The voyage had begun and I was part of it.

On our way to the Antarctic the catchers were hunting sperm whales and fin whales. This would continue until we reached the Antarctic, where the blue whale would be our most prized catch. I have experience only of the sperm, fin and blue whales, which I subsequently found to be beautiful and gentle creatures whose fate was to die gruesome deaths as the iron harpoons plunged into their bodies.

Evolution teaches us that, in the mists of time, the ancestors of these giant whales were terrestrial animals equipped with four legs. Gradually, over time, the sea started to encroach on their habitat, forcing them to adapt to their changing environment or die. They adapted. Their forelegs evolved into stunted flippers while their hind-legs, which can still be traced though their bone-structure, were absorbed.

The sperm whale, the 'Moby Dick' type, has a huge, blunt snout made up of hard blubber. Its diet consists mainly of fish, octopus and the giant squid, which can grow up to 33 feet in length. When the sperm whale tackles a giant squid it is a fight to the death. The squid will wrap itself around the head of the whale and block its blowhole in an attempt to drown it. The whale, now also fighting for its life, will use its thick, blubber-filled head like a battering ram and smash the squid into rocks on the seabed. All the sperm whales we caught had huge, deep scars on their heads.

Some of the sailors and workers on board had carved beautiful figures from the teeth of the sperm whale.

The blue whale, a dark slate-blue, sleek in body and massive in size, is the biggest mammal on earth and, possibly, the most defenceless. Instead of teeth it has baleen, which descend from its upper jaw. Baleen can, perhaps, be likened to the vertical slats of a venetian blind, except they are broad at the upper gum and narrower further down. Each slat of baleen overlaps the next. Behind the baleen is a mass of unruly hair. To eat, the whale opens its huge mouth, takes a mighty mouthful of water, and forces it out again through the baleen with its tongue. The baleen acts as a filtering system, trapping plankton and shrimp. An adult blue whale can consume a prodigious amount (around six tons) of shrimps and plankton a day. Again the marvel of nature is evident: the largest animal in the world lives on one of the smallest. The throat of the whale is relatively small. Its flukes are massive but its dorsal fins are small and look like stumps. Its eyes are large and soft, set in the sides of the head. Its underside has long grooves in its skin, with the sex organs situated below the stomach.

It was illegal to shoot undersized (less than 55 feet) and pregnant whales. If we did shoot either this would be noted by international inspectors berthed on the factory ship. If the shooting of undersized or pregnant whales occurred too often, fines would be levied on the guilty parties.

There were times when the body of a whale would be winched on board with milk shooting out of its breasts, situated each side of its vagina. This meant that, somewhere in that vast ocean, there was a baby whale, not yet weaned, which had lost its mother.

The fin whale is a replica of the blue, excepting it is grey and smaller.

The blue and fin whales' only enemy, besides man, is the orca, or killer whale. Orca are fearsome. On one occasion we saw six huge dorsal fins, each easily three times the height of an average shark's, screaming through the water at tremendous speed. They were intent on attacking the dead whales being towed by the factory ship. The captain shot at them with a rifle. The orca would go for the tongue of a dead whale, and also take huge bites out of its body, causing financial loss to the expedition.

The eardrum of the blue and fin whales is shaped like half a human face. If you placed two of them together and coloured in eyes and lips it would look just like a face. There was much competition to obtain those eardrums but the flenchers (men who used long-handled knives with curved blades to cut the blubber free from the whale's body) were in the best position to obtain them. A flencher with whom I had a good working relationship once gave me an eardrum while I was working on deck. I did not want to leave it lying around, and at the first opportunity I slipped into the locker where the harpoons were stored to hide it.

The harpoons were not lashed, as they should have been, but were leaning against the side of the locker. I bent down to hide the eardrum behind the harpoons when the ship rolled, and about 15 of the heavy harpoons crashed down on me. I could not move because of their weight. I hated calling for help, but I had no choice; I was trapped. After several calls, each one more desperate than the last, I was finally discovered and helped out. It seemed my rescuers initially had no idea where the calls for help were coming from.

The blue whale, found in the Antarctic itself, was the main prize of the whalers. The largest we shot was about 90 feet long. Estimated at a ton a foot, that whale weighed about 90 tons.

The blubber of the blue whale is extremely thick. When a whale was dissected on board, the flencher would make a few strategic cuts in its flesh, hook a wire sling into them, then attach the sling to a cable running from a steam-winch situated high above the deck. The flencher would give a signal to the winchman, and the winch would start up and tear one long strip of blubber from the carcass. This would be manoeuvred over a huge pot and dropped into it. The exercise would be repeated until the carcass was stripped bare of blubber. The deck was divided into two large sections: the meat deck and the bone deck, on which I worked.

When a whale was shot it was pumped full of air to keep it afloat. A staff with a flag and number attached to it would be plunged into it, indicating to which whaling company the whale belonged and the catcher responsible for shooting it. The skipper of the catcher would radio the towboats, which would tow the bodies to the factory ship. If the factory ship were close enough it would fetch the floating whale itself, and if there were no whales to tow the towboats would also hunt.

When the whales reached the factory ship they were tied to the stern until we on the deck were ready to receive the carcasses. When we were ready, two large hooks were lowered and manoeuvred until they hooked on to the large flukes of the whale. These hooks were attached to a very thick cable, which in turn was attached to the most powerful winch on the ship. This winch, situated on the fore-deck, would pull the body through a huge opening in the hull of the ship and up an incline. The winch would continue to drag the body of the whale the entire length of the deck, pausing at the various stations to allow the teams of workers to perform their different duties.

Because ours was a small factory ship we did not store the meat of the whale. Instead we dumped it over the side. There was an area on the side of the ship where the guard-rail could be removed. We would take cables from two winches situated either side of the gap in the rail, and connect them behind the huge mound of meat. When the winches pulled the cables taut it would force the meat over the edge.

We were about to dump one day when the foreman clambered up the side of the meat to clear an obstruction. The winchmen, not aware that he was there, started up their winches. As the mountain of meat slid towards the edge, the foreman came scrambling and clawing over the top in a desperate attempt to get clear. We all began shouting over the noise of the winches and waving our arms wildly, and the winchmen eventually got the message and stopped their machines.

Another potentially fatal mishap occurred when a whale on the deck broke its moorings in bad weather. Everybody scattered as it started to roll around on the deck. Eventually it rolled against the rail and was secured there until the storm abated.

Apart from those incidents it was pretty much smooth sailing. I was employed on the factory ship as a labourer. I had requested a transfer to a catcher but the request was refused because I lacked the necessary experience. On the factory ship the workers, as opposed to the sailors, were divided into two 12-hour shifts. One group did the nightshift for the first half of the season and then swapped with the dayshift for the remainder of the trip.

My job was to take the huge whale jawbones to a steam-driven saw, where they would be sawn into manageable chunks, and then take them to the pot openings around the perimeter of the deck. There were two pots under each opening, and these were rotated at four-hour intervals. Once the sawn-off parts of the jawbone or backbone were put into a pot the lid was securely tightened, and the oil in the bones extracted through the application of tremendous heat. When the bones were eventually discarded they had shrunk considerably. While we were filling one pot the bones in the other would be boiling away.

The tool I used to drag the bones was a light shaft of iron, a little thicker than a pencil and the length of a golf club, with a handle on one end and a hook on the other. During the latter part of the season, when I was on night shift and it was extremely cold, it was very painful handling this cold iron instrument. We could not wear gloves because with all the water and blood we were exposed to they would soon have frozen solid.

The food was plain but substantial. Sometimes, when working during the cold nights, we would cut a piece of meat from a whale and cook it on the winch.

We had no cash on the ship, besides what one came on board with. We were allowed to buy whatever we needed from the ship's shop on credit, to be deducted from our pay at the end of the voyage. Our currency on the ship was American cigarettes.

We would trade them for boots, jerseys, bottles of gin or whatever we could get. Every Wednesday and Sunday we were issued a fair-sized tot of gin, and on Sundays we were also issued a small bottle of beer. In addition we each received a tot of gin for every 10 000 barrels of whale oil produced. Some of the workers did not drink their rations, saving them instead in bottles that they would later trade. This was a boon to the drinkers because everything could be bought at the shop except hard liquor.

American cigarettes were also the main currency for gambling. I won tens of thousands of cigarettes. I used to daydream about how much I would be able to sell the cigarettes for, back home. (In reality I never sold one packet; I gave them away, mostly to friends.)

On Christmas Day there was a festive spirit aboard the ship. It was a holiday, and presents were distributed. Everyone on board received one of the gifts, which had been sent 'to those on the high seas' by anonymous donors. I got a blue scarf with a little note attached wishing me a safe journey home. I was thrilled with it. In my heart I thanked the unknown donor.

When a tanker came alongside to remove the oil we had obtained from the whales, or when a catcher came alongside to bunker, the bodies of two large whales would be placed head to head between the ships as fenders. As the swell rose the ships would part slightly and the bodies of the whales would expand to their normal girth but, when the swell receded, the bodies would absorb the tremendous impact of the weight of the two ships, preventing them from crashing into each other. This ebb and flow of the swells never ceased, and the two ships would sit alongside each other for up to 48 hours while the bodies of the whales continuously absorbed that tremendous pressure of thousands of tons of steel, crashing into them from either side. One can imagine the colossal strength and resilience of those magnificent giants of the deep.

Looking back now, I realise how cruel is the hunting of whales. If the whale was a dangerous or an aggressive animal then, perhaps, I could temper my conscience. But the whale is a gentle and peaceful creature. It harms nothing, except the plankton and shrimps it eats by the ton. Those stories about whales charging ships head on are, to my mind, an exaggeration. Any harpooned animal would rush around frantically in its pain and its desperate attempt to escape. If a boat or ship got in the way of a charging head or flailing flukes, it was just an accident.

The catcher, which was the size of a corvette (in fact, after the war corvettes were converted into catchers), was small, sleek, and built for speed. Below deck there was a great reel of nylon rope. This was led through the deck and attached to a harpoon. The hollow shaft of the harpoon was made of light metal while its head was of heavy metal. In the nose of the harpoon was a hollow in which a charge of explosives would be placed. On each of four sides of the head was a steel rod as thick as a pencil, and as long as an adult's middle finger. When the harpoon plunged into the body of the whale the charge in the nose of the harpoon would explode and the finger-like steel rods would open up, preventing the harpoon from pulling loose. This shot was known as 'die vas skoot' (the holding shot), while the final shot into the whale was known as 'die dood skoot' (the death shot).

A seaman would stand in the crow's nest, looking for telltale signs of water vapour. Before sounding, or diving deep, a whale takes in a huge gulp of oxygen. Resurfacing after about 40 minutes, it expels the carbon dioxide through its blowhole with gusto. The hot air expelled from the whale's body mixes with the cold air above the surface of the sea giving rise to a condensed column of vapour-to the joy of the whalers and the eventual despair and death of the whale.

When the lookout spots this water vapour he informs the skipper, who issues instructions to the helmsman. The rest of the crew stand by at their various stations.

The skipper, who is also the gunner, stands ready at the loaded harpoon gun and awaits further information from the lookout.

The lookout has to be sharp. If there is a pod of whales he has to be able to differentiate between those which are pregnant or undersize and those which can be legally caught. The whales might be swimming at speed, and as they swim they continually change positions within the pod itself.

The lookout identifies which whale is to be shot and informs the skipper accordingly, for example, 'third to the starboard'. The skipper braces himself against the rolling and heaving deck, gripping the gun handle and standing firm. When they get within range of the chosen target, he fires. The harpoon snakes though the air and plunges into the whale's body, the explosive charge going off a split second after impact.

There is wild commotion in the sea as the wounded whale reacts, and the rest of the pod dives for safety. The chase is on; the harpooned whale is played like a fisherman would play a fish. When the whale sounds the nylon rope is paid out, allowing it to 'run'. The angle of the rope indicates which direction it is travelling. The catcher follows, giving or taking in slack as the situation requires. When the whale breaks the surface the catcher thunders down on it, forcing it to sound before it has a chance to take in more air. The whale, weakened by its wound as well as its lack of air, is relentlessly pursued. Its dives become shallower, and its attempts to surface more frequent. Eventually the whale is so exhausted it just flounders on the surface. Even the roar of the engines bearing down on it fails to frighten the whale any more. It is beyond fear.

The skipper fires another harpoon (without an attached rope) into the body of the now helpless whale. If necessary, a third harpoon ('die dood skoot') is fired, ensuring the death of the whale. The whale is pumped full of air. A shaft bearing a flag and a number is plunged into its body. The towboats and factory ship are informed of its position. Whoever is in the best position to pick it up does so. The sea is red with blood. The gaping wounds in the body of the whale are ghastly. The skipper and his crew rejoice.

In the Antarctic, our captain received an SOS from some catchers trapped in pack ice, which was becoming harder and thicker as the winter became more and more threatening. We sailed to the pack ice and simply went crashing through it. I was sharing a cabin in the factory ship's bows, and as the ice broke apart and turned over it sounded like big guns being fired: 'Boom! Boom!'.

The underside of the pack ice was rugged and a dirty grey, quite a contrast to its upper side which was smooth and pristine white.

We eventually reached the trapped catchers and made our way to the open sea, with the catchers following us along the channel we opened in the pack ice. It reminded me of a mother duck in a pond being followed by her ducklings.

The pack ice was magic. It could transform a raging sea into a calm one. Whenever there was a big storm and we, and the catchers, were being thrown around like corks, making it impossible to work on deck, the captain would head for the pack ice. It might only be a short distance away, but the sea there would be relatively calm. I always marvelled at this sudden transformation of sea conditions and the influence the pack ice had on the mighty swells.

We encountered many huge icebergs floating around in all their glory. They were beautiful in their shimmering coats of purest white. Many of them had deep caverns on their sides. Delicate pastel shades would flow into each other, from the pristine white on the outside to gentle shades of blue and green, until the colours disappeared into the cavern itself.

On a sunny day the Antarctic was beautiful. The air was fresh and invigorating, and sparkled with cleanliness, while the majestic icebergs floated gently in the ice-cold sea. It was tranquillity itself.

There was one thing I seemed to miss seeing, and that was the Aurora Australis, or Southern Lights. I do not know if I saw it and did not recognise it, or whether we left the Antarctic before this phenomenon appeared. What I do remember seeing, however, was the sun setting partly below the horizon and then rising again. I was led to wonder if the Antarctic could be considered one of the wonders of the world.

On the way back to Cape Town from the Antarctic we ran into a tremendous storm in the notorious Roaring Forties. There was no pack ice here that we could run to for sanctuary. The factory ship was pounded by swells reported to be between 60 to 80 feet high. There were a number of catchers travelling with us, and we watched as they battled to climb the tremendously steep swells, slid down the other side, then disappeared. We would wait with gut-wrenching suspense for them to re-appear again. Time and again we saw them emerging from a watery chasm and climbing their way to the crest of the next huge swell.

We landed in Cape Town on an evening some time in March 1955, to a happy reception. I arrived home to a joyous reunion with my happy and loyal family. I immediately gave my father two boxes of Holland cigars I had brought ashore with me, and my mother a large whale's tooth I had picked up during the trip. I handed cartons of cigarettes to everyone who was present. I also gave my mother a substantial portion of my pay.

Shortly afterwards I contacted a Mr Adams, a taxi driver who operated in the docks, and told him that my friend Noel 'Connie' Conway and I had some contraband-cigarettes, cigars, boots and jerseys-on board the ship, and asked if he could smuggle it out the docks for us. He said he would arrange it. The next morning Connie and I went down to the Willem Barendsz, collected our contraband, and gave it to Mr Adams to take out. We met him outside the dock gates and compensated him accordingly.

I had fulfilled one burning ambition: to go whaling. Others were soon to arise. The most important one, by far, was to see a non-racial democratic government installed in South Africa. But that, as it turned out, was going to take another 40 years.

Chapter 6

Diamonds in the desert: 1955 - 1959

After a three-month stint on the whalers I was flush, and I painted the town red. But my money, like many good things, soon ran out.

I began to prowl the docks again, looking for a job on the trawlers, but the skippers had orders not to employ anybody who had left to do seasonal work. Many people, myself included, used the trawlers as a stopgap between seasonal jobs which paid much better. The owners wanted crewmembers who would work all year round.

Six weeks passed and I was still unemployed. I felt guilty, despite having given my mother a large amount of money when I returned from the whalers. I felt I was sponging on my family, expecting a plate of food every day yet making no contribution in return.

I told Maurice I was going to Johannesburg to look for a job, possibly on the mines, and he said he would come with me. I had enough money only for a single railway ticket to Johannesburg so Maurice, who was working as an agent for a cosmetics firm and had his own office, said he was going to sell his desk to raise money. He never did sell his desk; perhaps he could not find a buyer.

I said goodbye to my family and left on my own for Johannesburg, a place to which I had never been before. My sister Laura gave me about two dozen scones for the journey. On the train I bit into a scone and felt something hard inside it. I opened it up and looked inside. There was a shilling piece. I checked the other scones and in each of them found a sixpence or a shilling. In some, the money had been turned green by the butter. This money would prove useful later on.

When I reached Johannesburg I had nowhere to go, nor did I know anyone. I stored my kitbag in a railway station locker. Every time I wanted access to the bag I had to pay an official a 'tickey' (three cents).

That evening, and the following two, I slept on a bench on the railway station. At 5:00 a.m. the police would order us off the station. I would walk around the town until about 7:00 a.m. when I would return to the station. I would do my ablutions in the toilet, then go and collect my kitbag and take out a roast potato for breakfast. I went to the locker so often that after a while the guard stopped asking for a tickey. During the day I walked around Johannesburg looking for work, without any success.

The nights on the station were cold. There was a fountain on the station and throughout the night I would hear this fountain tinkling away. It made the nights seem even colder.

On the third night I was there, another 'lost soul' came to share my bench. He was shivering with cold. I was wearing a sports-jacket but I also had a suit of clothes in my kitbag. I collected my suit jacket from the locker and loaned my sports-jacket to this chap for the night. The next morning, when I awoke, he had disappeared with my jacket and my last pound note, which was in the top pocket. I just had to grin and bear it.

Towards the evening of the fourth day I remembered that my brother Ryland had asked me to pass on his regards to his sister-in-law, Edna, and her husband, Richard. I looked through my papers and found the address. It was in Smal Street, which I had come across previously in my wanderings through the city and had no difficulty in finding again.

I must have arrived at Edna and Richard's home some time after 6:00 p.m. Richard answered the door and invited me in. He had problems. He was trying to feed his two little children but was receiving no co-operation from them. They were kicking, screaming and spitting. I told Richard that Ryland sent his regards to him and Edna, and left.

I was almost at the front door when it opened and Edna came in. 'Eddie!' she said. 'How are you and what are you doing in Johannesburg?'

I said I was well, that Ryland sent his regards and that I was just leaving. 'No!' she said. 'You must come and have some soup with us.'

I was reluctant to stay, but she insisted. While we were eating our soup Edna asked me where I was staying. I told her that I was staying down the road. We continued talking. Then she asked me again, 'Eddie, where are you staying?'

I replied, 'Just down the road.'

This time she was suspicious of my answer. 'Where down the road?' she demanded.

I told her I was sleeping on the station.

'What!' she said. She told Richard to go down to the station with me, fetch my kitbag and return with me, because I was going to stay with them for a while.

I spent the next two weeks there, during which time I continued looking for employment. After numerous attempts to find work had failed, Richard suggested that I go make inquiries at the Anglo-American building in Commissioner Street. I did so, and was interviewed by a Mr Cairns. He then sent me through to another office where I met my namesake, a Mr Daniels. Mr Daniels asked if I would be prepared to work on the diamond mines in South West Africa. I said I certainly would, saying quietly to myself that I would be prepared to go to China, if necessary. He asked when I would be able to start, and I said, 'Immediately.'

He wanted to know when I would be leaving for Cape Town. I replied I did not know, as I had come up from Cape Town on a single ticket and had no money for the return trip. He said, 'Don't worry, the company will pay your fare to Cape Town by train and to Oranjemund by air. These expenses will be deducted from your pay.' I agreed.

I said goodbye to Richard and Edna, thanked them for their hospitality, returned to Cape Town for a quick hello and goodbye to my family, and flew to Oranjemund. From my first month's pay, which was far more than I expected, I sent Richard and Edna a sum which I felt was fair recompense for putting me up.

Oranjemund is a coastal desert town in the south of Namibia, close to the mouth of the Orange River, which forms the border between South Africa and Namibia. It is a diamond-mining town owned entirely by the Anglo-American Corporation.

After working for Consolidated Diamond Mines (An Anglo-American subsidiary) for about a month, I discovered that only whites and Ovambos were employed there: the whites to do skilled and semi-skilled work and the Ovambos the menial work. It seemed I was accepted as a white person. Because I was desperate for a job I decided to ignore this apartheid policy.

The accommodation in the town consisted of both married and single quarters. Those employees who were on the office staff stayed in slightly better quarters than their counterparts. At the mess, which was a large, spacious building, the office staff had their meals in the front of the mess while the workers had theirs at the back. There was also a squash court, two tennis courts, a swimming pool, a large shop catering to all tastes, a barber, a bottle store and a bar with a ladies' lounge and snooker room, and a cricket and a rugby field.

The skilled workers were mainly English immigrants, while the semi-skilled employees were mainly Afrikaners. Below the surface of the social relationships lurked a mutual antipathy, although the Afrikaners seemed more resentful of the English than the English of them. I worked mostly with the Afrikaners. If someone in the distance was driving badly or some machine had broken down or if the cat had kittens then the Afrikaners would say, 'Look at what that 'Rooinek' (redneck) is doing!'

The English in turn referred to the Afrikaners as 'hairy backs', but with less malice.

I mixed easily with either group. At work and where I lived, I socialised mostly with Afrikaners, but when in town or at the bar mostly with English and Scottish people. I was in the unique position of being able to poke fun at either group. Thus when I was with either group and an error had been made because of prejudice, I would poke fun at them, which both groups took in good spirit.

The social contrast between the British and the Afrikaners was pronounced. The British had recently emerged from the devastating war against Hitler. They had left a country where rationing was the order of the day and come to one that was, relatively speaking, flowing with milk and honey, and were more carefree in their lifestyle. After work, and at weekends, it was mostly the British who would frequent the pubs. The Afrikaners on the other hand were, by-and-large, conservative in their outlook.

The different religious denominations took it in turns to use the single church in the town. When it was the turn of the Dutch Reformed Church the church would be packed to overflowing. On other Sundays attendance was quite sparse.

At the end of the month, when we received our pay, there were ongoing parties, drinking and gambling. On one occasion a married couple was found swimming naked in the pool in the early hours of the morning. The situation was aggravated by the fact that, although they were married, it wasn't to each other.

I started work as a scoop operator. The scoop was a large machine built on the chassis of an obsolete Sherman tank. Its large tracks made it ideal for carrying heavy machinery across the desert sands. The scoop had a large wheel in front. Attached to this wheel were six scoops, each the size of a large bucket. As each scoop bit into the overburden (surface sand) it would take up a bucketful of sand and deposit it onto a conveyor belt on the side of the machine. This would carry the sand backwards and drop it onto another conveyor belt that led out from the rear of the scoop. This belt, in turn, would drop the sand into the 'catcher' of a 'stacker tank', another long conveyor belt that was also built on a Sherman tank chassis. Depending on how far from the area we were clearing we wanted to dispose of the sand, we could harness any number of stacker tanks.

The reason for shifting the overburden and depositing it elsewhere was to get to the bedrock. Beneath the bedrock were the diamonds. The story went that the diamonds had been carried from far inland by the Fish and Orange Rivers and deposited around the mouth of the Orange River, some two million years ago. However this story had been challenged, as strenuous attempts to discover a mother-lode along the upper riverbeds had been unsuccessful. The presence of diamonds in such abundance on the Namibian coast has yet to be explained.

Once the overburden had been removed and the bedrock exposed, a 'blaster' would drill holes in the bedrock and plant sticks of explosive in them. These would be detonated, blowing the bedrock apart and exposing the gullies and crevices in which the diamonds nestled. After the bedrock had been blown apart the bulldozers, excavators and other large earthmoving machinery would move in to clear the area of the tons of loose bedrock. Then sweepers would move in to clear the crevices and gullies of sand and stones. Any diamonds found in this process would be collected and sent to the Heavy Mineral Sorting (HMS) plant for sorting. From there they would be sent off for cutting and finally polishing, after which they would be sold.

Being a scoop operator was a pleasant job. Each shift was twelve hours, alternating between day and night shift every other week. Most of us took a radio with us when we went on duty. The radio was good company during the early morning hours of the night shift.

On the balmy summer nights and in the early hours of the morning the desert was beautiful. When I had a break I would wander around on the desert sands, shimmering eerily in the soft moonlight. One could hear the silence and the bright stars seemed so much closer. The huge bright lights on the scoop and on the stacker tanks, which enabled us to see what we were doing during the night shift, seemed almost obscene as they assaulted the soft night with their fierce lights. To appreciate the beauty of the desert night one had to move far away from the brazen lights into the soft embrace of the night itself. In this great sphere of nature one would feel humble and insignificant but one would also find an inner peace.

On some nights the wind roared and the onslaught of the stinging sand against the machinery sounded like sheets of rain. Then one sat huddled in the cabin, shivering and waiting impatiently for the shift to end.

When going on shift we would be taken to work by lorry. The driver would drop each of us near our respective machines and pick up the operators of the previous shift. Each operator would have a group of labourers working with him. These labourers were also transported by lorry if their compounds were far away, but otherwise they had to walk to and from their places of work.

Karlie Burger, the lorry driver, was a racist. At every opportunity he would be nasty to the Ovambos. If the cab of the lorry was full of scoop operators, all whites, and the next operator had to sit in the back of the lorry, then Karlie would demand that the Ovambos get off the back and walk the rest of the way home. He would do this even if they were still far from home or we were in the middle of a sandstorm.

I objected to this crude behaviour. I would often give up my place in the cab to an operator who had just been picked up and go sit in the back with the Ovambos. If the next operator to be picked up objected to sitting with them then they would still have to get off and walk the rest of the way home, but at least my action would have saved them a few kilometres.

One morning, returning from nightshift, I was sitting in the cab between Karlie Burger and Andries Dreyer. It had rained during the night and the potholes in the road had filled with water. There were lots of Ovambos walking on the side of the road on their way to work. Karlie tried his best to splash them by deliberately driving into the puddles of water. At first he was not successful, but then he spotted a chap who was almost level with a large puddle of muddy water. He accelerated, timed his move and crashed the left front wheel of the lorry into the pool of water just as the Ovambo was alongside it. Both Karlie and Andries burst out laughing as the fellow stopped and looked indignantly at his drenched, muddy clothes and the receding lorry

I did not laugh; I just looked straight ahead. When they realised I was not amused their laughter died down. I told Karlie it was a mean thing he had done. I pointed out to him that that worker was not in a position to obtain a change of clothes or wash the mud off, and would have to work in those muddy clothes all day.

Karlie hated me because I stuck up for the Ovambo workers. One day I smacked him for pushing a worker around, and he reported me to our foreman, Oom Tom (Uncle Tom). After giving me a dressing down, Oom Tom told me as I left his office, 'Next time give him one from me as well.'

About ten of us (the number varied at times) worked out in the desert and lived at Mittag, a small settlement of prefabricated shelters about 25 kilometres from Oranjemund.

There was a mess, with a kitchen attached, which doubled as a recreation room, and there were showers with hot and cold running water. But the place was desolate, and in the middle of nowhere.

For working out in the desert we received extra pay, called a 'field allowance'. Once a week a lorry-driver would bring post and any urgently needed supplies and, I suppose, check to see whether we were still sane and alive.

At weekends, all labourers were confined to their respective compounds unless they had received special written permission from their supervisors to go and visit others in the vicinity. Many of the supervisors would first humiliate their labourers before giving them permission. The labourers would have to crawl around on the floor, perform various antics, and would receive a few light kicks or smacks before receiving the all-important document.

I granted permission readily, but then the labourers of the other supervisors started to queue at my door every Sunday morning. After a while the other supervisors started to take exception to me granting their labourers permission to go and visit other compounds, and I had to abandon the practice.

While working at Mittag we were allowed one weekend a month in town, to collect our pay. And we would go to town, literally and figuratively. We would party from Friday night or Saturday morning (depending on when the lorry fetched us) right through till Monday morning. We would buy liquor to last us the rest of the month, drink it all over the weekend then buy another supply on the Monday morning before leaving. When we arrived in Oranjemund the whole of the single quarters would join us in a drinking spree.

While at Mittag I received an assessment from the revenue authorities, telling me I owed £40 income tax for the year. I thought to myself that I would get someone else to pay it for me, and on the next trip into town I joined a poker school. We played cards, drank liquor, smoked cigarettes, and swapped stories from the Friday night right through to 10:00 on Sunday morning when the pub opened. The final game ended with only two of us left, everyone else having dropped out of the bidding, and the table groaning under the weight of money on it. The other man's three queens beat my three tens. That finished me. I had lost my month's salary, had to borrow money to see me through to the end of the following month, and I still had to pay my £40 income tax.

This happened almost forty years ago, and I have never gambled since.

After some time at Mittag I was transferred to Oranjemund, where I worked as a gantry crane driver at a place called Central Fields. But my hectic lifestyle of drinking continued. It was the type of lifestyle that had led many a person to become an alcoholic. What saved me from becoming an alcoholic was sport.

I was considered to be the leading squash player in Oranjemund at the time, and was constantly challenged to play. I never refused a challenge, and played squash almost every night as well as at weekends. Sometimes we would play a system where the winner holds the court, and I would be on the court for most of the day. (I later discovered that the standard of squash in Oranjemund was pretty low, when I played a student from the University of Cape Town and he beat me in nine straight games.)

I met my wife-to-be, Eleanor, in Oranjemund. At the time she was married to Jack (Jock) Buchanan, a good friend of mine and my main adversary at squash. We would play squash every Sunday morning with the loser buying the first round of drinks. After that our drinking day would start in earnest.

One Saturday evening, after the club pub had closed, Jock, Eleanor, Sandy Lachlan and I went along with a mutual friend, Johnny Raul, to a place in Oranjemund called Texas. Johnny had told us that some friends of his were having a 'braai' (barbecue) and invited us to come along. When we arrived at the braai we found all of the people there were Afrikaners. We knew a couple of them, but felt we were definitely persona non grata. After a while Johnny disappeared. As the night wore on a huge chap by the name of Koos started to throw his weight around, and Jock, Sandy and I braced ourselves for trouble. Then Koos picked on Jock.

Earlier that evening we had attended a function at the club, and each of us had received a small ticket that was pinned to our lapels to show we had paid our entrance fee. Jock still had his ticket pinned to his lapel. Koos came up to Jock, ripped the ticket off, and said drunkenly, 'Wat is hierdie?' ('What's this?'). Then he tore it in half and threw it on the ground. Jock, who was half the size of Koos, grabbed him by the front of his shirt and told him to pick up the ticket.

Even though the music was blaring away it felt as if there was absolute silence. Everyone was tense and on the alert, and time stood still.

I do not know if Koos's guardian angel whispered to him that Jock was an ex-paratrooper, or if he noticed something else, but Koos bent down, picked up the bits of the ticket and handed them back to Jock. Suddenly we could hear the music again, everyone relaxed and the world started to turn again. Then Jock, pointing to his lapel, told Koos, 'Put it back!'

Again there was absolute silence, and everything seemed to be moving in a slow but exaggerated manner. Then Koos, in his drunken state, started to pin the two pieces of Jock's ticket to his lapel. He made a clumsy effort, but Jock did not pursue the issue.

Koos stumbled off. We realised we had overstayed our welcome and left. The following day I met one of the chaps who was at the braai and asked him if anything untoward had happened after we left. He replied that after falling about for a while, Koos had gone outside and tried to kick down a wooden fence.

Many attempts were made to steal diamonds from CDM. One generally heard only of the attempts that had failed. Perhaps those who succeeded are today living in obscure luxury, or have bought respectability.

Among the stories we heard was that of a prospector. Diamond prospectors were employed by CDM to go out to certain areas in the desert, sink holes into the sand and assess which would be the most profitable areas to mine. Their job was a lonely and isolated one, which made it ideal for diamond smuggling. The prospector and his helpers would be cut off from other human contact by the arid desert sands and the high, ever-changing sand dunes, until the supply lorry, or the foreman's four-wheel-drive, made its appearance, sometimes only once a month. One such prospector had hoarded a fortune in diamonds. He took leave from work and returned by plane to the spot where he had stashed them. He landed the plane on the Skeleton Coast, collected the diamonds, and taxied off. Unfortunately for him, one of the wheels hit a partially concealed rock and the plane overturned. Several days later he was found wandering in the desert. He was extremely glad to be rescued by the people who came to arrest him.

Another case was of the would-be thief who enjoyed playing golf. He would insert a diamond inside the golf ball then give the ball a mighty whack, over the Orange River and into South Africa. After hitting a number of balls over he would apply for leave and then go and collect them. He, in turn, was collected by diamond detectives who had earlier got wind of the scheme.

Then there was the case of the postmaster and the carrier pigeon. An exhausted carrier pigeon, with a small pouch filled with diamonds strapped to its back, landed at CDM's security section in Oranjemund. Security officers fed and watered the bird and released it, and followed it to its cage at the home of the postmaster. The postmaster was arrested and charged with illegal diamond dealing.

Security on the mines was strict. Before leaving the town one had to submit to an X-ray inspection. One would stand inside the open front end of the machine while a bar passed down from above one's head to slightly below one's feet. If a certain light started flashing this meant trouble, because now a thorough search of your clothes and body would be undertaken. In the meantime your luggage would be X-rayed and searched in another part of the security building.

An elaborate plan was uncovered which involved labourers. When their 12- or 18-month contracts expired, they would return to Ovamboland from where they would apply for a new contract.

Before leaving, they would hide diamonds inside tins of jam, meat or fish. The waiting room of the X-ray building had small, sealed windows that looked outside. The labourers prised a window loose, passed the tins to people who had already been through the X-ray machine, and then resealed the window. The scheme was uncovered when a security guard noticed that the putty on one window was much cleaner and fresher looking than on the others.

Many of the Ovambos claimed they had stolen the diamonds to help finance Swapo (the South West African People's Organisation), which at the time was at war with the South African government and its administration in Namibia.

The desert, like the Antarctic, had its own characteristic beauty and, like the Antarctic, could be awesome in its fury. The Atlantic Ocean lapped the Skeleton Coast, and the contrast between this vast stretch of water and the arid desert was stark.

The moonlight on the desert sand was beautiful and soft, but the sun was harsh and the glare of the sand could be blinding. In the still of the night one could hear the silence. The huge sand dunes had a life of their own and stealthily changed positions as they were gently encouraged by the breeze.

But when the storm raged and the wind blew hot the desert was fearful in its power. Huge sand dunes would disappear and reappear over night. The whole terrain of the desert would be altered. The stinging sands carried by the fierce, hot wind struck with blinding intensity. Like the storms in the Antarctic, a sandstorm could be frightening in its fury.

The plant life of the Namibian Desert was sparse, but there were areas dotted with bud-bearing bushes. Again the magic of nature revealed itself: those succulent plants with their hundreds of buds are the water reservoirs of the desert. When the animals of the desert required water they would consume those buds, quenching their thirst as well as their hunger. There are a variety of buck in the desert, with the Gemsbok, with its needle sharp horns, being the most numerous and well known. There is also an abundance of snakes, including the deadly Peringueyi adder. The side-winding movement of the Peringueyi adder enables it to have minimum body contact with the hot desert sand. It is about nine inches in length, well camouflaged in the sand and dangerous.

Life at CDM was tough and testing, but there was good companionship-my best friend in Oranjemund was Harold Lamprecht (Lampies), and I want to say 'Thank you' to him for his lovely friendship-and there were other interests and sport. I still remember a headline in our local newspaper after one of our cricket matches: 'Demon Danny takes six for ten.'

After some years there, however, I was fed up with the apartheid practices on the mines, particularly the job reservation law which prevented the Ovambos from working on machines they were fully capable of operating. I was also disgusted with the low pay the Ovambos received, and continually found myself in heated arguments or scraps with the racists who bullied and taunted the Ovambos.

Eleanor Buchanan and I had also found ourselves becoming increasingly attracted to each other. This gave me an added reason to leave Oranjemund, before things got out of hand.

However, Eleanor was to come back into my life in the years ahead.

Chapter 7

Peaceful change - a fading hope: 1959 - 1990

I returned to Cape Town, in late 1959, at a loose end. My brother-in-law, Jimmy Belford, was a keen amateur photographer, and over the years, when I came home on leave flush with money, I had helped him buy photographic equipment and set up his own darkroom. On my return to Cape Town he suggested we form a partnership and set up a photographic studio. I agreed. I put up the money and he provided the expertise and equipment. I suggested that we bring my brother Norman in as an additional partner, and Jimmy agreed provided Norman put up one third of the capital. As Norman was unemployed at that time I put up his share.

Jimmy gave me a crash course in photography, and we opened a studio in Athlone called Danford Photographic Studios-Dan from Daniels and ford from Belford. I worked full-time at the studio while Norman and Jimmy helped out at weekends. (Jimmy later set up his own shop in Manenberg, where he was killed by armed robbers.)

I enjoyed being a photographer. I was my own boss and I worked in a pleasant environment, taking photographs of happy occasions such as weddings, birthday parties, christenings, confirmations and the like.

When we first opened we had no work for a while, until we copied a popular idea. Every weekend for a month I would take photos of people in the street in Athlone, hand them a business card and invite them to come and view the photographs at our studio, and, if they liked, purchase them. The idea pulled in customers and put us on the map.

Ironically, the studio also got a lift from the government, which had made it compulsory for everyone to have an identification document. Each ID application had to be accompanied by two photographs of the applicant.

A number of our customers were pensioners who needed ID

to collect their pensions. Many of these elderly people could not make it up the stairs to our studio, or were house-bound by illness, so I would go to their homes and photograph them there. Some of them did come to the studio, but if I saw they were struggling to get around I would take them home. I did not charge for the additional service, but the goodwill it generated was good for business. Jimmy came in one day and asked if I was the person who was taking pensioners home and not charging extra for taking their photographs at home. I told him I was, and he said everyone was talking about it.

I started work at 9:00 a.m. on weekdays, and on my way in I would cross a bridge which overlooked the Athlone Post Office. Every now and again I would see a queue of elderly people, sometimes two or three abreast, stretching out of the post office and a good distance around the corner. I made inquiries as to why those people were waiting in such long queues, in any kind of weather and with no toilet facilities or water available, and was told they were there to collect their pensions. I also heard that they started lining up at 6:00 a.m. on payout days.

The pensioners themselves were reluctant to talk to me about their ordeal, fearing repercussions from the authorities. Nevertheless, I took photographs of the queue and sent them, with a letter, to both the afternoon newspaper and the Postmaster General.

A short while later, my friend Owen Luter, who ran a hairdressing salon next to my studio, told me he had heard the postmaster shouting blue murder, wanting to know who had complained to the newspaper about the pensioners.

Owen said the newspaper had not printed my letter but had incorporated it as the central point in an article about pensions and pensioners. I never saw the article. I tried to see the postmaster to tell him I was responsible for the letter but somehow we kept missing each other.

When I arrived at work the following payout day there was no queue. I checked inside the post office and saw that two additional clerks were behind the counter. It was lovely to see the pensioners arriving and going straight in, without having to stand on their sore feet for hours on end.

About four months later, with my arrest only a few months away, I noticed that a queue was again starting to form in front of the post office. I checked inside and discovered that one of the clerks had been removed. I continued to monitor the situation, but a short while later I too was removed from the scene.

The apartheid laws were hurting. Africans would come in to the studio and ask that their ID photographs be lightened, so they could be classified as 'Coloured' and would not have to carry a 'dompas'. Such a request might seem trivial to an outsider, but the pass system was an extremely oppressive one that hounded the African from the age of 16-when it became compulsory to register with the influx control office-to his grave. To be classified 'Coloured' meant he could stay legally in an urban area, he could have his wife and children with him, he could send his children to school, and he could perform certain types of work which Africans were, by law, not allowed to perform.

If a man was classified African, even if he had a legal passbook he was allowed in an urban area only under certain stringent conditions, and would have to live in the awful 'locations'. If he were an 'illegal' African he would sleep in the forest or elsewhere. He would always be on the run from the police. He would do any kind of work for a small wage just to survive. His wife and children would not be able to join him because they too would be illegal.

Elias Motsoaledi once told me, on Robben Island, how wives with their babies would join their husbands in the forests. When the babies started to cry the men would chase the women away, saying the crying of the babies would draw the attention of the police.

Similarly, so-called 'Coloureds' would come to the studio and request that their photographs be made fair so they could be classified as white. A 'white' ID for a so-called 'Coloured' person meant better job prospects, apprenticeships, better schools for his children, living in a safer neighbourhood, access to superior medical facilities, higher social status, and access to the beaches, camping sites, mountain routes, libraries, parks, and halls.

I was asked why I accommodated these requests. My reply was that these people who wanted a change of racial status were not responsible for the cruel apartheid laws which made them slaves in the land of their birth. If I could, in some small way, help break the chains of oppression that bound them then I certainly would.

The unfortunate aspect of 'crossing the colour line' was that it caused great agony and heartbreak among the marginal families, where those who crossed the racial barriers would literally disown their families and friends.

I had a strong urge to fight apartheid injustices, and supported all and any anti-government activities. I attended most of Cissy Gool's anti-government public meetings. She was highly militant. I remember one occasion when she and I were part of a committee of about 14 members who had to plan anti-Republic Day demonstrations. We met at her home near Castle Bridge and were supposed to report back the following week at the same venue on tasks that we had been allocated. During the week the government made threatening statements as to how they would deal with those who were planning to disrupt the Republic Day celebrations. At the following meeting only Cissy and I were present.

During this period a Cape Town City Council election was held with my brother Norman as one of the candidates, on a ticket of three. All three were elected to the council. Their terms, however, were short-lived. The government passed an apartheid law, which came into effect in 1972, prohibiting blacks from serving on the Cape Town City Council. There was a great outcry against this blatantly racist action, but to no avail.

Chapter 8

The Liberal Party of South Africa and the Emergency: 1960 - 1964

It was a Wednesday evening on a wet winter's night in 1959. A recent shower had taken place and Cape Town's Grand Parade was still wet, with puddles of water, resting in shallow hollows, reflecting the lights of the lamps. The Liberal Party had called a public meeting. I do not remember how I had got to hear about the meeting, but I was there.

There was a crowd of about 300 to 400 people. The speakers, who addressed the crowd from the back of a lorry, included Peter Hjul, Cromwell Nododile and John Duncan, brother of Patrick Duncan. They made fighting speeches and the crowd was enthusiastic. Peter Hjul ended the meeting by calling on people to come forward and join the Liberal Party of South Africa, to come forward and fight the apartheid government, to come forward and fight for democracy and justice in a non-racial South Africa.

Here was an organisation that tickled my fancy; it satisfied the criteria that I was seeking, being both anti-government and non-racial. Several party members with notebooks took down the names of people who wished to join. I stood in a queue and handed in my name. Several days later I received a notice from the secretary of the Liberal Party, inviting me to the meeting at which I became a member. It was a happy day that I joined the Liberal Party of South Africa (LP), because there I met some of the nicest and bravest people dedicated to the principles of non-racialism and justice.

The party was militant. We took part in marches, prayer meetings, protest meetings, and pamphlet distribution, among other activities. When the African National Congress (ANC) and the Pan-Africanist Congress (PAC) were banned, the LP gave them a platform by inviting members of those two organisations to address LP meetings in their private capacities.

One of our more successful local demonstrations was the Sit-

In Campaign. At the time, blacks could buy goods from any of the retail shops in the city, but could not sit down and be served in restaurants and tea-rooms. A 'mixed' group of LP volunteers would meet on a Saturday morning, go into a tea-room, and demand service. We were always refused service and ordered to leave the premises. On one occasion one of a group ordered four cooldrinks and was served (Advocate Lewis Dison, our legal adviser, had advised us to order cooldrinks and consume them standing up to avoid transgressing the Group Areas Act). When the waitress who had served this person saw he was part of a 'mixed' group, she pleaded with him to return the drinks, otherwise she would lose her job. He returned the drinks to her.

One Friday evening, at the Sea Point swimming pool, we went to the downstairs tea-room. We were told they were closing. We then went upstairs to the other tea-room, where we were told the same story. Going downstairs, we found the first tea-room had opened again. As soon as we walked in the staff started to pull down the blinds. The same thing happened when we returned upstairs.

Our actions drew large crowds, many of whom supported us. The security police had also got wind of our activities, and they followed us around as we went to various segregated tea-rooms. If we sat down at the tables they took photographs of us. I once went up to a photographer and asked him if he was from the press. He smiled at me, said yes, and showed me his security police card. He was Sergeant van Wyk, who later served me my first set of banning orders and was heavily involved in my inter-rogation when I was detained under the 90-Day Detention Act.

One Saturday morning about 16 of us were arrested. We were released at around 5:00 p.m. on bail of (I think) £25. Because the banks were closed, those who raised the bail on our behalf had to scramble around for the money. In the meantime other volun-teers had taken our place and continued with the campaign. They too were arrested, and a third group took over the reins. Some volunteers like Sylvia Neame took part in all three groups.

Charges against the first two groups of volunteers were with-drawn, but a Mrs Hendrickse of the Windermere branch was charged and used as a test case. She was found guilty and fined £50. After that the campaign petered out for lack of funds with which to meet these fines.

A lighter incident during the campaign occurred when I arrived late for a meeting at the LP office. The doors to the building were locked, and to gain admittance I would have had to go to a public telephone, ring the office and wait for someone to come down from the third floor to open the doors. I saw the lights were still on at the nearby parliament building, and decided that instead of bothering the meeting I would go and stage my own private sit-in.

I entered parliament on the white side, passed through the security check without any bother, and took my seat in the public gallery without being challenged. United Party leader Sir de Villiers Graaff was on his feet, speaking. Von Moltke, one of the National Party representatives of South West Africa, kept interjecting: 'Kafferboetie! Kafferboetie!' ('Kaffir-brother, Kaffir-brother'). Sir de Villiers Graaff complained to the Speaker, who warned Von Moltke to desist. No sooner had Sir de Villiers Graaff continued his speech than Von Moltke was at it again. Initially he was ignored but then the Speaker's attention was drawn again to this puerile behaviour. The Speaker reprimanded Von Moltke, who left his bench, walked to the middle of the floor, looked at the Speaker, bent his knee and said, in mock humility, 'Ek vra verskoning, Meneer Spreker. Ek vra verskoning, Meneer Spreker. Ek vra verskoning, Meneer Spreker.' ('I beg forgiveness, Mr Speaker.')

At this point the House rose for the evening. As people in the gallery got up to leave I turned to a man who had been sitting one seat away from me, and asked him: 'Who's that nut down there?'

He gave me a 'drop dead' look and, as he barged past, said, 'Ek weet nie!' ('I don't know!')

I left parliament unscathed, having had a glimpse of the sort of people who were making the laws we were fighting against.

If the South African MPs were a sorry lot, those from South West Africa were decidedly worse. Von Moltke was later invited by the LP to a lunchtime meeting to give the government's point of view on some apartheid measure. When Barney Zackon, a Jewish member of the LP, asked him an awkward question, Von Moltke told Barney he should not have been let out of the [Nazi] concentration camp.

The Sit-In Campaign was a grassroots affair that brought home to ordinary people in Cape Town the fact that apartheid was not sacrosanct, that the shops and cafés collaborating with it should be shown up, and that there was no shortage of people like us willing to stand up and be counted. For the tens and twenties of people who took part, there were hundreds who looked on, and thousands more who read about us in the press, who took heart and could see that we, at least, had not been beaten into submission to the government's race laws.

The Liberal Party fought other campaigns outside parliament, one of its greatest being that against the 'black spots removals', the ethnic cleansing which drove a million Africans from their homes into distant, soulless townships and 'resettlement areas'. The party campaigned against the Bantustans in the Transkei, Natal and the Transvaal, and worked to unite the opponents of apartheid, especially against Verwoerd's government, in the early 1960s.

The political climate was volatile in the early '60s. In January 1960, British Prime Minister Harold Macmillan made his famous 'winds of change' speech in Parliament in Cape Town. What he said was already obvious to us, as so many colonies in Africa were on the threshold of freedom and there was a new militancy in the liberation movements in South Africa.

A group of African nationalists had left the ANC to form the Pan-Africanist Congress, and it was the launching of their anti-pass campaign, pre-empting the ANC's campaign planned to start a week later, that was to usher in a new phase of the Struggle.

At Sharpeville, near Johannesburg, on the morning of 21 March 1960, the police shot and killed 69 people and injured hundreds of others. The victims were part of a large crowd who had gathered in front of the police station, defying the police to arrest them for not carrying their passbooks.

That evening thousands gathered in Langa and Nyanga townships in Cape Town and there were clashes with police in which several deaths occurred. The killings drew international condemnation of the South African government.

A few days later a front-page newspaper photograph showed ANC leader Chief Albert Luthuli publicly burning his dompas as a prelude to a three-day work stayaway called by the ANC. PAC supporters, particularly in Cape Town, had already embarked on a stayaway. The stayaway had support in some regions of up to 95 percent, and led to the declaration of a national State of Emergency. The government also passed special laws to try and stem the flow of international capital from the country, and-in an amazing attempt to placate both national and international condemnation of apartheid-briefly suspended the pass laws. (The pass laws were eventually scrapped in 1986.) During the uprisings that had taken place in the western Cape a number of PAC members and others had been killed, and a huge funeral was planned. There was also a placard demonstration planned, which we had agreed to support.

The morning of the funeral we met at our offices in Parliament Street. LP vice-chair Randolph Vigne volunteered to attend the funeral. Others and I agreed to take part in the placard demonstration. One snag was that we did not have many placards and some LP members were reluctant to use those made by Congress of Democrats (COD) members. I had no problem with working alongside COD, a white organisation in alliance with the ANC, and collected a placard which read, 'Down With Police Brutality.'

I placed myself opposite the gates of parliament, wondering why I was the only demonstrator at this strategic and highly visible point. (I later realised it was an area in which demonstrations were prohibited.) While I was standing there, somebody came out of the parliament gates and took my photograph. A little while later a police van stopped opposite me. The occupants pointed at me and held a discussion among themselves, then moved on. I did not realise at the time what a narrow escape I had had. I was unaware that a State of Emergency had been declared.

The funeral, at Langa, was solemn and peaceful despite the 50 000-strong crowd and the great feeling of emotion. Members of the ANC, PAC and other groups and church leaders took part. The police had undertaken not to be present, which mainly accounts for the lack of violence that day though tension was high and the people were angry. Among the thousands of black faces there were a few white faces, showing the world that there were some whites in South Africa who associated themselves with the Struggle and the aspirations of the oppressed.

On the day of the funeral my mother saw my niece, Pearl, who lived next door and worked with me at the studio, playing in the street. She asked, 'Pearl, what are you doing at home? Aren't you supposed to be with Uncle Eddie at work?'

'No, Ma,' replied Pearl, 'Uncle Eddie said there will be no work today.' My mother began worrying about me because she had heard on the radio that a State of Emergency had been declared. That afternoon several policemen trapped an African in front of my home and beat him viciously with long riot truncheons. That was the general pattern throughout the city. Africans were being chased all over and when caught were thoroughly beaten and then released. I do not know if the motive was to break every African's spirit and perhaps drive as many as possible out of the urban areas or just to put on a show of utter brutality, but the police carried out the task with relish. When my mother saw how brutally that African was beaten she imagined me being beaten in turn. When I arrived home that evening she was absolutely sick with worry.

The black townships of Langa, Nyanga and Guguletu were subjected to a furious onslaught by the police. Doors were kicked down and the occupants of houses badly assaulted. Hammington Majija, a Liberal Party leader in Guguletu, was so badly assaulted both his arms were broken. When he tried to lay a charge at the police station he was threatened with further assault.

The strike had gone on for ten days, Cape Town was paralysed, factories at a standstill and ships lying idle in the harbour. The government, however, knew only brutality as a bargaining tactic.

The day after the beatings began, a young student leader of the

PAC, Philip Kgosana, led a march on parliament to demand an end to apartheid laws. Around 30 000 people took part, coming in from the townships in long, dense columns along De Waal Drive and Main Road. They were disciplined and serious. By the time they reached the city the army had been alerted and mobilised to prevent them from marching on parliament. The marchers were persuaded to head down Buitenkant Street to Caledon Square, Cape Town's main police station, where Kgosana, Clarence Makwethu and other PAC leaders met with the police commander. After some negotiation they were promised that they would be allowed to meet the Minister of Defence, Frans Erasmus, later that evening. This promise was conveyed to the mass of people stretching up and down the road, and the crowd dispersed peacefully.

When Kgosana and his colleagues went to meet the Minister they were arrested.

The next day the army threw a 'cordon of steel' around the townships in an attempt to break the stayaway. No blacks were allowed to leave or enter, and were shot at if they tried. A terrible tragedy occurred when a soldier shot and killed a baby in its mother's arms as the mother was leaving the township. The army also tried to prevent food supplies from being taken in. However the Black Sash, led by LP activist Eulalie Stott, managed to deliver at least one truckload of food to the beleaguered townships. I still remember a front-page photograph in the evening newspaper showing a defiant Eulalie standing on top of the food-laden lorry. The Liberal Party raised large sums of money to support the strikers and also, led by Randolph Vigne, Tom Walters and others, went in with truckloads of supplies.

The stayaway was eventually broken by the mass detentions of the PAC and ANC leadership and others, both blacks and whites. Many were later sentenced to prison terms of six months or more. PAC president Robert Sobukwe was given a three-year sentence, at the end of which the government passed a special law allowing the prison authorities to hold him for an additional year. This law was renewed every year for the next six years. Robert was eventually released, a very sick man, in 1969. He died of cancer a few years later while under house arrest in Kimberley.

When the short-term prisoners who had been held on Robben Island were released, they were invited to the LP office where party members took affidavits on their treatment and conditions on the Island. There were frightening tales of suffering and brutality.

These were reported in Contact, a fortnightly newspaper owned by the LP. (The newspaper was originally owned and published by Patrick Duncan, an LP member who had defied the emergency regulations imposed after the Sharpeville massacre and continued to report fully on what was happening in the country. After Duncan was banned he left South Africa illegally for Lesotho. He sold the newspaper to the LP for a nominal sum.)

Under the editorship of John Clare, Contact published an article headed 'Devil's Island'. To bypass new laws forbidding any reports on prisons, copies of the affidavits were first sent over to England for publication by the sympathetic British press. Contact then reported on those overseas articles. In spite of taking this devious route to avoid transgressing the press gag, John still faced the possibility of three years imprisonment if charged. Thankfully he was not charged. To my knowledge Contact was the only newspaper in South Africa that published the information contained in the affidavits.

Contact was never banned, but every editor that took over was. Eventually it became foolhardy to continue running the newspaper.

Nearly 50 leading members of the LP were given banning orders, including the national chairperson, Peter Brown. I served for a while as chairperson of the Windermere branch and was eventually elected to the national committee, but I felt the only reason I had attained those lofty heights in the organisation was because of the spate of bannings.

In 1961 the Cape division of the LP decided to contest the Constantia constituency in the general elections. The seat was a safe one for the United Party (UP), which had previously always won it unopposed. Our candidate was Randolph Vigne. There was some disagreement among members of the LP around our participation in an apartheid election, but I supported Randolph's candidacy. I canvassed on his behalf and helped to put up posters that carried a large photograph of him as well as the then revolutionary slogan 'One man One vote'. Because we were strapped for cash, Randolph himself had to help put up the posters. It was quite funny when I had to sit on his shoulders to put a picture of him high up on a pole or tree.

The canvassing was an education in itself, as some of the arguments put forward by United Party supporters for continuation of white rule were absolutely pathetic.

Part of the area in Claremont that I had to canvas was known as 'Millionaire's Mile'. The houses were far apart and it was sometimes a bit disheartening to trudge all the way up a lengthy driveway only to discover that there was nobody home.

At one huge mansion I was invited inside. I asked the occupants to vote for the LP because it stood for non-racialism and justice, and backed this by pointing out the terrible injustices that prevailed. I received both a sympathetic hearing and a reply. As I was leaving the house my gaze was drawn to a large, magnificent painting on the wall. During the week the newspapers had reported that a large, valuable painting had been stolen from a French art gallery and that a big reward had been offered for its recovery. With my tongue in my cheek I asked the person I assumed was the owner of the house if that painting was the one that had been 'lifted' in France. He chuckled at this, but I do not know if he voted for the Liberal Party.

Our election meetings were, with a few exceptions, poorly attended. The most crowded was one addressed by LP president Alan Paton.

We lost the Constantia contest by a large margin. It seemed the great majority of white South Africans were not at all ready for a non-racial government.

Certain members of the LP, including Randolph, felt we were getting nowhere with peaceful political protests and decided to form an underground organisation to pursue other methods. In 1961 I attended a meeting in Johannesburg at which we established the National Committee of Liberation (NCL), later to be called the African Resistance Movement (ARM).

I felt guilty belonging to both the LP and ARM, as I felt ARM's objectives transgressed the LP's constitution on non-violence. I raised this problem with LP national executive member and fellow ARM member Adrian Leftwich, and said I wanted to resign from the LP. Adrian dissuaded me from resigning, saying that belonging to the LP was a good cover for ARM activities. I accepted this argument-if a large group of us had resigned it would probably have drawn the attention of the security police. Nevertheless, we reduced our involvement in LP activities in an attempt to lessen damage to the party in the event of our being caught.

The party also formally condemned illegal violent activities. This was a necessary step for the party to take, in order to distance itself from the activities of some of its members and ensure its survival as a legal political party.

In 1968 the LP, already severely weakened by the detention, arrest, banning or exile of many of its leadership, had to face a painful decision. The government had introduced the 'Prohibition of Political Interference Bill' which aimed at preventing political parties from having both white and black members. For the LP to survive it would have had to become either a 'whites only' or 'blacks only' party. To avoid this impossible choice, which would have been against its non-racial principles, the LP decided to dissolve itself.

The LP was founded in 1953 and survived for fifteen years. Much of its membership during these years was white. To be a white opponent of the apartheid regime at that time (and the same applies to members of COD) took immense courage. They were ostracised, threatened, persecuted, shot at, banned, detained, arrested, jailed and one, John Harris, was executed. They were people of high integrity, dignity and quiet courage.

I cut my political teeth in the Liberal Party, and it was there that I met some of the nicest people I know. I still think back fondly to those days.

Today I am a member of the ANC. I was approached by former LP members who wanted me to join them in resuscitating the party in the form of a new organisation, but I declined. I feel the ANC is the only organisation that can lead South Africa to peace and prosperity. It has come through a cruel and vicious struggle, yet both its quality leadership and powerful rank-and-file have retained their integrity, discipline and dignity.

After the 1960 State of Emergency a new organisation, the Coloured People's Convention,was established under the leadership of Dr Dickie van der Ross. In a relatively short space of time the Convention developed into a substantial organisation. Its public meetings were well attended and its support was strong.

At one point the government banned all the CPC's meetings within the greater Cape Town area. Eulalie Stott arranged for the organisation to have a meeting at the farm of a relative, Pieter Melck, near Malmesbury, which was outside the banned area. Delegates were told,. Through the grapevince, that they must take the first farm road to the left after a vehicle parked on the side of the road with its bonnet open. Everyone reached the farm shed safely, and the cars in which delegates arrived were screened from view from the main road because of the terrain of the land.

We met in a large barn in which chairs had been placed. Dr van der Ross's father was in the chair. Dennis Brutus was speaking when we heard that the barn had been surrounded by the police. A door opened behind Mr van der Ross and the head of the Cape Town security police entered the barn, accompanied by a number of other security policemen. Dennis stopped speaking. A strained hush fell over the meeting. Mr van der Ross turned around in his chair and looked at the security police who were standing behind him. Then without faltering, and with dignity, he turned back to the meeting and told Dennis to carry on. We scored a big moral victory, through the impeccable behaviour of our chairperson, over the security police who had hoped to intimidate us by their presence at our meeting.

When Dennis had finished speaking Mr van der Ross called on Rev Jooste to say a prayer. The prayer was so moving that some of the security policemen, who were slouching against some furniture behind Mr van der Ross, slowly came to attention. The meeting ended without any incident.

The 'Coloured' Convention faded away just as rapidly as it had come into being. The tailpiece is that it was in debt to the tune of about £400. No one would take on the job of secretary-the original one, Joe Daniels (no relation) of the LP, had fallen ill-until I was proposed and accepted. My only job was really to pay off the debt. I wrote to as many members as possible and asked each one to contribute £1 a month towards paying our debt. Some came up to scratch but many did not. When I met some of them and asked if they had received my letters they would tell me, with a smirk, that they had changed their address. I eventually managed to get 12 members to pay £1 per month. Over time that group dwindled down to Mr van der Ross, Dr van der Ross, Mr Ned Doman, my brother Norman and myself. We eventually paid off the debt.

Like other initiatives, the Convention did not achieve its objectives. However the presence of these initiatives had other benefits. When apartheid was finally defeated South Africa did not lack for well-thought-out, non-racial democratic principles on which to base its new form of government. We had put these principles forward and kept them alive through the Congresses, the Liberal Party and other groups, the Black Sash, the non-racial trade unions and sports organisations, Nusas and through many bodies that came and went like the Congress of the People and the 'Coloured People's Convention'. These ideals were needed when apartheid at last came to an end. They did not bring about its end, however. For that more extreme measures could not be avoided.

Chapter 9

The African Resistance Movement: 1961 - 1964

By 1961 a number of us were disillusioned with marches, strikes and protest meetings. We felt little was being achieved by such methods while parliamentary political activities, on the other hand, were totally ineffective. Something else had to be done to destabilise the apartheid government.

We formed an organisation known initially as the National Committee of Liberation (NCL), with a national executive concerned with political and overall strategic policy, regional executives, and cells.

After a brief and abortive attempt to launch an underground radio station-Freedom Radio-we decided to move into sabotage. Our primary aim was to attack government installations but avoid injuring or killing people.

We launched our first attack on 26 September 1961, almost three months before the ANC's military wing, Umkhonto weSizwe, went into action. Our attacks were mostly on electricity pylons but we also successfully sabotaged signal cables on the railways.

We were a small close-knit organisation with no informers in our midst. We had small cells in Johannesburg, Cape Town, Port Elizabeth and Durban. Johannesburg was initially our most active area but was later overtaken by Cape Town.

We were complete amateurs as far as sabotage was concerned. On our first 'pylon job' in Cape Town we took along spanners as well as explosives. We had already prepared four charges, each made up of six sticks of dynamite, in a garage that we had hired and used as a workshop. We had tested the electric flex we were going to use to connect the detonators to the charges, battery and clock, and although it did not work too well we were anxious to proceed with the job and decided to carry on.

Our driver, David 'Spike' de Keller, dropped Mike Schneider, Neville Hillman and myself on the side of a road near our intended target. We climbed over a low wire fence and crossed a section of open veld to the pylon.

At first we tried to weaken the structure by loosening some of its bolts, but soon gave up on that. I then climbed each leg in turn and attached a charge above a wire mesh that was there to discourage people from climbing the pylon. (We subsequently learned that all we had to do was place a charge at the bottom of two of the supports).

I climbed each leg again to place electric detonators in the charges, and lowered wires which the others connected to the battery and timer. Then I climbed down to collect the battery and timer. I intended climbing up again, to place the battery and clock with one of the charges so they would be destroyed in the explosion, when there was a tremendous bang: a short in the wiring had set the charges off prematurely.

I was enveloped in a blaze of bright light. I spun around and saw my two comrades, also bathed in light, holding up the tog bags in which we had brought the spanners and the explosives. They shouted: 'What happened,' and I shouted back: 'Run.'

We ran. I expected to be caught up in falling cables, if not crushed by the pylon itself, but nothing happened. In our haste we jumped one wire fence, then another, and found ourselves in another prohibited area. Because of the darkness we did not realise we had already crossed the road. We made our way back, placed a bottle at the edge of the road as a sign to Spike that we were in the vicinity, and waited for him to pick us up. From there we made our way safely home, grateful to have survived the night.

The next morning we drove past the site. The pylon was still standing, although one leg was completely cut and the opposite one bent. The other two were intact with the charges still attached. It was fortunate that I had placed the charges high up on the pylon. If they had been placed where we subsequently learned they should be placed I would have been subjected to the full force of the explosion.

Luck played a large role in many of our operations. Johannesburg had sent us several cases of dynamite-stolen from the gold mines-and we would unwrap the sticks of dynamite from their greaseproof paper and put the loose powder into plastic bags so it was flexible and easier to attach to a target. (I always felt very ill after handling the powder with my bare hands. I do not know whether it was from breathing in the dust or the chemicals entering through my skin, but I generally recovered after a few hours.) One evening we had completed our shaped charges and were left with a large amount of waxed wrapping. I suggested we burn the wrapping in a large dirtbin in our workshop, but Adrian, who was a member of the national executive, suggested it would be safer to dispose of it elsewhere. I agreed, and we drove in his car to Wynberg Park.

The pieces of wrapping were all curled up like wood shavings, and they made a large bundle. We had set the bundle alight in the park and were watching it burn when something behind me drew my attention: it was a police van. It had driven up so silently that neither of us had heard it.

'Wat gaan hier aan?' ('What's going on here?') asked one of the two policemen in the van.

Adrian, pretending to be cold and holding his hands over the fire, said we were just trying to keep warm. The policemen gave us a long hard stare then moved off. We breathed a huge sigh of relief. I do not know how they failed to notice that the flames were an unusual blue, or that the fire was making 'whoosh' sounds every time a remnant of powder caught alight. If they had noticed we could have been in serious trouble. To crown it all, when I got home that evening and emptied my pockets I found a short piece of safety fuse. How it got into my pocket I have no idea. If Adrian and I had been taken in for questioning that would have been damning evidence indeed.

An FM radio mast had recently been erected on Constantiaberge mountain, and we thought this would be a good symbolic target. We reconnoitred the site, which involved several strenuous climbs, until we felt we were ready to tackle the job. Robert Watson, an ex-British paratrooper who had given us some training in sabotage, and I were assigned to the operation.

We wore camouflage uniforms that Watson had procured.

Sheila Clare dropped us at the point where we would begin climbing and where we would be picked up again at a specified time. Besides the explosives, I was carrying a small semi-automatic pistol I had purchased legally in Namibia. After climbing for a while I suddenly realised I had dropped my gun somewhere. I immediately informed Watson, who was in charge. He said we would have to find the gun because the police could trace it back to me. We spent a long time retracing our steps and searching for the gun, which was difficult to find because it was black metal and the night was very dark. Watson eventually found the gun but we had spent too much time searching for it and had to abandon the operation.

The next attempt on the radio mast was undertaken by Adrian Leftwich and myself. In the meantime, we had been in touch with Johannesburg. They had explained that the best method to bring the mast down would be to blow one of the sets of steel cables that supported it. The mast was supported by four sets of three cables, therefore if we blew one set the weight of the other three would drag the mast down. Doing it this way would also enable us to determine the direction the mast fell, which was important because we had established there was a security guard on duty and we did not want to drop the mast on him. (Knowledge of the security guard came through one of those strange coincidences. I was on the upper deck of a bus with a friend, Enid Holmes. In the seat in front of us a somewhat drunken passenger was holding forth to his neighbour, who did not seem particularly interested, about overtime pay. He then turned around and focused on me and asked: 'Isn't it right that I should be paid overtime?' I said I did not know what he was complaining about. He then told me he was a security guard at the Constantiaberge FM mast and that on one particular shift his relief had either not turned up or had arrived very late. I agreed that he was entitled to overtime pay, and asked him what it was like working up there. My companion, unaware of my illegal activities, was not keen that I should continue the conversation, but I nevertheless asked the guard if it was not cold up on the mountain. He told me that it was nice working up there because one could always catch some sleep while on duty. And as for the cold, he said, giving me a knowing wink, one always had some 'liquid refreshments' handy to keep oneself warm. He said he was usually alone on duty until his relief came along and his superiors seldom checked on him.)

Johannesburg had sent us three custom-made charges for the task. The charges were oblong and made of light metal, and we filled each of them with powder from six sticks of dynamite. The underside of the charge was covered by a thin copper sheet, and it was through this that the main force of the blast would be directed. On top of the charge was a small opening in which to insert the electric detonator, and each charge had two metal bolts for attaching it to the cable.

Adrian and I were driven to the drop-off point by Mike Schneider, who was accompanied as a cover by Lyn van der Riet. We started climbing at early dusk. Night descended very quickly, but a pale moon, sometimes obscured by cloud, helped us pick out our route as we climbed. As we took a bend near the top of the mountain I got quite a shock: there were four bright security lights, attached high up on the mast itself, lighting the lower sections of each set of cables. At first I thought we might have been betrayed, because we had not noticed the lights before. However it was simply poor reconnaissance on our part-we had previously checked out the site only during the day.

The set of cables we had picked was a fair distance away from the guard's station. There was a heavy cloud mass pouring over the top of Constantiaberg, and this was a big help in that it diffused the bright security lights but left me enough light to work by.

My task was to climb some way up the three cables (which I did by stepping on the bottom cable, putting one hand on the top cable, and pulling myself sideways) place the charges in position, insert the detonators, and lower the wires down to Adrian. Adrian would attach the wires to the battery and the Zobo watch we were using. Whenever there was a break in the cloud I was clearly exposed on the cables, but the short breaks came often and I could not afford to jump down each time.

I had placed the first charge and bolted it firmly to the cable, and was busy with the second, when suddenly headlights appeared around a bend in the road leading up to the mast. I jumped down and Adrian and I ran into the darkness and watched from behind a rock. The headlights belonged to a police van. It made its way to the guardhouse where it stayed for a while. When the van left we returned to the cables and carried on. I finished attaching the two remaining charges, and Adrian wired them to the battery and watch. They were set to go off at 4:00am.

The appearance of the police van had delayed us quite a bit, and because it was pitch dark we were unable to move fast down the mountainside. We were supposed to reach the pickup at 11:30pm but only got there some time after midnight. Fortunately Mike and Lyn were still waiting for us. They were worried, but they were there. I was exhausted.

The next morning I stood on the back porch of my photographic studio and looked at Constantiaberge in the distance. I could not believe my eyes: the mast was still standing. I rubbed my eyes and looked again. Yes, it was still standing. I felt sick to the stomach. What could have gone wrong?

We had a quick emergency meeting. I offered to go up and dismantle the charges, but the others ruled against this.

The security police later told me, when I was in detention, that the charges were discovered three days after we planted them. A loose screw in the watch had prevented the charges from detonating.

The tailpiece to this little episode was on Robben Island, when I told Ahmed 'Kathy' Kathrada about the incident. He said, 'Oh, that was you! We [the ANC and Umkhonto weSizwe] were accused of that job.' We all had a hearty laugh.

We had a workshop in Dorp Street, Cape Town, where we prepared our timing devices and charges. Our explosives, which were in cases, were stored in a number of different places until we hired a storeroom in a block of flats in Rosebank. I was in charge of the explosives and detonators and would collect whatever we needed for a particular job.

Because the Zobo watches had let us down in the past we

gave up on them and started using Jock clocks instead. The converted Jock clocks looked just like normal clocks except they had two wires leading to a plug. Adrian hit on the idea of using plug connections while Watson was training us in the use of explosives. We had to connect the wires leading from the detonators to the battery and timer in the dark, wearing woollen gloves. This was quite a difficult exercise. After Adrian's brainwave, all we had to do once the charges were placed was insert a male plug into a female socket and the charges were set.

We arranged to meet at the workshop one evening. When we arrived we saw that the front door was open and banging in the wind, and the inside light was on. We gathered on the opposite side of the street, keeping the place under observation. We thought the security police might have raided the premises and, worse, might be waiting for us inside.

After a short discussion I volunteered to go and check it out. I entered the building with great trepidation. I pushed against the front door, but there was no one behind it. A long flight of stairs led from the front door to the two rooms on top. I gingerly climbed the stairs expecting to be challenged at any moment. As I entered the room at the top of the stairs I expected an unfriendly hand to descend heavily on my shoulder. Still nothing happened. I looked through the rest of the place and found no unwelcome visitors.

I called the others and they joined me in the workshop. After looking around we discovered that several of our Jock clocks and torches which we used for testing were missing, and realised we had been burgled. Anyone buying one of those 'electric clocks' from the burglar and plugging it into a wall socket would have blown the lights in their house, and this could have had all sorts of repercussions. We hastily abandoned that workshop.

Another incident occurred in which luck played a large part. One evening at my photographic studio I was demonstrating to Neville Hillman, among other things, how safety fuse could burn under water and still effectively set off a charge of explosives. I had filled the porcelain sink in the darkroom with water, attached a short piece of safety fuse with a detonator to a small piece of detonator cord, lit the fuse and placed the lot in the water. After checking that the fuse was actually burning underwater we lost interest in it and turned to other activities. We were rudely reminded of the fuse by a tremendous explosion that shook the place and plunged us into darkness.

My back was sopping wet. I was not sure if it was water or blood. I thought to myself if I could see stars it meant the wall had been blown out. I did not see any stars. Everything we touched was electrified and the acrid fumes in that confined space were overwhelming. We staggered out of the darkroom and hastily opened the windows of the studio to get rid of the smoke. I had some candles with which I had been experimenting to see if they could be used as timing devices. We lit a few and surveyed the chaos.

I had not realised, until then, how powerful an explosion a detonator cord could provide in such a confined space. The porcelain sink had been blown to smithereens, two shelves containing bottles of chemicals had been blown off the wall, and the dangling electric cord supporting the light bulb had been cut. There was water everywhere. I realised with relief that the wetness on my back was water and not blood.

We cleaned up and Neville fixed the light. Soon the place looked respectable once more. Fortunately there was no one else in the building that evening. I later explained to my brother Norman, who was not aware of my illegal activities, that I had stood on the sink to reach a bottle of chemicals. The sink collapsed under my weight and in trying to save myself I had hung on to the top shelf, which had pulled loose and gone crashing through the bottom shelf. I paid for the damage and the incident was forgotten.

One of our most successful efforts was the sabotage of railway signal cables, which brought Cape Town to a standstill. I did not physically take part in this operation. The cables were blown up at 3:00am and paralysed the railways for hours. Trains only started to run normally again towards the afternoon. Banks, shops, businesses and schools remained closed long after they should have opened, because those who had the keys to the premises could not reach their destinations or were delayed. There were a number of prominent reports of the incident in the newspapers. One woman who was interviewed said, 'This is just the beginning ...'

An incident that could have spelt disaster for us occurred after one meeting at which I suggested we should produce and distribute a 'Do It Yourself' sabotage manual. I argued that there were many people out there who might like to attack government property, but could not join sabotage groups because of the tight security practised by those groups. If we drew up and distributed a DIY sabotage manual then those people could use their initiative; they could organise their own groups and pick their own targets. I was asked to draw up a draft document and submit it for discussion to the next meeting.

At the next meeting the pamphlet was discussed and Randolph Vigne took charge of the document. The following day Randolph's house was raided by the security police, and he was taken to Caledon Square police station for questioning about unrelated activities in the Transkei. On his way to the station he realised he had the DIY document in the top pocket of his jacket. After being fingerprinted and booked he was put in a cell awaiting interrogation. He quickly tore up the incriminating pamphlet and flushed it down the toilet. If the security police had searched Randolph and discovered the pamphlet the situation could have been awkward.

There were a number of other incidents, including other attacks on pylons and a plan to blow up the Government Garage. Just about every one of them involved a fair amount of luck, which favoured us and enabled us to survive more than two years in the field. But eventually, our luck ran out.

On Friday 4 July 1964, Adrian Leftwich's flat was one of the targets in a general, countrywide raid by the security police. They discovered a notebook in his flat which recorded money paid into the organisation (each member had to pay a percentage of their income to the organisation and Adrian was keeping a record of these payments). When asked about the recordings he failed to give a convincing answer to the security police, and was taken in for questioning.

Lyn van der Riet was also present in Adrian's flat during the raid. The security police took down her name and address and detained her shortly afterwards.

ARM was on the rack.

PART
2

Chapter 10

Arrest and Detention: 1964

On the morning of 5 July 1964, I received a telephone call from Ann Tobias, a mutual friend of Adrian Leftwich's and mine, to tell me Adrian had been detained.

I was working at the studio when the call came through. Fortunately a friend, Sheaby Ndlumbini, had come to visit me that morning. I told him I had urgent business to attend to and asked him to run the studio.

My aim was to make sure the explosives were safe, so I went to check on Lyn van der Riet's flat in Rosebank. I parked in a spot on Main Road from where I could see the block of flats. I noticed Adrian's car at the end of the driveway and about six security policemen standing near it. Lyn's flat was on the ground floor, and I wondered if I could chance going to it. I decided to take the risk.

I made my way through the grounds, entered the building and walked down to Lyn's flat, right at the end of the corridor. I checked through her bathroom window to see if I could see the suitcases containing the explosives, but they were not there. I knocked on her front door. Looking back now, I realise how rash this was, as it was very likely that the security police were in her flat. Fortunately for me they were not, and Lyn opened the door. She was alarmed to see me. I asked where the explosives were, and she told me the police were around and I should go. I repeated my question, and she again told me to leave.

As I turned to leave I saw a black security policeman walking towards me along the narrow corridor. (It is necessary to use racial terms to put this incident in context: a white policeman would have reacted differently in the situation that was to follow.)

As Lyn's flat was the last in the corridor, and I was a few feet down from the door of the next, it was obvious that I was coming from her flat. However I braced myself, looked straight through the policeman, and brushed past him. He did not challenge me, as a white security policeman would have if he had seen me at the flat.

At the exit there were two white security policemen facing the street. I brushed past them too and continued to my car.

Lyn's flat faced onto a railway line, and I decided it would be better to keep it under observation from the other side of the line. I drove over the Belmont Street bridge and was approaching the area opposite her flat when I saw her emerge from a pedestrian tunnel. I drove up and invited her to get into my car. Again she begged me to leave. 'Please, please go away, they are following me,' she said.

The following morning, a Sunday, I called on Bill Hoffenberg for advice. He was not a member of ARM but a close confidant of our executive. He said if I was picked up I should avoid giving any information that could lead to the arrest of others, and we discussed ways of achieving this. (Bill was later banned and went into exile. He is now a distinguished academic, with a knighthood, in Britain).

On Monday I read in the Cape Times that Lyn had been arrested. I felt the situation was becoming a bit serious. I contacted 'Jacob' (Neville Hillman's code name) and asked him to meet me at 8:00pm that evening. I intended to find the explosives and do as many jobs as possible, to divert suspicion from those who had already been detained. I waited until 8:15pm for Neville, then left without him. I wanted to make contact with anyone who could give me a lead on where the explosives were.

I tried Millie McConkey's flat in Rondebosch, but there was no one there. After casting around aimlessly I decided to keep her flat under observation, and make contact with her when she returned. Around 11:00pm I saw a person behaving very suspiciously, slinking into the entrance of the block of flats. I thought to myself he looked like 'Luke' (Mike Schneider), but I was not sure. About half an hour later he emerged from the driveway, staying close to the wall, and crept away. As he passed under a streetlight I realised it was Mike. I got out of the car and called him. He was quite startled and told me I must not come near him because the cops were after him. I could see he was upset as he moved away from me. I shrugged my shoulders and got back into the car.

A few minutes later Mike knocked on the window of the passenger side of the car. I opened the door and he got in. He said, 'The game is up' and related how he and his girlfriend were returning to his flat that evening when they noticed two suspicious-looking characters hanging around the entrance to the block. As they went inside they glanced at a mirror in the lobby and saw these characters following them. Mike lived on the first floor, but they took the lift to the second floor. He ran along the corridor and down the fire escape while his girlfriend returned to his flat. The security policemen, for that was who they were, had raced up the stairs to the first floor. When Mike's girlfriend appeared they arrested her.

In the meantime Mike had got some distance away. He called his flat from a public payphone, and his girlfriend answered. She told him in an agitated voice that she could not see him that evening. Mike understood the message and started to look for shelter.

When I met him he was trying to make contact with Millie. He kept saying, 'The game is up' because the explosives were in his garage at the block of flats. They had been taken there earlier from Lyn's flat.

I dropped Mike in the city, and from there he bought a ticket and went to DF Malan airport. For some reason the security police failed to screen all the passengers, and he was able to fly out the country. (His girlfriend was briefly detained and released, and later joined him in London. Mike subsequently made a career for himself in the USA.)

I returned home in a state of apprehension and uncertainty, not knowing whether to go into hiding or not. I told myself I would make contact with Neville or anyone else I could warn, or assist, first thing the following morning. This was just rationalising, because I could not bring myself to run and hide. I preferred to face whatever was coming my way. I know better now.

I also felt I could not run because I had a responsibility to others. Again, I know better now. By this I do not mean one should abandon one's responsibilities in an emergency, but they should be handled in a way which allows one to take the necessary precautionary measures.

The security police came for me at about 1:30am on Tuesday.

I was boarding at the time, and my landlord opened the door in response to the banging. There were four Security Branch policemen, under the leadership of Captain Rousseau. They grabbed my landlord, thinking he was me, but he quickly rectified their mistake.

When I heard them at the door I knew it was the security police. I switched on the light and waited for them. They burst into my room. Captain Rousseau shouted, 'Staan op!' ('Stand up!')

I asked him why, and he shouted, 'Sabotasie!' ('Sabotage!')

I got dressed while two of them searched my room and shone a torch into the roof of the house. I was quickly handcuffed and bundled into a police car.

I was taken straight to Caledon Square Police Station and pushed into a room on the second floor. There on a table were our cases of dynamite, detonators, fuses and so on.

I was jammed up against the wall. Captain Rousseau stamped on my foot and, while standing on my foot (he was a large man), shouted in my face: 'Matt!'

I said I did not know what he was talking about. He told me they had got hold of someone's diary and found my telephone number next to the name 'Matt'. (Matthew was my code name.)

Lieutenant Van Dyk took over. Dangling an electric detonator in front of my face he shouted, 'What's this? What's this?' I said I had no idea.

I was under pressure. About 10 security policemen had crowded into the room. In my heart I prayed that the detonator Lieutenant van Dyk was shaking would explode, ignite the other explosives in the room and send us all into oblivion.

I was then taken to an adjoining room, which had been enlarged by the removal of a partition. Lieutenant van Dyk said 'Hier het ons baie plek. Ons kan hom nou lekker moer. ('We've got lots of space here. Now we can beat him up nicely).'

The policemen encircled me and I was shoved from one to the other. Occasionally I was thrown to the floor, picked up and thrown down again. At one point a brute of a policeman advanced on me. Captain Rousseau said 'Kyk sy hande!' ('Watch his hands!')

As this chap feinted with his hands he let fly a vicious kick at my groin. I parried the kick. During the melee Sergeant Sandburg had pulled on a black or dark brown boxing mitt. While the others were distracting me he hit me a stinging blow on the side of my face. Then later he positioned himself behind me and punched me just below the base of my skull.

My brain exploded, and I went down on my knees. I felt very sick.

Shortly afterwards I was taken to the charge office, signed for by uniformed policemen, and locked in a cell. Before being taken from the charge office I saw two security policemen leading in Mike's girlfriend. She was protesting vehemently: 'I don't know what you're talking about! I don't know what you're talking about!' Then she disappeared from view.

I was taken upstairs to the 'black section' of the police station. I was told to take a mattress and some blankets from one of the other empty cells, then locked up. I tumbled into bed fully clothed.

A few hours later the security police fetched me again, and I was taken, by now looking thoroughly dishevelled, to their offices. Lieutenant van Dyk and Sergeant van Wyk, also known as 'Spyker' (Nail) and 'Snake Eyes', recited from some book the number of times I could be sentenced to death for the offences I had committed.

A black security policeman came in, and to impress his superiors, told them I was the one who had been 'so cheeky' when he and Sergeant van Wyk served banning orders on me earlier in the year, and that I had refused to sign a document stating I had received the banning orders. Then another black security policeman arrived and confirmed I was the person who had brushed past him in the corridor outside Lyn's flat.

The four policemen escorted me back home and then to my

photographic studio, for a further search. While we were at my landlord's house more uniformed policemen came in. I was certainly an embarrassment to that poor family, who probably had never had a policeman in their home before.

The uniformed policemen wanted to know why I had not reported the day before to the Athlone Police Station, which I was required to do in terms of my banning order. I told them I had reported but possibly the officer in charge had not noted the fact. Lieutenant van Dyk interrupted and told the uniformed cops not to worry about me in future because I would not be reporting for a long, long time. (He was right: I began reporting again more than fifteen years later.)

While the security police were searching the house they left me standing in the corridor, handcuffed and bedraggled. As my landlady, Mrs Lewis, passed me I whispered to her that I was very sorry to have caused her so much inconvenience and embarrassment. She whispered back, 'It's quite all right, Mr Daniels. Please don't worry about it.'

Her response certainly made me feel a lot better. She had always been a kind person. When I first hired the room I had explained to the family that I was a member of the Liberal Party and therefore involved in politics. She said it was quite all right. When I was banned I told the family-the landlord was a schoolteacher and therefore a state employee-that if my presence were an embarrassment to them I would find other lodgings. Again they had replied 'It's quite all right, Mr Daniels.' And now this. However I know they did not suffer any repercussions for having had me in their home.

From the house we went to the studio, where the security policemen ruined my films by exposing them to the light in an attempt to find incriminating evidence. My brother Norman phoned while we were at the studio. He had been trying everywhere to trace me. I was not allowed to speak to him and was carted back to detention.

The first three weeks of my detention were possibly the worst. I made myself comfortable as far as sleeping arrangements were concerned by helping myself to an additional mattress and blankets from the neighbouring vacant cells, but my morale was low.

I tortured myself with the thought that the shock of my arrest must have killed my mother. Also, while I cannot remember now if I had been told that Randolph Vigne had been arrested, a picture of him sitting in a cell with his head in his hands kept entering my mind. I thought of his wife Gillian and their two sweet little children and my heart bled for them.

I had no change of clothing during this period and I can't remember being allowed to wash, except for hurriedly washing my face when I was allowed to go to the toilet.

There were no toilet facilities in my cell. I asked if I could have a bucket but the police refused, saying it was a dangerous weapon. Technically, the warders were supposed to check every two to four hours if prisoners needed to go to the toilet, but their checks were far less frequent and irregular. My cell was a long way from the charge office where the warders were on duty, and I found it difficult to attract their attention. I often had to urinate in empty milk cartons or cooldrink tins, which I would line up along the wall of the cell. If the warders waited too long between checks I would empty these containers, through a slight opening in the wire mesh that covered my window, and re-use them. The denial of toilet facilities was at times an excruciating experience.

These days I suffer slightly from emphysema. I do not know if this complaint came about because of detention, or was simply aggravated by it, but while in detention, particularly early in the morning and towards the evening, I often felt nauseous and dizzy. I could not fathom the reason for this. It was only later, on the Island, that I realised it had been due to carbon monoxide fumes. The second-floor cell I occupied in detention faced onto a busy road, and twice a day during rush hour the cars would line up outside, chugging and idling away while the drivers waited for the traffic lights to change. Quite a lot of the poisonous exhaust fumes must have seeped into my cell.

Towards the latter half of my detention I was joined on the second floor by detainees Sedick Isaacs, Achmat Cassiem, Manie Abrahams and James Marsh. They were each issued with three blankets. I cannot recall if they had sleeping mats as well.

However their cell doors had gaps of at least an inch between the bottom of the doors and the floor, and the winter of that year was extremely cold. One day when a magistrate came round to inquire whether we had any complaints, Mr Isaacs pointed out the conditions they were living in and asked, on behalf of the four of them, for additional blankets. He was told, 'This is not a health resort.' Nevertheless, after the magistrate had left, the sergeant in charge issued each of them two extra blankets.

My first break in detention came when the minister of my church was allowed to see me. One morning the door opened with a bang and there, flanked by two security policemen, was the Reverend McCrystal. He told me he had received permission to say a prayer with me. We stood where we were and he prayed, and we then said the Lord's Prayer together. As we said 'Amen' I quickly asked him, 'How is Mom?' He replied, 'Fine,' before he was ushered out the cell.

His visit boosted my morale. My mother was alive; the shock of my arrest had not killed her. It was all in my mind. Shortly after Rev McCrystal's visit I was allowed to phone Norman, who brought me a change of clothing, a shaving kit and toiletries.

While in detention I was shown statements made by other members of ARM who had been picked up. The first was a detailed statement on the attempted sabotage of the Constantiaberge radio mast. Only Lyn or Adrian could have made this statement. I initially denied all knowledge of the operation, but gradually came to admit my role. I said I could not tell who the other participants were, as we had all worn balaclavas and used only code names.

The next statement concerned a pylon job. Again I initially denied all knowledge but gradually admitted my role. I did so instinctively, feeling that if I grudgingly admitted my role then the security police would be more inclined to accept my denial of other events. I again insisted that I could not identify the others because of the balaclavas and code names.

That was the general pattern of my interrogation. I played the whole thing by ear, gradually admitting what they already knew, denying what they were unsure of and withholding information on or lying about what they did not know. In all I must have made and signed about five or six statements. I was surprised at the way I managed to lie so convincingly over and over again.

On one occasion I was questioned about Sheila Clare and Millie McConkey. I denied they were members of the ARM. The security police just laughed at me and filled in their names in a statement, which I subsequently signed. I felt cornered, especially as other statements shown to me by the security police contained their names. I thought the best thing I could do under the circumstances was play along, as I was not in a position to make an issue of it.

Increasing pressure was put on me to reveal the identity of Jacob, namely Neville Hillman. Whenever I was questioned about him I gave the usual story about balaclavas and code names. Often, during the early days of my detention, I would hear cell doors open and close on the floor where I was being held. I would call out through the small peephole in my door but received no reply. The following day, when I would be allowed to go to the toilet, the cells would once again be empty. I suspected people were being brought in by the security police in the hope that they would stumble across Jacob, and released shortly after they were cleared by someone who knew what Jacob looked like. Or maybe the cell doors I heard banging were on other floors, and I only imagined them to be on the floor where I was being held.

Whatever the case, the police eventually realised I was the only person who knew Jacob's identity. Adrian and Lyn had seen Neville during some jobs, and gave a very general description of him to the security police. The story I gave them was that I used to meet Jacob on a regular basis at a bus stop in Mowbray. I said I suspected he lived in Athlone because once or twice I had seen him approaching the bus stop from that direction. We would sit together in the bus, discuss whatever needed to be discussed and then arrange our next meeting. I only knew him by his code name Jacob and he only knew me by my code name Matt, and we made a point of never inquiring into each other's backgrounds. I also gave a vague description of him that had to tally with the description given by others.

My interrogation now consisted only of the question, 'Who is Jacob?' and my reply, 'I don't know. I've told you all I know about him.'

During one interrogation I was made to stand on a small patch of carpet for five hours and received no lunch or supper. During another Lieutenant van Dyk removed all the things in my cell, including fruit, clothes and a Bible, and I was not allowed to receive food or fresh clothing from outside. After three days Van Dyk had all my belongings returned, saying he felt sorry for me, and I was allowed to receive food and clothes from outside again.

On another occasion I was told that two investigators were coming from Pretoria with the sole purpose of questioning me. I was told they would not touch me but they would make me talk. I was certainly nervous at this threat. I was taken out of my cell at about 3:00 one afternoon, kept waiting till about 7:00, and then told, 'They'll be here tomorrow.' The same thing happened the following day. I never met those mysterious investigators.

One afternoon I was interrogated by Sergeant van Wyk, who was in charge, and Sergeants Sandburg and Olivier. They made me stand on a patch of carpet, fired questions at me concerning Jacob, and adopted threatening stances. I replied as I had before. Towards the end of the afternoon, possibly their knocking-off time, Van Wyk whispered something to the others. They looked at me and smiled. One of them went out and returned later with a flask and a large cake tin. Shortly afterwards another one went out and returned similarly laden. Olivier did not fetch refreshments, apparently because his home was too far away.

Van Wyk said, 'This is for us. There is nothing for you until you tell us who Jacob is, and you'll stand there until you tell us.' I shrugged my shoulders, and said I had already told them all I knew. The three sergeants began playing cards, glaring at me and firing an occasional question. After some time, having asked three times, I was allowed to go to the toilet. My left knee was troubling me and when Olivier saw me limping he gloated, saying, 'You are going to suffer.' (Incidentally, Sergeant Olivier behaved the best towards me out of all the security policemen.)

At around midnight, Sandburg and Olivier gave up playing cards, put their heads on the table and went to sleep. Van Wyk continued playing patience. After a while Olivier woke up and pleaded with me to tell them who Jacob was, so that they could go home to their wives and children. My reply was the same as before.

Later, the peace was suddenly broken by Sandburg, who stated loudly, 'As Daniels nou vir ons sê wie Jacob is, dan slaan ek nou hier dood.' ('If Daniels tells us now who Jacob is, I'll drop dead right here.')

At around 6:00am Olivier went to fetch coffee from the canteen. Van Wyk, indicating to me, said 'Nothing for him.'

By 8:00am they were all furious with me because they were officially back on duty. Van Wyk went to wash his face and came back shouting, telling the other two he was going to lose his temper with me.

Van Wyk and Sandburg left the room for a while and Olivier offered me two 'frikkadel' (meatball) sandwiches and a cup of cold coffee, which I accepted. Sandburg returned shortly afterwards looking for his sandwiches and got quite angry when Olivier admitted having given them to me.

Because all the other security policemen had now come back on duty they decided to take it in turns watching me. I asked one of them, Warrant Officer Olivier from the South African Railway Police, to tell me the time, estimating it must be mid-afternoon. He shouted, 'Why do you want to know the time?' and refused to tell me. Later I caught a glimpse of his watch: it was about 9:30am. I was feeling dizzy.

My ordeal eventually ended when Sergeant Olivier got irritated with the other security policemen who were watching me. They kept on asking Sergeant Olivier if he would relieve them for a few minutes, and then they would go out and not return. After this had happened a few times, Olivier took me to a room next door where the others were having lunch (I assume from this that it was between 1:00 and 2:00 p.m.) and playing cards, and told Van Wyk he was returning me to my cell.

Van Wyk said that was fine and they would fetch me again soon. When I got to my cell I climbed straight into bed and slept. They did not disturb me again that day.

Even though interrogation could be frightful, at times I welcomed it: once I was out of the cell there were always possibilities of escaping. A golden opportunity for escape presented itself one day, but because it was so unexpected I was caught off balance and the opportunity passed. I tried to manoeuvre for a similar set of circumstances but without success. For the same reason, I co-operated with the police when I was asked to point out the sites we had attacked. I came close to making escape bids on two occasions, but both times felt the odds against me were too great.

One day as we were driving out of the prison courtyard to go to a site, Warrant Officer Olivier looked in the car's rear-view mirror and said, 'Do you see who is waving to you?'

I looked back and saw someone who looked like a schoolgirl. I dutifully returned her wave, but said I did not know who she was. W/O Olivier reversed the car, and I saw it was Lyn. She was trying to be as cheerful and as brave as ever, but it was clear she had had a rough time and was under severe strain.

I met Lyn again while being taken for questioning. I greeted her and Sergeant van Wyk allowed us to say a few words to each other. We sympathised with each other in our mutual plight. She was surprised to find out that she was the first person I had seen from those of us who were detained. At that stage, except for the Rev McCrystal, I had seen no one other than those in authority.

I also met Millie once, after an interrogation session. A security policeman opened a door between the office I was in and another one, and there was Millie with about five or six security policemen. I instinctively bowed and greeted her, and she responded.

'Oh, you know each other,' one policeman said loudly, playing up to his audience.

I replied, 'Yes, we met at Liberal Party functions.'

They thought that was hilarious. I was led away to the sound of mocking laughter.

Neville was eventually caught more than 40 days after my detention. Some unfortunate factors led to his arrest. It seemed Adrian was giving the security police unsolicited information, including that he had met Jacob and myself on the mountain and on another occasion at the Tafelberg Hotel, and that Jacob's real name was Neville.

'We're not asking him for this information,' they said, 'He's sending for us and telling us these things.'

Eventually the security police said they were going to question my family about Jacob, as Adrian had told them he was a friend of the family. I tried my best to convince the police that Adrian was confusing Jacob with somebody else, but to little avail.

One day, in a cold sweat, I tried to get a message to my family. A common-law prisoner was cleaning the corridor that ran past my cell. I could not tell from looking through the peephole in my door if there was anyone else around, but I decided to take a chance and called the prisoner over. From the way he swiftly moved to my cell I gathered there were no warders in the vicinity, and I asked him if he could get me a pen. He said yes. From the peephole I could see the top of the stairs leading to the section where I was being held, and I watched as the prisoner crept stealthily down the stairs and disappeared. He reappeared, moving very quickly, with a ballpoint pen he had stolen from the warder's office.

I thanked him profusely for his brave action and frantically scribbled two notes on toilet paper. One was to my family telling them not to answer any questions about 'the fellow who built a desk for me' (whom they would know was Neville), and the other to a friend, explaining how she could get a hacksaw blade to me.

I gave the notes to the prisoner and asked him to get them to my brother-in-law, Jimmy Belford, who had an office nearby at Castle Bridge. I do not know what happened after that. Neither of the notes reached their destination, but I do know that the police did not intercept them either.

Following a later bout of interrogation I was being returned to my cell via the 'white' section of the charge office when I saw Norman, who had brought me something, standing in the 'black' section. I went over to him, with the intention of telling him not to say anything about Neville if the security police questioned him, but Sergeant Olivier was right at my elbow. I therefore asked Norman how Mom was and he said OK., and I asked him to tell her I was all right. As I was turning away, Olivier asked me whom I had been speaking to, and I replied, 'My brother, Norman.' Olivier asked Norman to wait there for him.

That evening, about 9:00 or 10:00, my cell door opened with a bang and a triumphant Olivier entered my cell. 'We got him! We got him!' he said excitedly.

I asked 'Who?'

He replied, 'Jacob!' and rattled off: 'Neville Hillman, address 21 Prospect Avenue, Cape Town, telephone number...'

I laughed, and told him they had the wrong chap. It was a desperate bluff. He put his fist against my chin and, in turn, laughed at me. Then he said, in a kind tone, 'No Eddie, we've got the right chap,' and left. I spent a very bad night thinking of Neville and his family.

The next morning the cell door opened again with a bang, and there stood van Wyk with two uniformed warders. 'Well Eddie, what have you got to say now?' he asked.

I replied, 'Congratulations.'

'You congratulate us?' he asked, in a surprised voice.

'Yes,' I said. 'Would you have betrayed your brother officer?'

He looked at me for a few seconds then said, 'Eddie, I admire you.'

He asked if I would like to see Neville, and I said I would.

About an hour later Olivier came to fetch me. I apologised for jeering at him the previous evening when I was trying to convince him they had arrested the wrong person; I told him I was very upset on hearing that Neville had been arrested. He accepted my apology with a smile.

I asked Olivier how they had caught Neville, thinking they may have intercepted the notes I sent out. But he related a different story, one that caused me great heartache. He said, 'I tricked your brother.'

Apparently, after locking me up the previous day, Olivier had gone back to Norman in the charge office saying he had a message from me for Neville, but had forgotten Neville's surname. Norman, in all innocence and thinking he was assisting me, replied 'Hillman.'

'That's it,' said Olivier, and rushed for a telephone directory.

To soften the blow, Olivier told me he had already apologised to Norman, which Norman later confirmed. On seeing Olivier's reaction to his answer Norman had felt there was something deeper involved. He had rushed to Neville's home and tried to clear the place of any incriminating evidence. But, unfortunately, all the evidence was already in the hands of the security police. I felt really bad. I had caused Norman so much trouble already; now this as well. I wished they had rather intercepted my letters, which would have made me directly responsible for Neville's arrest.

On our way to see Neville, Olivier told me they had asked him to make a statement but he had refused to do so. He said if Neville did make a statement they would release him. (Neville did eventually make a statement, but was not released. However I do not know if Olivier was intentionally trying to trick me.)

I met Neville in Van Wyk's office, and we shook hands. I told him to go ahead and make a statement because the security police already knew everything. I also told him that if necessary he must be a state witness against me as there was no need for both of us to go to jail. Neville objected strenuously to this. Van Wyk, who was present, was taken aback at my suggestion. 'You mean he must make a statement and not be a state witness?' he asked.

I replied 'No, he must be a state witness.' I did not push the issue, and was taken back to my cell.

That evening, lying on my bed and reminiscing, I thought back to when I had recruited Neville to ARM. He had also wanted to join the Liberal Party, but I advised him not to, pointing out that if the security police raided the LP's office and seized its books then his name and address would be known to them. That he accepted this advice is possibly the reason he had enjoyed an extra 40 days or so of 'sunshine'.

After Neville's arrest the pressure was off me and the rest of my detention was quite easy. Olivier brought me books to read. I was allowed a visit from my mother and my sister Laura. Later, Norman was also allowed to visit me. He had been invited by the British government to visit Britain, and very generously had come to ask me if I had any objections to his going. I told him I had none: we had never travelled overseas and I felt he should go. I knew he felt bad about leaving me, but I pointed out there was nothing he personally could do about my situation. Norman accepted my argument, and then told me, optimistically, that he was still paying my rent at the place where I had boarded. I told him to discontinue the payments because it was unlikely I would be using the place soon. A loudmouth security policeman chipped in: 'No, he won't be using that place for a long time again.'

Allow me at this point to introduce you, the reader, to my two sons. When I was arrested I had two lovely sons, Theodore and Donovan, from different mothers. Theodore was three years and six months old and Donovan was two years of age. I had not married either of their mothers, for personal reasons, but I had adopted Donovan when he was born. I had also offered to adopt Theodore, but his grandmother feared she would lose him to me and was not keen. I tried again from prison, writing to Theodore's granny offering to adopt him legally and promising not to interfere with their relationship. That was where the matter rested. Nevertheless, we embrace one another as father and sons, and Theodore and Donovan embrace each other as brothers.

Today Theodore has a lovely wife, Sharon, and four children, while Donovan is married to the lovely Marion and has three children. Before writing the above, I approached each of my lads separately and asked if they would have any objection to my writing about them. Each, without hesitation, said they would not. They are both fine lads and I love them.

Chapter 11

State Witness: 1964

I was asked to be a state witness on three separate occasions.

Early on in my detention, possibly in the first two to three weeks, I was told that Adrian and Lyn had offered to turn state witness in return for their release, and were planning to go overseas and get married. I ignored that statement.

At subsequent interrogations other security policemen told me the same story: 'the whites' or 'the Jews' were going to sell me down the river. Even the warders, who had nothing to do with the security police, said the same thing. I ignored all of them.

The first offer for me to become a state witness was made by Warrant Officer Olivier, who said if I gave evidence I would be ostracised by my comrades for, at most, six months, then the whole thing would be forgotten. I declined the offer.

On 24 July 1964 our situation became quite desperate. John Harris, an ARM member in Johannesburg who was acting independently as all his cell members had been arrested, placed a bomb on Johannesburg's Park Station. John informed the police, the railway police and the newspapers where the bomb was planted and the time it was due to explode, but no action was taken and the concourse was not cleared. The police later claimed he had not given them enough time to act.

Many people were injured in the explosion, and one of them, an elderly lady, died some months later.

Late that night, Lieutenant van Dyk fetched me from my cell. 'It's the death penalty for you now,' he said in a very agitated voice. 'John Harris, one of your members, planted a bomb on Park Station which has killed people. You'd better talk now otherwise it is the death penalty for you.' He scrambled around his office for a copy of the Sunday Times to show me pictures of the result of the explosion, but could not find it. He settled for a cartoon in the Cape Argus that depicted two hands, bloody up to the elbows, planting a bomb as if it were a seedling. It was captioned 'Red fingers?'

Van Dyk said the Sunday Times must be in the office next door, and that Adrian and Captain Rousseau were talking in there. He asked if I wanted to see Adrian. I declined.

The intervening door between the offices was closed, but I could hear snatches of conversation from the next room and I heard Adrian say, 'Bromberger.' I did not hear in what context Bromberger's name was mentioned.

I was very apprehensive when I was taken back to my cell. I was still being hammered about the identity of Jacob and now there was this new threat.

The next morning Lieutenant van Dyk said he had to go to Port Elizabeth, and would see me as soon as he returned. Three days later I was interrogated about trips I had made to Port Elizabeth and Grahamstown. After initially denying any knowledge of these trips I admitted having made them. Sergeant Olivier asked, 'Why must we first find out about these things before you tell us about them?'

At the end of my first 90 days in detention Captain Rousseau informed me I was being held for a further 90 days. A day or two later I was formally approached to become a state witness by Sergeant Olivier and another policeman. The argument they gave was that they wanted to release all the black men and white women who had been detained and charge only the white men. I declined. I was then approached by Captain Rousseau and, I think, Sergeant Sandburg, and they too asked me to become a state witness. Again I declined.

A while afterwards I was told by Olivier that Neville had asked to see me. When they brought him to my cell he said he had been asked to give evidence for the state and wanted to know my thoughts on the matter. I told him I was definitely going to jail, and that he should be a state witness as it was not necessary for both of us to go. After some persuasion he agreed.

Then I got cold feet. I told Neville the state would have to rely on state witnesses if they did not have enough evidence to convict. But Sergeant Olivier put the matter in perspective. He said, 'Look Eddie, what can Neville (who was a rank-and-file operative) say which Adrian and Lyn can't say?'

That was a fair point. I shook hands with Neville and, before we parted, made a short political speech. Sergeant Olivier had a hearty laugh at that.

Looking back on my experiences, from the time that Adrian was detained to when I was sentenced, I can say my attitude towards Adrian is that I bear him no ill will. He was in a difficult position and he took what he considered to be, at the time, the best way out. At the time of the trial I was certainly disappointed in him. Partly because he let the side down but more so because he saved himself at the expense of those for whom he was responsible. He was not responsible for me. I had joined ARM before he did. But he had recruited, I think, all of the other four who were charged with me. In this I feel he slipped up badly.

The fact that he gave evidence against me was unfortunate, but I can appreciate his position. Both he and I were members of ARM's national executive. From the day I fell into the hands of the security police I was threatened with the death penalty and so, I must assume, was he. With the Park Station bombing the situation became even grimmer. John Harris was subsequently found guilty of murder, sentenced to death and after an appeal, which was dismissed, executed. (It was reported that on the way to the gallows John sang 'We shall overcome,' noble words which proved prophetic.)

I do not know when Adrian decided to become a state witness, whether at this time or earlier, but I prefer to give him the benefit of the doubt and say it was at this time when the situation became so grim. Make no mistake, as far as Adrian was concerned he was fighting for his life.

It may be argued that I was in a similar position. Three offers to become a state witness had been made to me. I was continually being told by the security police, 'We want Adrian in the dock not you.' Why then did I not comply? I find it difficult to give a definite reason. I will put my thoughts down on paper and let others work it out.

I do not think it was because of bravery. I was very frightened of going to Robben Island. I had read some of the affidavits made to the Liberal Party by ANC and PAC members who had been imprisoned there. These affidavits were reported in the article 'Devil's Island' in Contact, and they were all very frightening.

I had had the opportunity of going into hiding. When I met Mike the night he was on the run and took him on the first leg of the journey that led to his escape, I too could have gone, but I had a terrible aversion to running away. Also I felt I had responsibilities to others in the organisation. Perhaps, in spite of my fear, there was a deep sense of loyalty in me. This may be a family trait because the loyalty of my brother Norman and my family to me, over time, has been tremendous. Or, perhaps, Adrian, because of his more fertile brain, keener perception of events and possibly more sensitive nature, could perceive the future better than I could.

My attitude to Lyn van der Riet, who was also a state witness against me, was one of sympathy. During the time we were active she was very brave, always cheerful and delightful. She and Millie McConkey had blown the electric railway cables in Observatory early one morning with a three-minute fuse-a brave job and a highly successful one. She had kept cases of explosives in her flat for long weeks; I had a nightmare after keeping explosives in my room for one night.

Under detention Lyn must have had a terrible time. Here was an Afrikaner girl (whose father, I was told, was chairman of a National Party branch in the Cape) in the hands of her Afrikaner captors. I can imagine the terrible pressure they must have put on her, calling her a traitor and treating her with contempt. I stated earlier how I saw her at the police station, when, in spite of her natural cheerfulness, I could see the strain written all over her face and in the way she held herself. Unlike Adrian, Lyn had not recruited any of the people who were in the dock. It is true that she owed loyalty to the organisation but the pressures she was under were tremendous. I can understand her succumbing to those pressures.

On the Island there was a warder named Van der Riet who told me Lyn was his cousin. He was slightly hostile towards me. One evening, after lock-up, I realised I had not filled my water bottle. When Van der Riet passed my cell on his rounds I asked him if he would be kind enough to fill it. He did so, and on his return he said to me: 'Almal van ons Van der Riets is nie die selfde nie.' ('Us Van der Riets are not all the same.')

I wrote to Lyn from prison in 1969. Believing she was being terribly ostracised, and in an effort to try and console her, I pointed out that she could not expect people to condone what she had done. I realised she must have been in a terrible position. Her family hated her for bringing disgrace upon them and betraying 'the Afrikaner nation', while her former comrades and friends were ostracising her for giving evidence. She had nowhere to turn to. I said to her, although she might not relish my letter because it perhaps raised memories she would rather forget, that if she needed a friend she should let me know. She never did. Perhaps she did not receive the letter or, perhaps, she did not need a friend.

There were other state witnesses who were not called. One was Neville, a fine and dedicated person. He was initially very reluctant to be a state witness against me but I managed to wear him down. Whether I was right or not in doing so I leave to the judgement of others. Then there was Millie McConkey, an attractive young lady and, like Lyn, very brave. She too has my sympathy for the ordeal she had to undergo. I have no hard feelings against any of them. As a matter of fact, I still have a sneaking admiration for those two women. They were tremendous.

All of the above tried to do something positive to bring about a non-racial democratic society in our country. We were amateurs fighting against professionals. We were playing for high stakes and when we lost we got hurt badly. But we did try.

Initially five of us, Stephanie Kemp, Alan Brooks, Anthony True, David 'Spike' de Keller and myself, were charged with sabotage against the state. After some legal argument a separation of trials was agreed to. Stephanie, Alan and Anthony were charged with 'Furthering the Aims of Communism'. They were found guilty and sentenced to five years imprisonment. Three years of Stephanie's sentence and two of Alan's and Anthony's were suspended.

Spike and I were charged with 'Sabotage against the State'. I was Accused Number One and he Accused Number Two.

The trial was pretty straightforward. Only the first and last days of the trial were open to the public. The rest of the time it was held in camera, though our parents were allowed into the court. My mother declined to attend; the only time she came to court was on the last day, when sentence was passed.

It was sad indeed to see Adrian, who had been like a son to the De Kellers, in the witness box giving evidence against Spike. Spike's father sat with a bowed head while the tears flowed silently down his mother's cheeks. Our representatives, Advocates Gibson and Snitcher, had little with which to defend us. The evidence against us was overwhelming. In fact when Advocate Gibson got up to cross-examine a witness, presiding judge Beyers wanted to know if he was already pleading in mitigation of sentence.

Defending me, Advocate Gibson emphasised my poor social background and lack of education (Standard Six), in contrast to that of my comrades, implying I was unduly influenced and misled. I could appreciate his efforts-he was desperately trying to play down my role to avoid a possible death sentence.

However I drew the line when he gave me a prepared statement to read from the dock. I drew up my own statement, which, with a few alterations, he approved. He asked if there was anyone I could call to testify on my behalf, such as my mother or church minister. I said I did not want anyone to testify for me. This was the right decision: Spike's uncle came to give evidence in mitigation, and Judge Beyers just humiliated him from the bench.

The evening before Spike and myself were to be sentenced, I heard Manie, a fellow detainee, calling across to Spike in the white section of the cells. I could not make direct contact with Spike because of the position of my cell, so I just relaxed on my mattress and listened to their shouted conversation. Suddenly Manie broke into song with 'The Longest Day.' It was appropriate to the occasion. It certainly was the longest day for Spike and myself. Manie sang that song with such gusto it reverberated throughout the police station.

The next morning, when Spike and I were brought up from the cells below the court, the courtroom was packed. I heard an urgent voice behind me calling, 'Eddie! Eddie!' and turned around. It was my eldest brother Ryland (now deceased). He had fought his way through the crowd. We shook hands in what was both a greeting and a farewell gesture.

As I looked round the courtroom, I caught the eye of René Hillman sitting in the public gallery. I mouthed to her the words 'How is Neville? Okay?' She smiled, nodded, and held up her hand with her index finger and thumb forming a circle. I again mouthed 'How is your Mom?' Again she gave me the reassuring sign. I was glad for this reassurance because the Hillmans were like family to me, and it was I who had recruited Neville into ARM.

'Stilte in die hof. Staan op.' ('Silence in the court. Stand up.') The court usher's voice rang out. Everybody stood up. There was a hushed, expectant silence. What was the sentence to be? The judge appeared, looking rather festive in his scarlet robe and somewhat out of place in this grim situation.

He sat down, produced a sheaf of papers from his flowing gown and started to read his judgement.

'You can blow up every pylon in the Western Cape ...'

And in ringing tones: 'You will never intimidate us ...'

He went on: 'Accused Number One tells the court about the skolly [street thug] menace which plagues the townships. What does he know about skollies? I know about skollies! He is a super skolly! A skolly only walks around with a knife in his pocket while he walks around with dynamite'

While he was in full cry, a solitary sheet from his sheaf of notes suddenly floated down from the bench. It lightly wafted through the air, made one or two dainty little half-circles, threatened to make a complete somersault, changed its mind, reversed its motion, being gently guided and cushioned by some unseen air currents. It seemed utterly incredible that this sheet of paper would have the temerity to play innocent games in this ominous atmosphere, while the judge thundered on with his vicious polit-ical judgement.

Though my fellow accused and I were the central figures in this drama being enacted in the court, at times I felt quite detached from the proceedings. I have read of cases where persons undergoing surgery spiritually detached themselves from their bodies and dispassionately view the proceedings from a distance. Others have viewed weeping relatives round their 'dead' bodies. With me it was not quite so dramatic. I quickly abandoned my spiritual detachment when I heard the judge say I was a super skolly. I was angry. I wanted to shout at the judge from the dock. My definition of a skolly is a parasite who preys on the weak, helpless and the poor. I did not consider myself to be in the same category. In the public gallery my mother's reaction was the same; she got up to chastise the judge and Ryland had to pull her back into her seat. The moment passed.

The judge carried on with his judgement, 'I sentence Accused Number One to 15 years imprisonment and Accused Number Two to 10 years imprisonment'

Amid whistles and wails the judge left the courtroom. My mother shouted from the gallery, 'My boy, Mommy will never see you again.'

I shouted back from the dock, 'Don't worry Mom. Everything will be all right.'

Inside, I felt it was the end of the road. I could not see myself surviving 15 years on Robben Island. I had read those other prisoners' affidavits. I knew about the beatings, the torture, the dirty food, the starvation diets, the punishing labour, the exposure to the harsh elements, the scanty clothing and the threadbare blankets. All this and more made my future seem rather bleak.

During the awaiting-trial period my mother had come to visit me, and to put her mind at ease I had told her there was a possibility I could be sentenced to 15 years-a lawyer had estimated 20 years, trying to keep my mind away from the possibility of the death sentence-but as a political prisoner it was unlikely I would serve even two years. She seemed satisfied with my assurances at the time. Actually hearing sentence being pronounced in that pervasively grim atmosphere, however, destroyed any hope I might have given her. She broke down and wept.

This had always been my one great inhibition in my fight against the apartheid system: the repercussions of my actions on my loved ones. I and others were prepared to take our chances, doing what we saw as our duty, and whatever happened to us we would accept as the price one had to pay in the interest of a cause greater than oneself. But the repercussions on one's very loyal family could be harsh indeed. But, I suppose, one just had to clench one's teeth and carry on regardless. It is always the individual who suffers in the Struggle and it is the Struggle that always benefits from the suffering of the individual. One must also bear in mind that everything that is done for the Struggle is done voluntarily.

Unlike the perpetrators and defenders of apartheid, we had no big brass bands, public acclaim, pay, pensions, medals, or state funerals. Instead, we had to operate clandestinely inside the country and risk all the sanctions we were exposed to for daring to challenge the might of the apartheid state.

I am sure none of us who were seriously opposed to the government considered ourselves infallible. Many of us, through what some may consider foolhardy actions, had laid ourselves open to harsh criticism. But all we can say in our defence is, 'We tried.' Perhaps we failed and failed badly, but we did try. And here I will make the same statement I have made elsewhere: at no time in the history of mankind has a powerful oppressor been overthrown overnight by the oppressed. Often the Struggle has taken decades, centuries, or longer. But ultimate victory over the oppressor has been achieved through the sacrifices, suffering, blood and tears of those who over the decades, centuries or more, have tried and 'failed'.

After being sentenced we were kept for a while in the cells below the court, until the large crowd that had waited around to cheer us on our way had dispersed. In spite of the lengthy delay, there were still some hardy souls outside as the large truck containing the two newly-sentenced prisoners roared out of the court gates. Peeping through the narrow slats of the truck I saw some familiar faces, among them one of my closest friends of former years, Maurice Hillman. Would I ever see them again? Some I have. Others I have not, because they have died, have left the country or have failed to make contact.

The epithet of 'super skolly' which the judge hurled at me was very hurtful. I wanted to write to him from the Island pointing out to him that, from the point of view of statistics, he might know more about skollies than I did, but when it came to practical experience I knew more about them than he did. He lived in broad, well-lit, protected areas. I lived in the heart of District Six. I had been robbed more than once, and on one occasion was kicked unconscious by those skollies. I had seen the results of the cowardly and brutal acts they perpetrated on the weak and defenceless. I doubt whether he ever had any physical contact with this terror of society. Possibly the nearest he had ever come to them was when he was on the bench and they in the dock. I discussed the idea of writing to the judge with Nelson Mandela, but he advised me that a letter written in that vein had little hope of being passed by the prison censors.

Today it is no longer relevant because the judge is dead.

Chapter 12:

To the Island: 1964 - 1979

Robben Island lies just off the coast of Cape Town, in Table Bay, at the foot of the African continent. It is somewhat oval in shape, 1,5 km at its widest, and surrounded by the waters of the cold Atlantic Ocean. The Island, which is 6 to 10 km from different parts of the mainland, can be seen from a number of places along the coast, but it is best viewed from the mountains around the city of Cape Town.

As a young boy, the first time I viewed Robben Island from the top of Table Mountain, it looked quite innocuous, more of a shipping hazard than a place of cruelty. I did not know at the time of its terrible history, of the brutality evinced by political rulers of the day towards those who were banished there.

The Island's history was characterised by the imprisonment of leaders of slave revolts; the imprisonment of African chiefs who challenged the advance of the colonists into their territories; the banishment of lunatics and lepers; and, from the 1960s onwards, the imprisonment of black political adversaries of the National Party and its apartheid policies.

Since the 1960s the Island has become internationally both notorious and famous. Notorious because of the brutal manner in which the government dealt with its political opponents, and famous because of the calibre and character of those imprisoned there: people such as Nelson Mandela and Walter Sisulu.

The prison truck in which we were taken from the courthouse stopped first at Roeland Street Prison (now a national monument) to deliver Spike de Keller to this whites-only institution. We shook hands and parted company. I was taken to Pollsmoor Prison, which was for black prisoners.

At Pollsmoor I changed into prison garb. While waiting to be booked in, I asked to be allowed to go to the toilet. The warder told me to 'go through that gate there', pointing towards a cell. Clutching my worldly possessions-a little plastic bag containing a face cloth, a toothbrush, a tube of toothpaste, a tube of shaving cream and a razor-I went to the gate. I got a sickening feeling in my stomach when I saw the mass of unkempt and demoralised humanity behind that iron grill. They were all sitting on their haunches, lined around the walls of a large cell that housed 60 or more prisoners. I steeled myself to walk through this menacing crowd. Clutching my little plastic bag even tighter than before, I pushed against the iron grill. It was locked. I quietly returned to my place and forgot about the toilet.

I was given lunch, a miserable-looking tin plate of mealie rice, which I refused. (This squeamishness of mine towards prison food would, in time, disappear.) While still waiting to be taken to a cell I watched other prisoners being booked in or discharged.

One old black gentleman was being discharged. His relatives had paid part of his fine, so he did not have to serve his full sentence of six months. He was changing into his civilian clothes, which had been kept for him in a bag by the prison authorities, and as he was standing on one foot pulling on a threadbare pair of long underpants, the loose leg of the underpants flapped near the food I had abandoned. A prison trusty immediately rushed in to assault him. I intervened, telling the trusty I did not want the food and that the old man had not deliberately tried to contaminate it. The trusty glared at the old man, who cowered away.

There was another trusty there whose sole job, it seemed, was to assault the incoming prisoners. As the warder called out the name of a prisoner and the prisoner moved forward to be booked in, this trusty would hit him in the face. I suppose it was some sort of softening-up process. The trusty reined in his enthusiasm, though, when one prisoner who looked like an old jailbird pre-empted his strike by threatening to 'get him'. However it was frightening that the trusties could assault other prisoners with impunity, and with the full approval of the warders. It seemed as if this was normal procedure.

I was put into a very large cell by myself. There was another prisoner there when I arrived, but he was removed. I looked under the few blankets lying around in the cell and found a picture storybook with which I whiled away the time.

At about 3:00pm I was fetched by the warders, handcuffed, put in leg-irons, and driven to the Cape Town docks. I was escorted from the prison van to the boat by two warders, one of whom walked behind me with a Sten gun trained on my back. I was on my way to Robben Island.

On board the Issi-named after the wife of General Jan Smuts-the shackles were removed from my ankles and I was taken, still handcuffed, down to the hold. Perhaps I was too wound up to notice the stench of the bilge oil, but on later trips to and from Cape Town it affected me to the extent that I vomited. The small portholes in the hold were blacked out, which added to the gloom. The paint had peeled off in places on a few of the portholes and as we travelled to the Island I squinted through the holes, but because I was so low down all I could see was the grey sea.

I was alone in the hold. I thought to myself how often I had been alone in my life: I had gone by myself to attend political meetings; I was alone when I joined the Irvin and Johnson fishing trawlers; I was alone when I joined the Dutch whaling fleet; I was alone when I went to Johannesburg; I was alone when I went to work on the diamond mines of Namibia; I had joined the Liberal Party of South Africa by myself. And now, I was once again alone, in the dirty hold of a prison boat on my way to the Island. I had no one with whom I could share my fears.

In later years I use to think of prison visitors, some that had never even seen the sea before, being forced to sit in this stinking hold. Add to this the frequently rough seas, and one can appreciate the courage and love of those who braved these unpalatable conditions over and over again to come and visit us, even if it was for only half an hour.

On arrival at Robben Island I was picked up at the docks by the prison van and taken to the isolation section. The prison gates were opened with a flourish by the warders and clanged shut behind me. At the isolation centre the warder accompanying me banged on the door. Another warder inside peered out through a large peephole, accepted a key through the peephole, and unlocked the door from the inside. The section was cold, bleak and grim and deathly silent. I was hurried up the corridor, placed in a cell, and the iron grille slammed shut behind me. The double-lock key grated in the lock, and the outer wooden door to the cell was closed. I heard the warders' footsteps fading away. I was alone with my thoughts and my fears. About an hour later the wooden door opened and a warder handed a quarter loaf of bread covered with fat through the bars. That was my supper and my introduction to Robben Island.

I was to remain in the isolation section for the next 15 years, until my release. The section then consisted of about 70 single cells, and contained both common-law and political prisoners. Some of the political prisoners were placed there on the instructions of the security police while others were put there by the prison authorities.

On my first morning in prison I was whistling quietly to myself in my cell when a trusty came to tell me I must not whistle. I stopped, but after a while I started whistling under my breath. This trusty once again sidled up to my cell and said, 'You must not even whistle softly.' Strict silence had to be observed at all times.

I was kept inside my cell, except for a daily brief period for exercise, for the first three days. I was then allowed to join my fellow prisoners in the prison yard breaking stones.

I had been there for little over a week when I heard that one of the older prisoners, Mr Filani had been sentenced to three days 'spare diet' (i.e. rice and water) for having soap other than the regulation prison issue in his cell. Mr Filani was serving a life sentence for his part, which he vehemently denied, in the Bashee Bridge murder case in which a white foreman, his wife and two daughters were murdered by alleged members of Poqo, the PAC's armed wing. .

I felt bad about the old chap starving there and decided to smuggle him some food. At lunchtime I was locked in my cell with a plate of cold mealie rice. I ate about two-thirds of it and wrapped the rest in toilet paper and slipped it inside my shirt. After lunch we were let out and I made my way to my place in the yard, where we sat in rows and hammered big pieces of slate into gravel. The old man was in a cell about ten paces from the end of the row in which I was working. While banging away at the slate I explained to Mac Maharaj (12 years), who was sitting next to me at the end of the row, what I intended doing, and requested that we change places. We pushed our pieces of slate around until we were in a position to swap places. There were four warders patrolling the yard and one on the catwalk, and I asked Mac to let me know when they were looking elsewhere. He gave me a signal, and I raced off. I took the mealie rice from inside my shirt, pushed it between the bars of Mr Filani's cell, and headed back to my place in the line. But it was mission impossible. Before I got there two warders had hold of me. There was much confusion and noise. Some of the warders rushed over to search Mr Filani's cell. A prisoner sitting nearby, Clarence Makwetu (five years), shouted to Mr Filani to throw the mealie rice out of his cell, which he did. I could hear the heavy key grating in the lock as the grille to his cell was opened and he too was placed under arrest.

I was immediately marched to the head of the prison, Chief Theron. When he heard what I had done he shouted loudly that he would show me, and others like me, what would happen to us if we stepped out of line. He was sitting at his desk and turned round to take some papers from the cupboard behind him. Without thinking, and bemused by what I had got myself into, I started to walk around his office. This led to another torrent of abuse being hurled at me. He then asked if I had anything to say. I explained to the chief that what I had done I had done on my own initiative, that the other prisoner was unaware of my intentions and was therefore an innocent party to the affair. The chief made some notes then told the warders to take me back to the yard, where I continued to work. That was the last I officially heard of the incident; I was never charged or penalised for it. However my fellow prisoners subsequently reprimanded me: they already had their own system, of which I later became part, for supplying food to prisoners on 'spare diet'.

The African prisoners on the Island were worse off than the Indian or 'Coloured' prisoners, in that they were given only sandals, short pants and a shirt each while the others had shoes and socks and, in winter, were issued with long trousers and jerseys.

Some of the 'Coloured' chaps argued we should show solidarity with the African prisoners by refusing to wear long trousers and jerseys in winter, but I was one of those who argued that our aim should be to fight for all prisoners to be issued the same clothing. We felt that if we refused to accept the clothing issued to us we would be prejudicing our case for improved clothing for all. However at least two prisoners did refuse to accept additional winter clothing when it was issued to them.

We started off, if I remember correctly, with three threadbare blankets and a sisal mat. We slept on the cement floor. Years later the situation improved considerably, and all political prisoners were then allowed six blankets, a bed and a mattress. All prisoners were also later issued with a pair of shoes, two pairs of long pants and two pairs of short pants, two long-sleeved shirts, a safari shirt, two jackets, overalls, a short raincoat, a hat, two jerseys, socks and underclothing. We kept these clothes all year round.

In the early years food was scanty, dirty and very poorly prepared, but again this situation improved in later years. Rations were increased and the food was prepared by other political prisoners, who did a magnificent job with the limited rations and ingredients at their disposal. Just prior to my release I wrote an illegal letter of appreciation to the kitchen staff. I pointed out that one of the methods the prison authorities had used, in attempt to break our spirits, was to give us bad and insufficient food. This had failed. They, my fellow prisoners in the kitchen, made a positive contribution to the maintenance of our morale. Dirty, ill-prepared food, theft and smuggling of food had become a thing of the past, an unpleasant memory.

In those early years the African prisoners received no bread and the others did not receive Puzamandla (a powder which, when mixed with water, makes a healthy drink). Later African prisoners were given one slice of bread three times a week and the non-Africans were given a quarter of a loaf every day. We pooled these discriminatory rations and shared them out equally among us. (I must make it clear that I speak with authority only about the section in which I was kept. We never had any access to any other parts of the prison, except when Ahmed 'Kathy' Kathrada and I were in the prison hospital for short periods in 1967 and 1968 respectively. Kathy had surgery for piles on the Island and I had a hernia operation in Cape Town. We were allowed a brief period of recuperation in the prison hospital. After that, for 'security reasons', we were no longer allowed access to the hospital regardless of how ill we were. However we did receive reports from time to time about conditions in other sections.)

Initially I did not know that African prisoners were not receiving bread. It was brought to my notice when Dr Pascal Ngakane mentioned it in passing during a conversation. He also mentioned that day was his wedding anniversary. That evening I tried to smuggle my bread to Pascal as an anniversary gift, but the warders locked us up so fast I was unable to. Speaking about Pascal brings a joke to mind. Africans were not allowed liquor in South Africa, and so-called 'Coloureds' could obtain liquor only under stringent conditions. As we were waiting in a queue for something or the other I whispered to Pascal that my brother had a bottle store on the mainland. He looked at me and said, 'Oh?'

'Yes,' I said. 'But he hasn't got a licence.'

Pascal burst out laughing and started to repeat the joke to those around him. Everybody had a good chuckle.

In the early years, with few exceptions, our cells were very bare. Besides clothes, bedding and our ballies (chamber pots), we had nothing else in our cells. We had to observe strict silence in our section. At weekends and on public holidays we were locked up for 24 hours at a stretch, with 30 minutes of exercise in the morning and another 30 minutes in the afternoon. During the week we would break stones in the yard, or work in the quarry, from 8:00 a.m. to 4:00 p.m. We were locked up at 4:30 p.m. and would have our supper in our cells. By 8:00 p.m. we all had to be asleep. The lights remained on throughout the night, and a warder locked in the section with us kept us under observation throughout the night from the corridor.

Here too changes occurred later. Those of us with study privileges were allowed to keep books in our cells. We also had access to censored books from the prison library. We were no longer forced to sleep at 8:00 p.m. and some warders turned a blind eye if we read throughout the night. But we still spent long periods in our cells. On weekdays we were locked up from 4:30 p.m. to 6:00 a.m., and on weekends from 3:00 p.m. to 7:00 a.m.

As I mentioned earlier, we shared the section with common-law prisoners up to about 1966 or 1967. There were 70 or more prisoners in the section, and the warders divided us into three groups. One was the Rivonia group, from the famous treason trial, which included Nelson Mandela, Walter Sisulu and five others. Two was members of the National Liberation Front (a radical offshoot from the Non-European Unity Movement called the Yu Chi Chan Club), and comprised of six prisoners. Group three, the riff-raff, made up the rest. I was among the riff-raff.

We were allowed to shower twice a week, on Wednesday afternoons and Saturday mornings, and on Saturday mornings would receive a change of clothing. The Rivonia group would be let out first to shower. They would take their time while washing and have first choice of the change of clothing. They would be followed by the NLF group. By the time we were let out to shower it was often already almost lock-up time on a Wednesday or lunch-time on a Saturday. We were harassed and provoked to hurry up by the warders. Some of us would not even get to the showers, and would give up trying in disgust. As we were herded into the yard to get dressed, threats, pushes and sometimes a blow from a warder's baton would cause terrible tension and strain.

Educated prisoners were often the worst treated by the trusties and the warders. Dennis Brutus (three years) was systematically and vilely persecuted, so badly that at one stage he became psychologically disorientated. On his release he gave a press conference in London in which he gave an account of the brutalities on the Island. Unfortunately, he was accused of exaggerating. He was not exaggerating, but telling the unvarnished truth. Andrew Masondo (12 years) had his shoulder blade forced out of position in an assault by warders. Mr Mlambo was made to dig a hole, forced into the hole and then urinated on by a warder. He was also assaulted with a baton.

Amongst the worst of the warders were the three Kleinhans brothers, who were later removed from the Island.

In our section we had a committee made up of representatives of all the political organisations represented in the prison. The function of this committee was to maintain peace and harmony among the different groups, organise the general running of the place-for example, cleaning the areas in which we were housed, dishing out food, and so on-and take up complaints with the authorities. The political organisations took responsibility for maintaining discipline among their own members.

The prison authorities never recognised this committee, or any subsequent ones except for a sports committee, and it operated illegally.

Because of some inter-organisation disagreement the committee collapsed in about 1968/1969. For about three years after that we lived an uneasy existence, trying to keep down tension and strain as best we could by engaging one another only on a personal basis and not a political one.

In the early 1970s the authorities started to increase the pressure on us. They pushed us hard and instructed us to maintain strict silence at work. This meant we had to maintain a 24-hour silence, because we were not allowed to communicate or make any noise in the cells. I remember one prisoner, Johannes Dangala (five years) singing quietly to himself at work, and the warder shouting at him, 'Silence, you must not talk.'

Johannes shouted back, 'I'm singing, not talking.' The warder told him loudly he was not allowed to sing, and that ended that little fracas.

We were charged with petty offences and trumped-up charges, and sentenced arbitrarily to loss of meals, isolation and loss of studies. The Namibian prisoners, who were housed in the opposite wing of our section, had a particularly rough time. They were persecuted by the warders under Sergeant Carstens, Sergeant Meyer and one other, who were in turn subordinate to some very bad officers.

This persecution and provocation by the authorities forced us once again to set up a committee to co-ordinate our activities, and to avoid strife we elected this committee from the body of prisoners. This general committee took responsibility for co-ordinating the running of our section. We also agreed that any political issues would be handled by another committee comprised of representatives of the political organisations.

The first act of the political committee was to call a hunger strike in protest against the persecution of the Namibians. One Friday we refused to eat lunch or supper. That night a gang of warders under Chief Fourie sneaked into our section after 8:00 p.m. We were forced to strip naked and face the wall of our cells, and our cells searched.

Once the warders had passed our group, they started to beat prisoners. The screams of terror, fear, anguish and pain reverberated down the corridor. Looking through my cell window, I could see the batons bouncing off the bodies and heads of my fellow prisoners in the opposite wing. Andimba Toivo Ya Toivo and Jeff Masemola were beaten unconscious by the warders while a prisoner named Chilwane had his testicles crushed till they bled.

The next morning we elected Walter Sisulu to raise the matter of the assault with the officer who would routinely come around to hear complaints and requests. Unfortunately it was the same officer who had led the assault, Chief Fourie. He and Walter had a stand-up slanging match, but it was the last organised assault launched against us.

About a week later Chief Fourie said he would grant us an interview at which we could raise matters relating to prison conditions. Four of us, Walter Sisulu, Neville Alexander (10 years), Kwedi Mkalipi (20 years) and myself, represented the prisoners. We received a good hearing from Chief Fourie and Chief Van der Westhuizen. A few days later the four of us were sent for by the Commanding Officer, Colonel Badenhorst. He saw each of us individually, and furiously bawled at us, telling us that we could speak only for ourselves and for no one else. Then he dismissed all our complaints.

Prior to my arrest I smoked about twenty cigarettes a day and double that number at weekends. Being a poor social mixer at parties, I would use cigarettes as an 'ice breaker' by offering them to those in my vicinity. We were not allowed to smoke in prison, but those in 'A' group were entitled to several squares of compressed tobacco. This was really vile stuff. In the early years we were all in 'D' group and none of us was allowed access to any kind of tobacco. We would barter with the common-law prisoners, exchanging soap and toothpaste for tobacco that they smuggled into our section or brought to our place of work.

The common-law prisoners took great risks in smuggling tobacco and newspapers to us. They usually stole these from the homes of the warders. Some prisoners did it because they supported us in our opposition to the authorities and, perhaps, also liked to cock a snook at the authorities, while others did it simply for mercenary motives.

To supplement our smuggled tobacco we would pick up cigarette ends in the street while walking to the quarry. We would also raid the ashtray in the warder's office for butts and even collect the dregs from his pipe after he had cleaned it. We really smoked poison.

Nelson Mandela pointed out to the authorities that there were only two reasons why they raided our cells and continually subjected us to body searches, and these were to search for tobacco and newspapers. He said these raids and body searches caused unnecessary strain between prisoners and the prison authorities. He suggested that if we were allowed legal access to tobacco and newspapers then the reasons for continually raiding us would fall away.

In about 1968 we were officially allowed to smoke. Prisoners were allowed to order 300 cigarettes a month or two packets of tobacco. The first time that we placed our orders for tobacco it took two months to arrive. This happened a few times with the warders making all kinds of weak excuses to us as to why it had not been delivered, and chuckling to themselves. I got so fed up with this type of blackmail that I told the warders to keep the cigarettes and tobacco, and I quit smoking.

About a year later I was busy cleaning the shed at the quarry, while everyone else was at the quarry face, when I came across a still-smouldering pipe belonging to Lalu Chiba (18 years). I took a puff on it. The taste was horrible; I spent the rest of the day spitting, trying to rid my tongue of that vile taste. That experience sealed my distaste for tobacco.

It was fortunate that I gave up smoking at that time, because a short while later I was diagnosed by the prison doctor as suffering from emphysema. Besides this touch of emphysema I am also slightly asthmatic, a hereditary condition, but otherwise my health is good.

One day the boilers in the kitchen broke down. We were locked up without supper and told that as soon as the boilers were repaired we would receive our food. We were woken in the early hours of the morning and told that our food had arrived. There was excitement in the section, I suppose because it was something outside of the rigid routine to which we were subjected. We were unlocked and some of us went to fetch the food at the gate. The area from where the food was fetched and dished out was ablaze with light, but when I moved out of the glare of the lights to the far end of the yard, I suddenly appreciated the softness of the darkness of the early summer morning.

I had not experienced darkness since coming to prison, because we were locked up all night and the lights in our cells were always on. The stars were big and bright and glorious. They seemed so close to the earth. For a few minutes, those of us who had moved out of the harsh light into the sweet darkness, felt so free, gloriously free, enjoying the spectacle of the beautiful, glittering stars against the dark backdrop of the early morning summer sky in all its glory.

It soon came to an end. We were locked up once again in the glare of our cell lights, cut off from the dark, tender night with its glittering jewels.

On my release I often stood in the garden of my brother's home and drank in the beauty of the night and the dazzling stars.

Chapter 13:

Work, Study, Visits: 1964 - 1979

We worked in the prison yard, knapping (breaking) stones, until a couple of years after I arrived on the Island. We all felt very cooped up in this space and repeatedly asked if we could work in the open. Permission to work in the quarry was granted in about 1966.

Even so, the work remained hard and soul-destroying, with the warders pushing us to meet arbitrary quotas. We also complained of continuous glare from the lime walls and exposure to the elements. Eventually, in about 1974, we were transferred to sawing and chopping wood and, finally, to collecting seaweed on the beach.

The provocation of the warders in trying to force us to work harder often led to protests in the form of hunger strikes or downing of tools, or individual arguments with warders. Some of us were charged for these protests and arguments, and sentenced arbitrarily to the loss of food, loss of studies or isolation. (Those of us who challenged the charges in court usually won our cases.)

From around 1977 onwards we no longer went out to work but remained in our section. There were two reasons for this: we were given only work that we considered soul-destroying, and some of us were getting on in years, among the most senior being Govan Mbeki, Walter Sisulu and Nelson Mandela.

In the early years of my imprisonment the medical orderlies and doctors made it seem as if they were doing us a big favour when they examined us or prescribed medicine. In latter years their attitude underwent a pronounced change and, although we still encountered the occasional doctor or orderly who was a bit bumptious and overbearing, if we were provoked too far we could report them to their superiors who would give an attentive ear to our complaints. In the past we were seldom given the opportunity to raise complaints, and if we were those complaints were usually dismissed with utter contempt.

Security on the Island was extremely tight, and we were allowed no opportunity for contact with outsiders or even prisoners in other sections. In 1968 I had to go to a hospital in Cape Town for a hernia operation. As soon as the operation was over I was whisked from the operating theatre, driven to the docks and, despite the bad weather and rough seas, taken straight back to the Island. (While I was lying on a stretcher in the hospital foyer waiting for the police van that would take me to the docks, a nurse walked over, straightened my blankets and tucked them under my chin. The warders who were guarding me made no objection. A few minutes later the nurse returned and again fussed over me, but this time she slipped a packet of cigarettes under the blanket. It was really a lovely gesture. We were not allowed to have cigarettes in prison at that time, but I managed to smuggle them in undetected.)

I recuperated in the prison hospital, as did Ahmed 'Kathy' Kathrada after his operation there. Following that no further prisoners who underwent operations or were seriously ill were allowed to stay in the prison hospital. We had to recuperate in our cells and were nursed by our fellow prisoners. We had some serious cases among ourselves. One, Mobbs Gqirana (six years) became so ill we thought he was going to die. We appealed to the authorities to take him to the hospital where he could receive proper medical care, but they refused to budge. They did not want prisoners from our section to meet any other members of the prison population.

Those of us who had the financial means to study and applied for permission to do so were given a form to sign stating, among other things, that we would forfeit the study privileges if we were found guilty of abusing them.

On Nelson's advice we refused to sign the form because its conditions were too stringent. We later signed a modified form.

Initially only a few prisoners were allowed to study, among them Ahmed Kathrada. He ordered study materials in excess of his requirements and distributed the surplus, including ballpoint pens, pencils and scribbler pads, among his fellow prisoners. I was one of the fortunate beneficiaries. It was a generous and brave gesture on Kathy's part, in that his study privileges would have been revoked if we had been caught in possession of the material and the prison authorities had traced it back to him.

We quickly used up the scribbler pads we received from Kathy and had to find other sources of paper. My favourite source was Sunlight soap wrappers, which were large compared to the wrappers of other items. I went around and booked those wrappers from my fellow prisoners well in advance of them placing their orders for toiletries. In the main section, where conditions were worse than in ours, the prisoners used cement bags as writing paper.

The lime quarry was our classroom. We had to be careful with written notes, because we ran the risk of losing study privileges if we were caught with unauthorised notes. Usually we tried to memorise points, or made cryptic notes on our hands and arms.

Our history class, for example, would consist of about six prisoners. We would assemble at the quarry face and have an hour or so of discussion while working with picks and shovels, then surreptitiously form different groups for other subjects such as English, Afrikaans or Geography.

We were never allowed to order just any book from the university library. Every book had to be censored first, and often the recommended readings were turned down. At times we were even denied prescribed books. Some of the warders in the study department tried to help us by speeding up stationery orders, posting assignments and dispatching orders for library books, but others deliberately dragged their feet and made things as difficult for us they could. Many warders resented us studying and improving our academic qualifications. Up to the early '70s we were allowed to register-at the University of South Africa (Unisa)-only just before registration closed. Over time, as improvements occurred, we were allowed to register fairly soon after registration opened each year, and the handling of our study materials improved.

Studying was very important, especially to the long-term prisoner. It meant he could occupy his time and exercise his mental faculties, and that when the time came for him to rejoin society he would find it so much easier to adjust. Studying involved drawing up a disciplined and meaningful programme; it distracted our minds from our narrow environment, tempered our yearnings and gave us common ground.

At a latter stage the authorities forbade any prisoner registering for subjects beyond matriculation level, although those already registered for tertiary subjects were allowed to complete their courses. This action was a big blow to us. We pointed out to the authorities that allowing us to study was in their interests as well as ours, because when prisoners were meaningfully occupied the chances of frustrations and tempers overflowing into violent behaviour were minimised. They remained firm in their decision, though when I left the Island there were rumours floating around that tertiary subjects would be allowed again.

Even though the conditions for studying were primitive, with the help of our more learned fellows a number of prisoners learnt to read and write, while others obtained diplomas and university degrees.

I arrived at jail with a Standard Six education, having not studied for some 22 years. I was given permission to study in July 1965, and obtained my matriculation certificate the following year. In 1967 I enrolled through Unisa for a BA degree. In March 1971 I was arbitrarily sentenced to six-month's isolation and my study rights revoked. Three years later I was once again allowed to study and I completed my BA, majoring in Sociology and Economics. I then registered for a B. Comm (Administration), which I completed in February 1979, majoring in Business Economics, Industrial Psychology and Economics.

I owe my academic success to two factors: my very loyal brother Norman, who financed my studies, and my fellow prisoners, who so unselfishly and diligently helped me to understand the subjects to which I was introduced.

Although the general prisoners had organised field games since about 1972, we played no sport on the Island other than table tennis and teniquoit, which we ourselves had organised, until about 1976. After that we were able to enjoy tennis, volleyball and soccer. We also relaxed with more sedentary games such as scrabble, chess, ludo and Q-kerm-a game similar to snooker in which short cues are used to pocket wooden discs on a square board.

In the latter part of my imprisonment we had a weekly film, taped music, and censored news. We were allowed to subscribe to a number of magazines such as Reader's Digest, National Geographic and Huisgenoot. The magazines seldom reached us intact; they were censored and any 'undesirable' parts removed. Towards the end of my imprisonment we were also allowed to receive Time magazine and approved books from the provincial library.

Access to privileges depended largely on a prisoner's classification, an issue that became of great importance to us. All political prisoners started as 'D' category, while common-law prisoners such as rapists, murderers and robbers started off as 'B' category. 'D' category prisoners were allowed only one letter and one visit every six months. 'A' category, on the other hand, were allowed to have a radio, newspapers, four contact visits and four letters a month, and were allowed to buy groceries.

When I arrived on the Island all political prisoners were classified as 'D' category, and only grudgingly promoted to higher categories. In my case it took five years to get to 'C' category. We were not aware that the authorities were denying us privileges that were a basic part of prison regulation. Nevertheless we agitated for promotion to other categories to ease our environment and to gain access to newspapers. We used to dream about the newspapers we were going to subscribe to when we were eventually promoted to 'A' category.

I was eventually promoted to 'C' category in 1968, but was demoted in 1971 for some misdemeanour. I eventually became 'A' category in 1976, however even then I was never allowed a radio, newspapers or a contact visit. By this time there was not a lot of difference between the A, B and C categories, it was easier to get promoted and privileges had increased.

Some of the younger and much later arrivals to the prison objected to the system of classification and called for it to be abolished, but the authorities refused.

Letters and visits were our only meaningful contact with the outside world. They were also our most sensitive spot. Any vindictive or small-minded warder could make a prisoner's life a misery by interfering with this contact under the all-powerful and sweeping guise of 'security'.

Any letter we wrote to the outside world had to go through the censor's department. There were certain people we were not allowed to write to or receive letters from, and also subjects and incidents to which we were not allowed to refer. These subjects changed, depended on whoever was doing the censoring at a particular time. If we wrote to an 'undesirable' person the letter would not be posted, and might be noted in our personal file. We might or might not be informed of that fact. If a letter was handed in for censoring and exception was taken to a phrase, then that letter was returned to the prisoner with the offensive words underlined, with instructions that the prisoner must rewrite the letter without them. One prisoner had the same letter returned three times for rewriting, because each time it was submitted a new fault was found. In addition he had to alter the original date on the letter to the present date.

This sort of censoring caused us much frustration. Those who did the censoring seemed to rely mainly on guesswork, and often ruled out quite innocent phrases. Also the content of our letters was often out of date or irrelevant by the time they came back from the censors. One could refuse to rewrite a letter, but this meant forfeiting it. The alternative was to eat humble pie and rewrite it, but then one also had to alter the date, giving the recipient the impression the letter had been recently written. This could give rise to misunderstandings, particularly if one was contacting family members to raise personal problems.

Visits were another sensitive issue. We were told that we were allowed visits from immediate relatives only, which in my case limited the potential visitors to two very loyal brothers, an elderly mother and an invalid sister. In other words there were, in real terms, only two people who could visit me regularly.

A number of other people wanted to visit me on the Island but their applications to do so were not considered favourably, either because they were seen as a security risk or they were not immediate family.

When Jimmy Kruger, then Minister of Justice, met Nelson Mandela on the Island they discussed, among other things, the question of immediate relatives. Kruger told Nelson that the criterion for visits was not family ties but security. Anybody, he said, could apply to visit and if they were not a 'security risk' then the application would be granted.

The authorities used either argument as it suited them. The blanket term 'security risk' also applied to all white friends and relatives, regardless of whether they were politically involved or not.

When a visit did take place it did so under stringent conditions. Both the prisoner and visitor would be warned that any discussion outside family matters would cause the visit to be cancelled. There was no physical contact between the visitor and the prisoner. They were divided by a partition and could see only each other's head and shoulders through a piece of thick glass, and they had to speak to each other through a telephone system with a warder listening in on a third telephone. If anything was said which the warder did not like he could immediately stop communication by throwing a switch.

The fact that they had all these security arrangements and yet still denied us visits by certain people made us come to the conclusion that the authorities were acting vindictively when they refused visits. We felt it was, like the censoring of letters, an invidious attempt to destroy our morale.

A further frustrating point was that many of the prisoners on the Island came from areas beyond Cape Town. Their family members had to undergo long and costly journeys, sometimes from more than 1000 kilometres away, to visit them. Even so they would not be allowed to visit for more than half-an-hour.

Chapter 14

News, the garden, the earthquake: 1964 - 1979

The authorities had two aims in their handling of us: one was to get the world to forget about us; the other was to destroy our morale. One of the ways of destroying our morale was to deny us information about the outside world. News, particularly political news, was our life's blood, and some of us took desperate risks to obtain it.

Despite the tight security measures in place to prevent us receiving information, we heard of the assassination of Prime Minister Dr Hendrik Verwoerd, the 'architect of apartheid', on Tuesday 6 September 1966. Verwoerd was stabbed in parliament by Dimitri Tsafendas, a parliamentary messenger. The news, shocking as it was, gave us renewed hope that the government would now come to its senses and change, or at least modify, its cruel apartheid policy. But that hope was dashed with the ascendancy of John Vorster to the premiership. (One morning, looking out across the yard from my cell window, I saw Tsafendas on the opposite side of the yard. He was standing in the sun with his back pressed against the outside wall of his cell trying, I assume, to get as much warmth from the wall as possible because of the coldness of his cell. We saw him for a few more days during his two daily half-hour exercise periods. Then we saw him no more.)

After a few months in prison I was allowed to receive the Reader's Digest. A few months later we were denied access to all magazines. When I was again allowed to receive the Reader's Digest it was regularly censored in fact, mutilated.

The one magazine we were allowed to order that was hardly censored at all was the Farmer's Weekly.

When one of my fellow prisoners, Dr Masala Pather (18 months), reached 'A' group status he applied, as was his right according to prison regulations, to subscribe to newspapers and purchase a radio. He was given the 'horse laugh' by the authorities, and told he would be allowed to order one magazine.

He had to submit a list of six, from which one would be chosen. When Masala reported back to us there was an immediate huddle, by those who had knowledge of magazines, as to which should be put on the list. Mac Maharaj called for the inclusion of The Economist, but his suggestion was pooh-poohed by the others who felt the authorities would never allow it. Eventually a final list was drawn up. However Mac continued to agitate for the inclusion of The Economist, arguing that it would be only one of six possibilities and that we had nothing to lose by including it. Finally, the others relented, and magnanimously dropped one of the other titles.

The authorities chose The Economist! There was utter disbelief, mingled with joy, that we had made a breakthrough as far as news was concerned. Mac was congratulated by all for his insistence on its inclusion.

Masala went ahead and ordered the magazine. When it arrived, for some reason the authorities never bothered to unwrap it, and for the first time we received uncensored world news. Masala was released from prison about three months later, but Mac coincidentally became an 'A' group prisoner at the same time and immediately asked permission to take over the subscription. The authorities granted his request, and we continued to receive the uncensored publication for about a year. (Mac ordered the publication by airmail, so we also received it quicker than we had previously.)

Unfortunately one issue was left lying around in a cell, and a warder on duty idly paged through it. He suddenly realised it was packed full of news, and took it to the office. The next issue of The Economist was handed to Mac by Lieutenant Naude (the officer in charge of studies) personally. It consisted of the cover only; the rest of the magazine was 'censored'. That was the end of The Economist, but we did have a good run, thanks to Mac.

On our way to the camp where we chopped wood we would pass a rubbish dump, and one day we saw lying among the rubbish what appeared to be an intact newspaper. At the camp, which was about half a kilometre from the dump, Hennie Feris (six years) and I discussed ways of getting hold of that newspaper. Hennie volunteered to go and fetch it while I kept watch. This was a great risk because he could be shot for 'trying to escape'. The camp was surrounded by a wire fence, with horizontal strands joined by vertical strands. Hennie and I loosened two of the vertical strands, enabling him to push two horizontal strands apart and slip between them. He reappeared about 30 or 40 minutes later, moving furtively between the bushes and taking occasional shelter behind a tree. I gave him the 'all clear' sign and he slipped in quickly between the wires. While he passed the newspaper to Kathy I reattached the vertical wires.

Wilton Mkwayi (life) and Siegfried Bhengu (10 years) were in charge of cleaning the 'ballie' (toilet) at the wood camp every afternoon just before knocking off. The warder who accompanied them on this task usually kept well clear of them. Whenever we got newspapers they would hide them in the cleaned toilet and retrieve them first thing the next morning.

Kathy, Lalu Chiba (18 years) and myself were the best news suppliers to our section. If any one of us went out of the section, say to see the doctor on the Island or a trip to Cape Town to see an optometrist or dentist, we usually returned with a current newspaper or magazines like Time and the Financial Mail. We were so successful on these excursions that on the rare occasions we failed to bring back any publications a general air of disappointment would pervade the section.

Occasionally we were able to make contact with common-law prisoners and persuade them to trade newspapers that they had obtained from warders' homes. The price was a full packet of Boxer tobacco for an English newspaper and a half-packet for an Afrikaans newspaper. Because the exchange had to take place quickly and we did not have time to examine the newspapers we bought, we would sometimes later discover we had been sold a dummy- that is, the classified advertisement section. More often than not, though, the common-law prisoners dealt with us fairly.

Perhaps our biggest scoop as far as newspapers were concerned was when a missionary preacher, Brother September came to give a church service in our section. About 12 of us attended the service, which was held in a corner of the prison yard, and sat in a semi-circle around a table we had provided for Brother September.

Hennie Feris and I were sitting opposite each other and we both noticed at the same time that a thick newspaper was sticking out of Brother September's satchel, which was leaning against a table leg. Our eyes immediately locked. I raised my eyebrows in the form of a question and indicated the satchel with a quick glance. Hennie nodded ever so slightly and held his hands in front of his chest, indicating prayer. From there on we played it by ear. The warders were patrolling the yard keeping an eye on us as well as on the other prisoners in the yard. I edged as close I could get to the satchel without raising suspicion, and waited to see what Hennie did. He asked if he could say a prayer, and Brother September, pleasantly surprised, agreed. Hennie gave me a sharp look, and began to pray. He was very eloquent. Assuming that Brother September, with his head bowed, had his eyes closed, I edged over further. When I noticed that his eyes were open I slowly retreated back to my original position. Hennie, not being aware that Brother September's eyes were open, looked at me questioningly. I shook my head slightly. A short while later Hennie ended his prayer, and I thought we had lost a golden opportunity. However a while later Brother September said his own prayer, and closed his eyes. I moved over and prised out the newspaper (the Sunday Times), slipped it under my jersey and moved back against the wall. When the service ended, a few prisoners said goodbye to Brother September while the others gathered around me to obscure my rather wide girth from the gaze of the patrolling warders. I made my way safely back into the section.

The authorities tried desperately to prevent us from obtaining news and jumped at anything that appeared remotely suspicious. During the Christmas holidays we would divide ourselves into teams and compete against each other in various games, and Elias Motsoaledi (life) was elected president of one of the domino teams. The title stuck, and afterwards we always addressed Elias as 'Mr President'. As time passed the nickname was shortened to Mr Pres. An alert warder heard us using the name and reported this fact to the office. Brigadier Aucamp, who was in charge of security, sent for Elias and accused him of smuggling newspapers into our section. Elias was nonplussed, and said he knew nothing about smuggling newspapers.

'Yes you do,' said the brigadier, 'That's why they call you Mr Press!'

We all had a hearty laugh when we heard this story.

But the reaction of the authorities when they did find something was far from funny. Following the discovery of a radio battery in the main section, the section was raided and a number of prisoners put in straitjackets, and viciously beaten. Then they were frog-marched over to our section, which also contained the punishment block. One of the prisoners who were very badly beaten was Peter Maganu (10 years). Nelson Mandela and I were together in the yard that day and saw Peter standing nearby. Nelson went over and walked slowly around Peter, gazing fixedly at him as he stood shivering with pain. When Nelson came back over to me he said he had taken a good look at Peter so that if he were called to give evidence about the beatings he would be able to describe his condition.

We were given permission to have a garden in the prison yard, and we put Lalu Chiba in charge of it. Lalu really had 'green fingers', and grew peppers, cucumbers, chillies and even watermelons. Unfortunately the warders would raid our garden after dark when we were all locked up. One afternoon one warder was in too much of a hurry to wait for nightfall. He came into the yard, went straight to the garden and helped himself to a watermelon. Billy Nair (20 years), whose cell had a window facing onto the yard, let out a howl of protest when he saw the warder. We never got our watermelon back but the thieving by the warders of our garden produce stopped after that.

In 1968 the Ceres-Tulbagh region was the epicentre of a tremendous earthquake which affected much of the Western Cape. The Island was shaken like a terrier shaking a rat.

Our cell windows facing the corridor had hollow bars with steel rods dangling inside them that would move and make a noise if one tried to saw through the bar with a hacksaw blade.

Otherwise one had to hit the bars quite hard to obtain even a small tingle. When the earthquake struck the clanging of the bars sounded like the very loud ringing of church bells. Nelson, whose cell was diagonally opposite mine at that time, stood at his window asking what was happening. I shouted back that I did not know.

The earthquake struck in waves. In the distance we heard what sounded like the steady beating of drums: Boom! Boom! Boom! Boom! The noise got steadily louder as it approached the Island, rising to an overwhelming volume. The cells tilted, the Island shook and the clanging of the bars was deafening. We were plunged into pitch darkness and feared that the sea would overwhelm the Island and drown us in our cells. The two warders who were on duty at the time fled from our section.

The next day we complained that we had been kept locked up under those dangerous conditions. The authorities assured us they had aircraft standing by in case things got out of hand. We accepted that explanation with a kilogram of salt.

One warder told us about a chief warder, whom we knew to be a habitual drunk. Apparently when the earthquake struck this chap and his wife ran through the town in their pyjamas shouting, 'Die wêreld vergaan! Die wêreld vergaan!' ('The world is ending! The world is ending!') They felt quite sheepish when they discovered that the world had not come to an end after all.

The earthquake was, nevertheless, a terrible experience for us locked-in prisoners.

Chapter 15

Warders; release hopes: 1964 - 1979

There were numerous incidents of assault and brutality on the Island, but I will relate three here which give an insight into the kind of prison officers we were dealing with.

One night in October or November 1969, while I was studying for examinations, I heard what I thought was singing well after 8:00pm. I wondered what was going on. The next morning I raised the matter with another prisoner, who told me what I had heard was not singing but screaming. Some common-law prisoners who were painting our section told us what had happened.

A few days previously, two warders, Nothnagel and another, were bullying the common-law prisoners, who lived in a large communal cell. Eventually one elderly prisoner got down on his knees and begged the warders to leave them alone. The reply from one of the warders was to hit the prisoner in the face with a baton. This so incensed the other prisoners that they attacked the warders, who fled followed by a few stones. One of the warders was slightly injured on the hand.

That night a gang of warders under Chief Fourie crept into the cell while the prisoners were sleeping, and viciously assaulted them. The following night there was another 'carry on' (assault), and again the next night. Once the warders were in the cell one would shout: 'Staan op!' ('Stand up!') Those who were slow to jump up were immediately attacked, and then others were picked on. The prisoners were saying they were afraid to go back to their cells, and when in their cells, they were afraid to sleep. They showed us bruises from their beatings.

Chief Fourie, then a Lieutenant, left the prisons service soon after, but this was not necessarily connected to the assaults. There were rumours that he was forced to leave because of involvement in homosexual affairs.

Another incident also concerned the bullying warder Nothnagel. A common-law prisoner was attacked by another while sitting on the toilet. A friend came to his assistance and a slight fracas ensued. The two antagonists were taken to the office by a warder so that the trouble could be investigated. Nothnagel was in the office and decided to investigate the matter, although he had no authority to do so. After listening to each of the prisoners, he told one to go into the other room. As the prisoner turned his back, Nothnagel hit him twice viciously on the head with his baton, then dismissed the case.

The prisoner showed Nelson Mandela and myself the two terrible gashes, which had been stitched, on his skull. On my release I could have identified the prisoner who was so brutally assaulted by Nothnagel, but refrained from doing so in case he was still in prison and was victimised.

The third incident involved Mr Mbekwa (five years), a prisoner who lived diagonally opposite me in isolation. He was called to the office one day, and on his return I noticed the back of his head was bleeding. I asked him what had happened, and he said he had been speaking to Lieutenant van der Westhuizen, who had become increasingly hostile. When Van der Westerhuizen opened his desk drawer and took out a baton, Mr Mbekwa realised that the Lieutenant intended assaulting him and made a dash for the door. Before he could reach the door, the lieutenant landed a blow on the back of his skull. We hid Mr Mbekwa's blood-stained shirt and later showed it to a representative of the International Red Cross, but heard nothing further about the incident.

Lieutenant van der Westhuizen, whose nickname was Bongola (Donkey in Xhosa), was quite a sadist. He would walk up and down our corridor, ostensibly speaking to his subordinates and saying in a loud voice that he did not believe in 'one meal' because 'three meals' were more appropriate. What he meant was that if we appeared in front of him for any contravention of prison regulations we could expect to suffer the loss of at least three successive prison meals.

Many of the assaults on us took place while a Colonel Badenhorst was commanding officer of the Island. One day three judges, Judge Steyn, Judge Corbet and Justice Martin Theron, vis-

where we worked on the Island, and spoke to Nelson Mandela in the colonel's presence. When Nelson spoke of the colonel's brutality, he took exception and threatened him. The judges warned the colonel that he was threatening Mr Mandela in their presence and that they could not tolerate that. Subsequently, I saw Nelson conversing with the three judges. A short while later, a matter of weeks, I think, Colonel Badenhorst was removed from the Island.

Brigadier Aucamp should not escape mention here either, because he was in overall charge of security and Head of the Prison Board for many years. We suffered much under him.

Not all warders were bad and brutish though. Some actually showed a kind face to us. Once or twice warders had sidled up to me and told me it would not be long before we would all be released. As it turned out they were mistaken, but it was good of them to say so. Another warder once invited Joe Qabi (12 years) to the office to listen to a tape of Mama Thembu, a popular song at the time. But such gestures were rare indeed.

The officers and warders who were cruel were really only carrying out the policy of the government, which was to destroy us both mentally and physically. They also wanted us to be forgotten by the outside world. All forms of intimidation and pressures were brought to bear on us. However I am happy and proud to say that they failed to destroy us or make the outside world forget us. We survived, and our morale remained as high as it ever was.

Because of my particular circumstances I could have been released from prison at any time. Four of my fellow accused had been released before the completion of their sentences, including Spike de Keller who was sentenced with me for sabotage. A number of legal attempts had been made to get me released from prison, and my fellow prisoners were very optimistic about my early release. Because of this, I decided to keep a diary to record the assaults and other forms of persecution taking place and the names of the warders/officers and prisoners involved, so I could report them when I got out. Unfortunately, during the height of the harassment in 1971, my diary was confiscated in a raid and I was arbitrarily sentenced to loss of studies and three months solitary confinement for abuse of studies.

During this time my brother Norman came to visit, and I was warned by Chief Fourie not to inform Norman that I was being held in isolation. I ignored the warning, and told Norman I was being punished illegally. Chief Fourie immediately cancelled the visit. While the warders were dragging me out of the booth I continued shouting and told Norman I wanted to see a lawyer.

I was sentenced to another three months solitary confinement, and when I demanded to know why was told it was for possession of an illegal diary-for which I had already been sentenced to three months isolation and loss of studies.

Lawyers soon contacted the Island on my behalf, but were informed by the prison authorities-without my knowledge-that I no longer required their services. For the next three months my brother was prevented from visiting me through one pretext or another: he was sent permits late; he received the wrong permits or other impediments were introduced. He took up the matter with the Commissioner of Prisons who instructed the prison authorities to allow him to see me. When he next came to visit I asked what had happened to the lawyers. He was surprised, and said I had informed the lawyer, through the authorities, that I no longer needed their services. I told him I had done no such thing, but we could not pursue the issue because the authorities justified any of their actions by saying they were 'in the interests of state security'. (It was only three years later, after MP Helen Suzman had taken up the issue with the powers that be, that I was allowed to study again. Dr Alexander (10 years), Andrew Masondo (12 years), Joe Qabi, Lalu Chiba and I pointed out to the Commissioner of Prisons, General Steyn, that we had suffered financial losses because of the arbitrary cancellation of our studies. He promised compensation, but up to today we have not received a cent.)

As I mentioned previously, a number of attempts were made to secure me an early release. I had originally been charged along with four other people, but because three of them pleaded guilty to an alternative charge of furthering the aims of communism, as opposed to sabotage, there was a separation of trials. All of us were found guilty under the different charges and received various sentences. Subsequently, the then Minister of Justice, John Vorster, made a statement to the effect that he felt the other four (who were all students) had been misled, and that the government would favourably consider any representations made on their behalf.

Representations were made, and the four were released prior to the completion of their sentences. Vorster had emphasised 'students', which ruled me out. I was approached and asked if I would have any objection to my mother making representations to the government on my behalf. I said I did have objections, and I would prefer it if she did not do so.

Because my fellow accused were all white and had been released, and I was black and was still imprisoned, sympathetic people argued that the government was acting unjustly and racialistically towards me and agitated for my release.

I think the first attempt to get me released was made by Helen Suzman. Then my brother Norman approached me in 1968/9 and asked if I was prepared to accept an exit permit. I said, yes, but only if there were no conditions attached to it. Further attempts were made by lawyers and, I think, by Tom Swartz of the Progressive Federal Party. All of these attempts came to naught.

In 1969 Judge Steyn and Judge Groskopf came to see me. Judge Steyn was acting in his capacity as chairman of NICRO (National Institute for Crime Prevention and the Rehabilitation of Offenders). After we chatted about my attitude towards the government, the judges told me they were prepared to intervene on my behalf, provided I gave an undertaking that I would not advocate or participate in violence against the government. I declined to give such an undertaking, saying if I did so I would be sentencing my own children to slavery in the land of their birth. The interview was terminated and the judges left.

A few weeks later I wrote to Judge Steyn, asking him if parole could be considered as a basis for my release, pointing out that if I broke any of the parole conditions then I could be re-arrested. I did not receive a reply to this suggestion. The authorities might not have sent the letter off.

In 1971 or 1972, Judge Steyn again came to see me. We had a long heart-to-heart chat. Again I was asked to give an undertaking, without which the judge felt he could not intervene to obtain an exit permit for me. I told him I could easily tell him a lie, obtain the exit permit, and refute my undertaking once out of the country, but I did not wish to do so. I would not want him, on some future occasion when he was negotiating on behalf of somebody else, to say, 'You know Daniels-Eddie Daniels-he gave me an undertaking, but he let me down.'

I pointed out to the judge that giving such an undertaking would be compromising myself. He then said that even if I gave him a verbal undertaking, just between him and myself, he would accept it. I replied that I could not do so. We shook hands and parted.

After Judge Steyn's second visit I approached my fellow political prisoners individually, and asked each of them what their reaction would have been in similar circumstances. Half of them said they would have given an undertaking and refuted it once they were out of the country, as they were under no obligation to honour an agreement with a government of the calibre of the South African government. The other half felt I had acted correctly. It was important, they said, to show the government the integrity of the people opposed to it.

On analysing their replies, I came to the conclusion that both points of view were valid. It all depended on one's own personality and values.

A few years later a lawyer came to see me with the idea of pursuing my release. During the discussions he showed me, and I was allowed to read, a copy of a newspaper report headlining the fact that Judge Steyn and Judge Beyers (the judge who sentenced me) had appealed to the government to release me.

I asked the lawyer what it would cost to petition the government, and he replied, 'About R600, but your brother won't minding paying for it.' I felt a bit sick about this, wondering how my poor and loyal brother would pay such a large bill.

After discussing the issue, during a lunch-break, with both

Nelson Mandela and Walter Sisulu, I asked the lawyer what chance his law firm had, if two senior judges, with influence and relatives in the cabinet itself, could not get me released?

I told him it was best that he dropped the matter, and he agreed. I went on to complete my full sentence.

After my release I learned that the International Defence and Aid Fund (IDAF) would have met the costs of the petition. My family could not tell me this because IDAF was banned in South Africa.

Incidentally, Mr Pelser, who was Minister of Justice at that time, told one petitioner that I would be released unconditionally when I had served my sentence. When I was eventually released it was not unconditionally. But by then Pelser was no longer Minister of Justice.

Criticisms, which I consider unfair, have been levelled at ARM members who were released from prison prior to completing their sentences, as well as those who escaped arrest by fleeing the country in 1964.

With regard to the first group, I felt that if there were any criticisms of their early release they should have been levelled at the government, and not them. The government had the power to lock them up and to let them out. If some of them gave undertakings as a precondition to being released, that was understandable. No one wanted to remain in jail unnecessarily. What was important regarding any undertaking was the context in which it was made. Somehow the critics felt it was unfair that those people were released prior to the completion of their sentences, while I had to serve my full sentence. If there was any unfairness, then it was on the part of the government, and not them. It would not have helped me one iota if those four had served their full sentences.

With regard to criticisms of those who fled the country, I personally am happy that so many escaped. I mentioned in a previous chapter how Mike Schneider managed to fly out of the country, and one of my biggest thrills while in detention was hearing that Randolph Vigne had escaped in a similar fashion. I believe escaping, provided it was not done at the expense of others and that one did not evade one's responsibilities, was important to perpetuating the Struggle. It was a morale-booster for others, and also meant fewer people in the hands of the police, which in turn meant less evidence at the trials of those who were caught. To those members of ARM who succeeded in escaping from the hands of the police, I give my heartiest congratulations.

Eddie Daniels' elder brother Norman.

Eddie Daniels.

Eleanor Daniels in front of an exhibit at the Robben Island exhibition.

Eddie Danliels with his sons Donovan (left) and Theodore (right).

Eddie and Eleanor Daniels.

The Methodist Church of Southern Africa

INNER CITY MISSION, CAPE TOWN

16th August 1984

TO WHOM IT MAY CONCERN

This is to confirm that <u>EDDIE DANIELS</u>
and <u>ELEANOR BUCHANAN</u> were married
before Almighty God on 29th July, 1983
in the Buitenkant Street Methodist
Church. Although the un-Christian
regime of the Republic of South Africa
does not recognise their marriage,
they have been married in the sight
of God and before a supportive congre-
gation who had no doubt that their
marriage has been blessed by God.
It was a privilege for me to participate in this Christian celebration.

REV. DERRICK F. JOLLIFFE M.A.

SUPT. MINISTER.

Eddie and Eleanor's marriage certificate not recognised by the ara-
partheid state but recognised by the church.

The Cape Argus on the day of the sentence.

Groep B / / /	No.864/64. Raad No.4/1039.
Group	Board No.
Geloof	Naam Edward Daniels.
Religion	Name
OPMERKINGS	Misdnad Sabotasie
REMARKS	Crime
	Vonnis 15 Jaar G/S.
	Sentence
DUIMAFDRUK—THUMB IMPRESSION	Datum van vonnis 17/11/64.
	Date of senteace
	Datum van ontslag 16/11/79.
	Date of discharge

Eddie Daniels' prison ticket..

Telegramadres: "LANDDROS"
Telegraphic Address: "MAGISTRATE"

Telefoonnommer 41-1711 - 15
Telephone No.

Privaatsak 9017
Private Bag No.

Poskode 8000
Postal Code.

DEPARTEMENT VAN JUSTISIE—DEPARTMENT OF JUSTICE

REPUBLIEK VAN SUID-AFRIKA—REPUBLIC OF SOUTH AFRICA

Verwysingsnommer
Reference No.

11/5/2 - 294

LANDDROSKANTOOR
MAGISTRATE'S OFFICE

CAPE TOWN

1981:02:09

Navrae/Enquiries: Mrs Esterhuyse

Mr E J Daniels
165 - 11th Avenue
KENSINGTON
7405

Sir

RELAXATION OF RESTRICTIONS

With further reference to your letter dated 1981:02:09
permission is hereby granted to visit your son at Groote
Schuur Hospital, Observatory subject to the following
conditions:-

(a) That you take the shortest route from your residence
     to the Groote Schuur Hospital and back;

(b) That you do not communicate with other listed com-
     munists or restricted persons;

(c) That you adhere to all other conditions of the res-
     triction orders in force againste you;

(d) That you reapply for permission to visit your son at
     673 Lansdowne Road, Lansdowne, after the latter
     has been discharged from hospital.

Yours Faithfully,

MAGISTRATE OF CAPE TOWN

Permission granted Eddie Daniels to visit his son, Donovan, in hospital.

Nelson Mandela with Eddie Daniels at a private breakfast.

Eddie Daniels with from left to right, Mama (Albertina) Sisulu, Eleanor Daniels and Walter Sisulu.

At President Mandela's inauguration. Back row from l to r are Ahmed Kathrada, the author and Lalu Chiba. Front row from l to r: Eleanor Daniels and Barbara Hogan.

Mr Mandela and Mrs Machel visiting Eleanor (who was recovering from a major operation) and Eddie Daniels at Somerset West.

PART
3

Chapter 16

Politics and improvements;
Section B: 1964 - 1979

During my years in jail I acted as a representative of the Liberal Party of South Africa. When I told Walter Sisulu how I had joined the LP he was quite astonished. He gave me that quizzical look of his when he was not sure if a person was pulling his leg or being serious. Then with his heart-warming little chuckle he said, 'Eddie, are you serious? Do you mean to tell me that you just walked forward and joined the organisation on the basis of it being non-racial and anti-government?'

I said, 'Yes.'

Walter just shook his head in amazement. But I must point out I was not the only one who had joined the LP that evening, lots of other people did too. As a matter of fact I had to stand in a queue.

What Walter did not know was that I took all my political decisions on my own. None of my friends joined in any of my political decisions and activities, except for Neville, who joined me in ARM, and his elder brother Maurice, who joined me in the Torch Commando march. My other friends, by and large, distanced themselves from me because of my keen interest in the exciting political activities that were taking place in my country. And, as I knew no one in the political world that could advise me, I really had to find my own way around.

As a member of the LP in prison I met with political opposition from the National Liberation Front (NLF), the African People's Democratic Union of South Africa (Apdusa)-a wing of the Unity Movement, and the Black People's Convention (BPC). They accepted me as an individual, but not in my political capacity. The PAC accepted my political status.

However I received 100 percent support from both the ANC and Swapo (South West Africa People's Organisation). Members of both these mighty organisations were tremendous to me both in my political capacity and as an individual. Without their support my position would have been difficult or perhaps impossible, but they helped me to survive.

The opposition used various arguments to undermine the LP. They argued that I was an individual, representing only myself; that I had been expelled from the party (I only recently learned that LP members who were also members of ARM were not expelled, although many people believed we had been.); and that the party had been dissolved, it no longer existed.

I countered that the expulsion of ARM members had been political expediency, and was necessary for the party to survive. Regarding the dissolution of the LP, I pointed out that the Prohibition of Political Interference Bill, which prohibited people of different races from belonging to the same political organisation, had made it impossible for the party to function legally as a non-racial organisation. This therefore put the Party in the same position as the Communist Party of South Africa (CPSA), ANC, PAC etc. It was true that the LP had never been banned as such, but making it illegal for it to function had the same effect. Therefore, as far as I was concerned the party, because of its illegality, had gone underground. I was therefore its representative in jail. The Liberal Party was, at least, still alive in me.

The opposition never liked it, but that was my stand, and in that stand I had the full support of the ANC and Swapo. Many ANC members spoke in glowing terms of the role the LP had played in the Struggle, and the close co-operation that existed between the LP and the ANC. Swapo also acknowledged the LP's role in the Struggle.

When former LP president Leo Marquard died, I organised a commemoration service on the Island. The ANC, including SACP members, Swapo and PAC attended. The NLF and Apdusa felt they could not attend.

I must point out, though, that on the day John Harris was executed I called on all prisoners who were present to stand and observe a minute's silence in salute to a great freedom fighter, who had just paid the supreme penalty for his opposition to apartheid. I made the call during a lunchtime break at the quarry. All members of all organisations complied.

When members of the Black Consciousness Movement (BCM) arrived at the prison in 1977, one of their leading members informed me, first in writing then later verbally, that they believed that all whites who were opposed to the government were symbolically black. I accepted this point of view. But later, after a few had lived in our section for a while, the organisation adopted a more hostile approach towards me. The same person who had told me that anti-government whites were symbolically black, now told me their constitution stated that they could not work with the Liberal Party and similar organisations, such as the National Union of South African Students (Nusas).

I also had a political discussion with another leading member of the BCM, in which we exchanged the history and policies of our respective organisations. Towards the latter part of his delivery he said the BCM would accept a black communist as a member, but not a white communist. At that point I told him I did not judge a person on the colour of his skin, but on the quality and sincerity of his ideas, and terminated the discussion.

Quarrels arose between the BCM and the ANC over recruitment of members. The BCM claimed jurisdiction over all organisations affiliated to the movement, including the South African Students Organisation (SASO), and the National African Youth Organisation (NAYO). The ANC objected to this, pointing out by way of example that people like Winnie Mandela and Lindi Sisulu were supporters of the BCM, an amorphous concept, but were also members of an organisation, namely, the ANC. The ANC said they would respect members of the Black People's Convention (BPC), but members of student and worker organisations were free to decide which political organisations, if any, they wished to join in prison. The BCM was supported in its stand by the PAC and Apdusa. The ANC was supported by Swapo and the Liberal Party.

In the general section of the prison an attempt was made to set up a committee, comprising representatives of all political organisations, to welcome new arrivals and find out which organisations they claimed membership to. Those who were not committed would be given time to decide whether they wished to join an organisation.

The ANC felt they could not be part of the committee, saying that short-term prisoners and those due to leave the prison soon should not indicate they were members of an illegal organisation, as this could expose them to further charges on their release. The committee soon ceased to function.

Subsequently, violence broke out between members of the BCM and ANC. A number of BCM members and one ANC member were arrested and charged. But because the ANC members, who had suffered injury as a result of the violence, refused to testify for the state, the court cases collapsed.

At the time of my release the relationship between the BCM and the ANC was warming up, and the hostility and animosity between the organisations seemed to be evaporating.

Members of the BCM did well in prison. They fought physically when the authorities tried to persecute them, and their resistance caused the authorities to be more careful in their approach to us, which in turn, contributed to the easing of the tensions and strains in our environment. However I did not agree with the political approach taken by the BCM. I found it narrow and shallow. This approach, I felt, was due to the fact that a large majority of its members had not been exposed to the variety of factors that could be utilised in our opposition to the government. I found the large majority of BCM members I met to be fine, upright persons who had courage and were dedicated freedom fighters. All they required, in my opinion, was a broader and more flexible approach to the Struggle.

Regarding Apdusa, in which I include the NLF group, I can speak only about those with whom I actually lived in the section of the prison that we occupied. I found them all, socially, very pleasant persons, and I got on very well with them. They also made a solid contribution to maintaining community morale. I am personally indebted to some of them for the substantial and unselfish academic assistance I received from them. Politically, however, we disagreed. They were not so much anti-white as anti most organisations that were opposed to the government, as well as being anti-government. The attitude of most of them was unfortunate, in that they would often belittle the efforts of others, particularly white liberals. Some, unfortunately, found this a popular pastime.

This attitude completely disappointed and disillusioned me. I pointed out to them that in their opposition to apartheid the liberals had been second to none. Over the years they had been harassed, persecuted, banned, exiled, tortured, jailed and even executed. The majority of ARM members were Liberals with a capital L, and ARM was the first organisation to launch an active campaign of sabotage against the South African government. The LP had launched political demonstrations against the South African government, and Contact, the LP-supporting newspaper, was the only newspaper in the country which had defied the Emergency Regulations in 1960, and, in defiance of the law, referred to the atrocities being perpetrated on Robben Island. Also, the LP was the only really non-racial organisation at that time.

Gradually my political identity became tolerated, if not fully accepted. In all fairness to the Apdusa members, we did work together politically where necessary. But they drew the line at serving under the chairmanship of the LP.

The PAC fully accepted my political status. I got on well with most of its members and some have won my admiration.

The Swapo members I met were people of calibre and character. Most of them were peasants. They were honest and brave, and very dedicated to the Namibian struggle for independence. They won my admiration and respect. This organisation, over time, unreservedly supported my political stand.

The ANC was, in my opinion, the most powerful foe of the South African government. Its members were of high calibre and character. They were dedicated and disciplined members of their organisation. Over the years I got on very well with possibly all of them. The ANC from the very earliest years had recognised and supported my political status unreservedly throughout my stay in prison. I remember that in the late 1960s the ANC and the LP submitted a petition to the government calling on it to release us from prison, and failing that, to recognise us as political prisoners. The other organisations represented in prison declined to be party to that petition for various reasons.

Much, though not all, of the political wrangling among the organisations in my section was due to my presence. After I was released it should have been much easier for the organisations to come together and show a common, united front to the authorities, and to have single delegations when meeting with the International Red Cross, parliamentarians and others.

I made the point earlier that latter prison conditions were a great improvement compared to earlier years. These improvements came about not because the authorities wanted to improve our conditions, but because of pressure from different quarters. We, the prisoners, fought for changes from inside the prison and suffered in the process. Outside prison, pressure from MP Helen Suzman, the South African Council of Churches (SACC), political and other organisations, churches, judges, students and individuals all contributed to the positive changes.

Then there were the international groups-the United Nations (UN); the Organisation of African Unity (OAU); the World Council of Churches (WCC); Amnesty International; the International Defence and Aid Fund (IDAF); individual governments; the International Committee of the Red Cross (ICRC), and many other anti-apartheid organisations. All of them exerted pressure, to various degrees, on the SA government to treat its prisoners more humanely and improve their living conditions.

Even though the prison conditions improved, relative to 1964, there was always much room for improvement. Our major demands were that:

We should be recognised officially as political prisoners, and be accorded the status that goes with this.

All persons taken in combat with the forces of the South African Government should be recognised and treated as prisoners of war.

A non-racial administration should be in charge of us. The prison staff should be selected on merit, with the ability to handle people, and not on the colour of their skins.

We should be allowed to mix freely with our fellow political prisoners. (Our small world had a population of around 30, with only an occasional change of face. Over time, we were denied meaningful contact with the rest of the prison population, among whom we had brothers, friends and even sons. The psychological pressures that we endured were enormous.)

We should be allowed to study any academic subjects and pursue them to their highest levels.

Other demands included the scrapping of classification of prisoners, contact visits, newspapers and radios for all prisoners, that all prisoners should be allowed to buy groceries, and that the prisoners in Pretoria should be allowed to join those on the Island. None of these demands were met.

Our environment was extremely claustrophobic. Around 30 of us were cooped up in a small, narrow area. We bumped against each other twenty times a day. So if there was any friction, tension or anxiety among the prisoners it was aggravated by this proximity to one another. We were simply unable to keep out of each other's way. It was only because of the high discipline prevailing in that section that physical conflict was kept to the minimum.

Under these restrictive conditions, and being locked up alone for 14 or 15 hours at a stretch, people tended to brood over things. Any unpleasant incident or remark, imagined or otherwise, could be exaggerated or distorted out of all recognition overnight.

Speaking from personal experience, if I suffered some mental strain or anguish, the next morning I would find it difficult even to look my fellow prisoners in the eye.

One must take into consideration the fact that of the 30 or so B Section prisoners, at least nine-including the Rivonia crowd-had been in the section since 1964. Over the years we demanded to be removed from this section because it was built as a punishment block. We were put there on the instructions of the security police, not because we had transgressed prison regulations, and we insisted we should not be housed there. Our demands were ignored.

The older men, I know, preferred the single cells as they had a little privacy, but they also wanted to be allowed to mix with the rest of the prison population, which would certainly have broadened their environment. The younger chaps clamoured to leave the section because of its stifling environment. The authorities allowed a few people to transfer to the main section, and reports we received about those people indicated that the change to a wider environment had a beneficial effect on their behaviour and mental state.

At the time of my release we were being kept inside the section all the time. We were only allowed outside the high surrounding walls once a fortnight, to take a walk around a field. Other prisoners were not allowed access to this field when we were there. One or two of the younger chaps would kick a ball around but the majority of us just walked and chatted. Otherwise, we remained inside the section, and were locked up at least 14 hours a day, and at weekends and on public holidays for more than 16 hours a day.

The authorities asked if we wished to work, and we took a vote on the issue. About 10 people were willing to work two or three days of the week, but the rest were not keen because of the soul-destroying nature of the work available to us. We did, however, request that we be allowed to go for walks on weekdays. The request was turned down on the grounds that we might meet other prisoners.

Chapter 17

Five who helped us survive: 1964 - 1979

In our long, long years on the Island, living conditions, both practically and psychologically, were difficult. There were a number of people who helped make life bearable in these very bleak conditions, but I want to mention five in particular who won my respect and admiration.

Johnson Mlambo (20 years) was an educated person and a gentleman who refused to allow himself to be humiliated or degraded by the prison authorities, though he was one of the most persecuted prisoners-I mentioned previously how he had once been made to dig a hole, forced into the hole, and urinated on by a warder. His courageous behaviour was an inspiration to us all. I will give two examples.

In the 1960s, stealing and smuggling of food from the kitchen was rife. Both warders and prisoners, political and common-law, were involved. The stolen food was used, among other things, to barter for tobacco and to obtain sexual favours. A number of prisoners took a stand against this behaviour, but it was difficult to stamp out. One evening Johnson accosted four prisoners who had stolen food, and he was attacked and very badly assaulted. He was rushed to hospital in Cape Town, where his life was saved, but he lost an eye. Today he wears a glass eye.

On another occasion, Johnson was found guilty of throwing soup over a warder's trousers and sentenced to six lashes. On the morning the sentence was to be carried out, we were working in the prison yard, breaking stones. Every time the large brass knocker was banged from the other side of the door to our section, indicating to the warder inside that the door was about to be opened, our eyes swivelled in that direction. A number of times it was only warders coming or going. Then Johnson entered the yard, dressed in a short-sleeved shirt, a pair of short trousers and wearing sandals. All eyes were fixed on him as he walked, with dignity, along the paving that bordered the yard to his place diagonally opposite me. He sat down on his hard brick seat, picked up his hammer and started to break stones. Throughout his ordeal he showed no pain or even discomfort. The warders who were hoping to see him wince were sorely disappointed, and we, the prisoners, were inspired by his brave effort.

I was thrilled when, on the day I was to be transferred from the Island to Pollsmoor Prison, I saw Johnson waiting in the corridor in front of the office. He had asked special permission to say farewell. That was a very touching moment for me. Johnson later became president of the PAC in exile.

Andimba Toivo Ya Toivo (18 years) arrived at the prison in 1968. He was a strong, resolute person who made a valuable contribution to our community in prison. He also showed great loyalty to me.

The Swapo leader, who was kept apart from the other Namibians on the Island, was adamant that Namibians should not be held in a South African prison. He refused to speak to or acknowledge any prison officials, visiting VIPs, and even the ICRC when they came to the Island. Nelson Mandela advised him to engage all and sundry in conversation, during which he could make political points, but he refused.

One evening during a raid on our section he smacked a warder who was pushing him around. This resulted in several warders attacking him with their batons and beating him unconscious.

Ahmed 'Kathy' Kathrada (life) was a very tolerant person and got on well with everyone. Even if he became involved in a heated discussion the discussion would always end without friction. Kathy proved to be a good friend to me over time. His presence in prison, his tolerant nature, his dedication and his lovely personality made a positive contribution to the morale of his fellow prisoners.

Kathy was in charge of 'intelligence', ably assisted by Mac Maharaj and Lalu Chiba. Codes, the smuggling of messages to other sections of the prison, and the dissemination of news from the outside world all fell within his ambit. This function was vitally necessary to us because strategies such as hunger strikes, downing of tools etc. could then be co-ordinated. Also the obtaining of reports from those who had just been imprisoned in the other sections of the prison and news from any other source. All of this was necessary to keep us informed as to what was happening beyond our section, and played a very important part in keeping up our morale. It was also the most dangerous function, because the authorities tried desperately to keep us in ignorance of what was happening outside our section. Any discovery of illegal material by the authorities meant punishment for the prisoner or prisoners concerned.

(Kathy told me a story while we were together on the Island, relating to Abram Fischer Q.C. Bram's grandfather was President of the Orange River Colony, his father Judge President of the Orange Free State, and his wife, Molly, was the niece of General Jan Smuts. Bram, however, was the leader of the South African Communist Party. While on trial he was granted bail of R10 000 and the return of his passport to enable him to appear before the Privy Council in London in a case involving patent rights. He won the case and returned to South Africa to face trial and eventual life imprisonment.

The incident in question occurred in 1964: Bram and Molly were travelling to Cape Town to consult with Bram's clients on Robben Island, including Nelson Mandela. Bram, who was driving, swerved to avoid hitting a cow and the car went into a river. Molly was trapped and drowned. A week later Bram continued his journey to Robben Island. On arrival at the Island he asked the Commanding Officer of the prison not to tell Nelson and company about the tragic loss he had suffered until he had completed his consultation and left the Island.

I include the above as a salute to the memory of Abram Fischer).

Walter Sisulu (life) was the most loving personality in our section. He represented everything that is good. He was compassionate, kind, tender and understanding. Anyone from any organisation could come to Walter and find a sympathetic and understanding ear. He always saw the lighter side of a remark or an argument. The younger chaps would offer to wash his clothes, or to take his place in the cleaning team, which included polishing floors and scrubbing the yard, but he refused all offers and insisted on doing his stint.

Walter could also take a joke at his own expense, and would always see the funny side of the leg-pull. I discovered that during his early soccer-playing days his nicknames were Boiling Water and Joko Tea.

Because of his ill health, Walter was prescribed a hot-water bottle by the doctor. Nine times out of 10 he would forget to fill this hot-water bottle before lock-up in the afternoon. Suddenly, we would hear Walter's agitated voice, 'Hi chaps, I forgot to fill my hot-water-bottle!' followed by a soft, embarrassed laugh. One of us who had not yet been locked up would take the bottle through the cell window and rush off to the bathroom to fill it. This almost-regular incident usually raised quite a chuckle throughout the section, and the occasional teasing comment.

Walter was fond of mischievous questions such as, when we were cleaning our area, 'Should we sweep before we dust or should we dust before we sweep?'

If one answered, 'We should sweep first,' he would say, 'If you sweep first then when you dust the dust will settle on the floor.'

If one answered, 'We should dust first,' then Walter, with a quiet smile, would say, 'If you dust before you sweep then when you sweep the dust will settle on the tables and window sills.' This typified Walter's gentle sense of humour, which further endeared him to us.

But the bottom line was that Walter had immense spirit. He was a tremendous inspiration to all of us and was loved by all of us.

Nelson Mandela (life) was revered by most of the prisoners and respected by everybody, including the prison authorities. A noble person, he was humble and modest but could also be resolute. He carried a perpetually heavy responsibility and carried it well, and with ease. All prominent visitors made a point of seeing him. He was never informed beforehand of a visit, just suddenly confronted with it, but he always rose to the occasion. He was a great inspiration. In times of stresses and strains, whether it was inter-organisational or concerned the authorities, he was always at the forefront in solving problems.

Nelson once told me that, while he was addressing one of the many public meetings held by the ANC, the police opened fire on the crowd and a bullet passed close by him. I can't imagine what kind of history South Africa would have had if that bullet had found its mark.

In 1962 Nelson had left South Africa illegally to organise training facilities and camps for Umkhonto weSizwe in Africa and abroad. After he attended an Organisation of African Unity (OAU) meeting, some African heads of state tried to dissuade him from returning to South Africa, saying he would be arrested, tortured, and possibly die in prison. Nelson replied it was his duty to return, which he did. After being underground for about 17 months, he was arrested and sentenced to five years imprisonment for leaving the country illegally. Subsequently, while still serving his five-year sentence, he was charged with High Treason and, along with the other members of the Rivonia Group, found guilty and sentenced to life imprisonment.

Both Nelson Mandela and Abram Fischer left foreign, friendly soil to return to South Africa and life imprisonment. When they returned they were unaware what fate had in store for them. It could have been the death penalty, yet, they returned.

Nelson was very studious. He was even prepared at times to forego the two half-hour exercise periods we had in the early years, when we were locked up for 23 hours at a time. In the evenings Nelson was allowed to study and read only up to 10:00pm. He then had to go to sleep, despite the fact that our cell lights were on all night anyway.

At the time he was studying Afrikaans, and had received permission to subscribe to Huisgenoot, an Afrikaans magazine. When the warder came on duty in our section he was not allowed to have a radio or any reading material, and would soon become very bored. Nelson would place the Huisgenoot in a conspicuous position so the warder would notice it on his rounds. After passing Nelson's cell once or twice, the warder would ask if he could borrow the magazine, and Nelson would duly oblige. The warder, now being obligated to Nelson, would allow him to study and read throughout the night.

There are a few incidents I would like to relate about Nelson as they apply to me personally.

I do not know how the practice started, but during our long years together Nelson and I shared personal letters which we received from home. When he received a letter written in Xhosa he would translate it for my benefit. I do not know if he shared his personal letters with other prisoners, but I was deeply touched that he did so with me.

In the late '60s I was rather ill for a few days, and one morning was too weak to get up to empty my ballie (chamber pot). Nelson looked into my cell to check on me, and when he saw how ill I was he stooped down, picked up my ballie and set off down the corridor with a ballie (his own and mine) in the crook of each arm, to go and empty the contents and wash the pots. To appreciate this gesture one must realise that, even then, Nelson was an international personality. He was also the most important prisoner and the leader of the most powerful political organisation, the ANC, on the Island. He could have instructed any member of his organisation to assist me but, instead, he stooped down personally to assist me.

I have already mentioned the diary I kept-recording, among other things, assaults on the prisoners, the names of the perpetrators and victims, and the dates of the incidents-and how the diary was discovered during a search for a radio. When the news flashed around that I had been keeping a diary and the authorities had captured it, it sent a flutter of panic around the section. I was approached by a number of prisoners, anxiously enquiring if I had mentioned them in the diary. Because I had been recording in the diary for several years I could not remember all of the entries, but I promised to play down whatever entries I could.

I was deeply worried and quite frightened. There had been a number of recent assaults on prisoners, and Lieutenant van der Westhuizen, who had led the attacks, had informed me he would be seeing me that afternoon. I waited anxiously to be called. Eventually, we were locked up, and I was informed the lieutenant would see me in the morning. That night I slept very uneasily, if at all.

The next morning I got up and collected my plate of pap (mealie meal) from the yard. On returning to my cell I received a tremendous thrill. There, sitting in my seat with his plate of pap on my table, was Nelson. He consoled me, without directly referring to the diary in any way, and said, 'Danny, I know that you will handle this matter.' The mere fact of seeing Nelson there and chatting to him boosted my morale, which had been at very low ebb until then. (The strange fact of this incident is that I was never summoned by Lieutenant van der Westhuizen. I assume word had got out about the assaults to the outside world, and the authorities had called a halt to them, just in time for me.)

Nelson also showed tremendous respect for my political position. Whenever he had met with an important personage, and he met quite a number while on the Island, he would first give a report to the ANC and then report to me, individually. This concern for me touched me deeply. After a few of these reports, I suggested it would save time if I sat in on the report to the organisation. However I had sat in on only one when the leader of another organisation accused me of being an ANC member. Therefore, to maintain my political integrity, Nelson once again began giving me individual reports.

The important point to remember here is that Nelson had no need to give me reports at all. He did so out of the goodness of his heart.

From about 1976 onwards we were allowed to go to a separate soccer field once a fortnight where the young chaps would kick a ball around while others walked around and chatted. To get to this field we had to pass the main sections. Fellow prisoners would rush to the fence to cheer and salute their leaders. When walking past the sections Nelson would often walk with me, emphasising, I feel, the non-racialistic approach of the ANC.

This non-racialistic stand was emphasised in statements Nelson made in two political trials.

When found guilty of inciting people to strike and of leaving the country illegally in 1962, he stated from the dock 'Your

Worship, I hate racial discrimination most intensely and in all its manifestations. I have fought it all my life. I fight it now, and will do so until the end of my days.' (Long Walk to Freedom, Nelson Mandela, p313)

After having been found guilty of High Treason and facing a possible death sentence in 1963, Nelson stated from the dock: 'I have fought against white domination, and I have fought against black domination. I have cherished the ideal of a democratic and free society in which all persons live together in harmony and with equal opportunities. It is an ideal which I hope to live for and to achieve. But if needs be, it an ideal for which I am prepared to die.' (Long Walk to Freedom, Nelson Mandela, p354).

While Nelson was in prison, some people dismissed the possibility of him contributing to the future of the country. They argued that because he was out of circulation and unable to communicate freely he would have no idea whether the sun still rose in the east and set in the west. Past and present events have proved those soothsayers wrong: here we have a man who has not only demonstrated great leadership qualities, but who can hold his own, and better, in discussions, debates, and negotiations with local and international political, economic and social leaders.

Both Nelson Mandela and Walter Sisulu are men of great stature. Besides making a major contribution to the maintaining of high morale in our section, and beyond, their integrity was tremendous. I lived with these two men for 15 years in a very barren and demoralising environment, but they transformed it into a wholesome one by just being there.

To appreciate the depth of their integrity, one has to look at it in the context of the relationship between them and me. Both of them were internationally recognised figures. Both were leaders of the most powerful organisation opposed to the South African government. But who was I? I was a nonentity compared to these two great men. The organisation I represented in prison, the Liberal Party, had dissolved. I was the only member of this dissolved organisation on the Island. Yet I was treated with respect by both the ANC and SWAPO in my political capacity. So why should Nelson and Walter be so honest and truthful to me? It was because of their great integrity, which often surfaced in their interaction with others. When I think back to those days I marvel at the integrity of these two great men.

Messrs Mandela and Sisulu are personal friends of mine. They have inspired me by their tremendous courage and dedication in the face of terrible adversity.

They are kind, humble and modest but are dedicated to the cause they believe in, and can be resolute. These two men should have been in the highest seats of power but were instead in the lowest possible position that any citizen of any country could be in-prisoners in the jails of their own country.

Adversity, at times, often brings out the best in people. It always brought out the best in these two men. These two great men, over time, showed great personal loyalty to me. I shall always be indebted to them for their beautiful gestures of friendship. Over 15 long years, they lifted me, and others, by the way they handled problems and carried themselves in adversity. To have lived with them was both an education and an honour. These two men are noble, noble in courage, in character and in spirit.

Over the years a number of political prisoners passed through what eventually became known as the B section on Robben Island, the section in which I spent my full 15 years of imprisonment. I pen the names of those whom I have not mentioned in the body of the book but to whom I wish to pay tribute. Among the names I can recall are: James April; Theo Cholo; Fikile Bam; Samuel Chibane; Frank Anthony; Ziteh Cindi; Saths Cooper; Don and Lionel Davis; Thompson Daweti; Michael Dingaka; Samson Fadana; Jackson Fuzile; John Ganye; Kader Hassim; KK.; Mosiuoa Patrick 'Terror' Lekota; Jeff Masemola; Andrew Mlangeni; Strini Moodley; Zeph Mothopeng; Justice Mpanza; Peter Mthembu; Louis Mtshizana; Dennis Brutus; Themba Mvelase; Muntu Myeza; MD Naidoo; Pascal Ngakane; FT Ngendane; John Nkosi; George Peake; Herbert Phinde; John Pokela; Poppies; Sandy Sejake; Sylvester Skota; Vusile Tole; Townsend; Zifozonke Tshikela; Leslie van der Heyden; Sonny Venkatrathnam; Brandsi Vusani;

Bobby Wilcox; Joshua Zulu and Moffat Zungu. To all of my fellow prisoners I wish to say 'Thanks, for the memories.'

Chapter 18

Escapes that never were, 1: 1964 - 1976

From day one of my arrest I dreamt of escaping. Several opportunities arose when I was in detention, but because the chances of success were low I had to abandon them.

Then there was the occasion when I tried to bribe a warder. Because there were no toilet facilities in my cell at Caledon Square police station, warders had to check the cell every two to four hours, in theory, to see whether I wished to use the toilet. In this instance, when the warder opened up my cell, he was alone. This was unusual: since the escape from a police cell in Pretoria of Arthur Goldreich, Harold Wolpe, Mosie Moolla and Abdulhay Jassat in July 1963, it had been standing orders for a head warder accompanied by a warder to check on prisoners. Possibly the head warder was otherwise engaged.

I seized the opportunity. I told the warder how rich I was, and said if he would allow my friend Neville Hillman, who was being held on the first floor, and myself just to take 'a walk around the block', I would pay him R2000. My brother, I told him, had my power of attorney and would give him the money. After a long hesitation, he said he felt the risk was too great for him to take such a chance.

After appearing at a pre-trial hearing-with Spike de Keller and the others-at which a separation of trials was ordered, I was transferred to Pollsmoor Prison. I was welcomed into a large cell, which normally accommodated 50-60 prisoners, by Sedick Isaacs, Achmat Cassiem, James Marsh and Manie Abrahams. They were also awaiting trial for sabotage. (They were found guilty. Sedick was sentenced to 12 years and the others three to five years apiece.)

When I told them of my attempt to bribe a warder at Caledon Square, Manie pointed out a warder whom he felt might be favourably inclined to assist us in going AWOL. I approached the warder, 'Mac' MacDyllan and offered him R2000 if he would help us to escape. He agreed. I felt ashamed of myself because I did not have that kind of money, and at the next opportunity told Mac so. I said I would give him R200 when we were outside. He accepted this. We did not know then that Mac was helping common-law prisoners escape for as little as R10 a time.

Mac eventually procured a few hacksaw blades for us. We had no experience of sawing through iron bars, nor any idea of how long it would take. Arrangements had been made for a car to pick us up on a Wednesday evening, so we began sawing on the Tuesday morning.

Manie and James kept a watch on the corridor while Sedick, Cassiem and I took turns to saw. We sang to cover the noise of the sawing. We soon discovered that breaking the hacksaw blades in half gave us a better grip and more leverage.

While I was sawing, I saw what I thought was the badge of a warder's cap, shining through the opposite cell's window. My stomach gave a triple flip and I felt quite sick. It seemed we had been discovered. I looked again, and realised it was a mark on the window, reflecting the sunlight. I felt very relieved.

We completed two cuts, one at either end of a bar, in good time. We left just enough metal to keep the bar in position. We disguised the cuts by filling them with butter and cheese, which we smeared with dirt. We decided to leave the next bar until the following day.

The next day, to our horror, the cell opposite us was filled with common-law prisoners. We were in a quandary. Do we saw or not? But we had to cut another bar if we were going to leave that night. We discussed the matter and decided we had to go ahead.

We tried to cover with our bodies the windows through which we could be seen by the prisoners opposite us. But they soon noticed our activity. When we finished sawing some of them asked us to pass the blades over, as they were being transferred to Robben Island the following day. I told them we had no blades, and that they must have been imagining things if they thought we had been sawing through the bars.

That evening Mac came on duty, very agitated. He said something had gone wrong and there would be no pick-up that evening. Now we were in a pretty pickle. The bars were cut, there was no pick-up available and the prisoners in the opposite cell knew we had sawn through our bars. We told Mac to make other arrangements for a pick-up as soon as possible, and asked him to get rid of the hacksaw blades.

The following evening we received a terrible fright. We heard the tinkling of chains and the shuffling of bare feet. Then we heard a voice saying 'Kom verby' ('Come past') in menacing tones. This was followed by thuds and agonised screams. We rushed over to the window to see what was happening. Two rows of warders were lined up on either side of the corridor. Naked prisoners, handcuffed, in leg irons and chained to each other, shuffled between the warders as vicious blows from batons, fists and feet rained down on them.

The warders saw us watching and ordered us away from the window as the assault and screaming continued.

We found out shortly afterwards that there had been a mass escape, with Mac's assistance, the night before. The prisoners who were beaten were ones who had participated in the escape bid but had not made it.

That evening we slept very badly, thinking of our own cut bars, and what was going to happen to us if and when those bars were discovered. The next morning we looked across at the communal cell in which the beaten prisoners were housed. They were a miserable lot. Each prisoner had only a thin blanket with which to cover his nakedness. They were cold and shivering. They came to the window to show us their wounds. Black and blue weals ran across their bodies. That day, at least, they received no medical attention or food. The thought of our own cut bars put us in a cold sweat.

Then the first raid took place. It seemed one of the prisoners who was in the opposite cell had informed on us. The warders swarmed into our cell armed with long canes. We were ordered to strip naked, and the cell was thoroughly searched for incriminating evidence. Failing to find any, the warders struck at the window bars with their long canes. However they failed to discover the cut bars.

We breathed a sigh of relief but were still filled with keen anxiety. We were put under closer observation. The acoustics were very good in this section and one evening, while Sedick was brushing his teeth, a warder came to investigate to see if we were sawing through the bars.

Our days and nights were filled with apprehension.

Then the authorities struck again. Again we were made to strip. The warders once again went around banging at the window bars with their long canes. One warder approached the window that contained the cut bars. When I saw he was about to start banging away at those bars I rushed over and told him to mind the food that we had placed under that particular window (as awaiting trial prisoners we were allowed to receive food from sources outside the prison). The warder was so surprised he just moved around the boxes of food and went to bang away at the window bars further down. Once again we had survived.

The third and final raid took place a short while afterwards. This time we were removed from the cell and placed in a cell diagonally opposite. After about 20 to 30 minutes of intense anxiety and apprehension, I heard the two most frightening sounds I have ever heard in my life. They sounded like the end of the world. Boooommm! Boooommm! The two cut bars were dropped, deliberately, one by one, on the cement floor of the cell. The sound travelled to us and through us, filling us with dread.

We were fetched and marched back in single file. I was the first to enter the cell, and saw the commanding officer standing there looking very angry indeed. Next to him stood the head of the prison, Chief Bosman, a cruel and sadistic person. As we walked up to the Colonel, still naked, I saw the bars lying on the ground through the corner of my eye. Pointing at them, the Colonel shouted, 'What is the meaning of this?'

I pretended surprise at his question and tone, and looked startled when I saw what he was pointing at. I told him we knew nothing about it. He said, 'You are responsible for that!' again pointing to the bars. I emphatically denied that we knew about or had anything to do with the cutting of those bars. I said they must have been cut before we were put in the cell.

We were removed to the cell opposite, which was empty at the time. About twenty warders milling around, adopting hostile stances. In the cell we had just vacated, welders went to work to replace the cut bars.

Amid all this fuss, a common-law prisoner was brought in. He went up to Bosman, then, indicating the window bars, climbed on to the window ledge and pointed out how a strip of welding had been filed smooth, ready for the hacksaw blade. (If the bars are reinforced by a strip of weld then, so I was told, the weld must be filed away before a hacksaw blade can be used on the bar itself. The bars in the cell we had just vacated had not been reinforced, enabling us to use the hacksaw blades on them straight away.)

After a warder had clambered on to the window ledge to inspect the filed bar, so did I. I turned around to Bosman and told him I was glad he was here when the prisoner pointed out the filed bar, otherwise we would have been held responsible for that as well. This threw the prison officials a bit off balance.

The next morning Sergeant Olivier of the security branch came to investigate. We continued to deny all knowledge of the cut bars, but Olivier said he knew we were responsible. 'When the criminals cut the bars', he said, 'they put soap into the cuts. You put butter and cheese in them'.

That day we were removed from Pollsmoor Prison and again placed under detention conditions, despite the fact that we were awaiting-trial prisoners.

The sequel to the above episode was that Mac, Jill Jessop (the Cape Town secretary of the Liberal Party who, with others, had arranged a safe place where we could lie low for a while if we managed to escape) and Manie's aunt and uncle were charged with helping prisoners to escape. All of them were discharged except for Mac, who was found guilty and sentenced to three years on Robben Island. (Mac managed to visit me while I was recuperating from my hernia operation in the prison hospital. We had a nice chat and there were no hard feelings.)

Meanwhile my very loyal brother Norman heard about our

failed attempted escape in England. He was worried because he had supplied Mac with the cash to buy whatever was necessary for the escape. On his return to South Africa a short while later, he carefully scanned the airport for any 'strange' characters. Fortunately there were no members of the Special Branch waiting to arrest him.

Another opportunity arose when a lawyer, who was assisting my advocate, came to see me about my case. While we were talking I noticed that we both smoked the same brand of cigarette. Later, lying in my cell, I thought if he slipped half a hacksaw blade under the silver paper in his cigarette box, then while we were talking and offering each other cigarettes we could arrange to swap boxes. I put the idea to him the next time I saw him, but he, very sensibly, declined.

On the Island, escape from the section in which I was housed was virtually impossible. We were counted in the morning before we left our section to go to work. We were counted at each of the three gates on our way out. Outside in the street we were counted once more. At work we were counted almost every half-hour. At the end of the working day we would be told to fall in and counted. On our return to the section we would again be counted through each of the three gates. Once in the yard, we would be forced to strip naked and counted while our clothing was searched for any contraband. Finally, when we were locked up in our individual cells, we would be counted again.

For the rest of the day and the whole night, a warder would be locked in with us. He would lock the gate to our section from the inside and hand the key to the officer in charge through an observation hatch in the gate. The lights in our cells were kept on all night, and the warder would patrol our corridor throughout his shift, checking our cells as he passed. In addition to all this, our cells were double-locked and the key handed to the officer in charge, who would keep it in a safe overnight.

At one point I managed, through the ANC, to smuggle a letter to Sedick Isaacs, who was in a different section and was also very keen on escaping. He had taught both science and geography, and I asked him when would be the best time of the year to escape, taking into consideration the tides around the Island. His reply, via the good offices of the PAC (of which he was a member), was that the best time would be during winter, because the tide would carry me towards the mainland. I kept this information in the back of my mind for future use.

Sedick hatched his own plan, which was to poison the water reservoir in the hope that all prisoners on the Island would be taken to a mainland prison from which it would be easier to escape. However the prison authorities discovered the plan. Sedick was sentenced by a prison court to six cuts and an extra nine months imprisonment, in addition to his original sentence of 12 years.

Of all the escape plans I dreamt up on the Island, possibly the best one was worked out in collaboration with Joe Qabi and Siegfried Bhengu. At the quarry, because I had a bit of a bad knee, I had been put in charge of maintaining and cleaning the shed in which we ate our lunch. In an attempt to make the place look nice I had built a small birdbath, consisting of a washbasin in a sandpit. The sandpit was bordered by four, large, sturdy logs.

The idea was that if the opportunity occurred, that is if we could get at least ten hours before we were discovered missing, we would trundle one of those logs down to the nearby beach in a wheelbarrow from the tool-shed. Using spades as oars, we would paddle across to Bloubergstrand on the mainland, about 7km away. We would tie the spades to our bodies with strips of blanket, to prevent us losing them, and also wrap strips of blanket around our legs, so we would not cut ourselves while paddling.

The problem with the plan was we had no way of testing it. We did not know if the log would support all three of us. However we were prepared to take our chances.

Time passed, though, and we could never find the required period to put the plan into operation, so in the end it was abandoned.

It was ironical that here I was trying so hard to escape, when in 1969 and again 1971 I had been offered a legal discharge from prison, providing I gave an undertaking that I would not advocate or participate in any violent activities against the government.

I felt then, as I feel now, that my refusal to give such an undertaking was a matter of honour.

Chapter 19

Escapes that never were, 2:
The Mandela Rescue Plan: 1976 - 1981

After 10 years on the Island I had abandoned all plans to escape because of the tight security, and settled down to complete my prison sentence. But, I suppose, thoughts of escape were always on the back of my mind.

In 1976 I noticed that helicopters were flying over the Island with impunity, and with increasing frequency. The choppers were delivering goods to the increasing number of oil tankers sailing around the southern tip of Africa because of trouble in the Suez Canal region. At times these helicopters would pass over-head with a large basket or net attached to their underbellies con-taining, I assume, supplies for the tanker. It was the basket that, to my mind, increased the possibilities of a successful escape. The important point here is that there would be no need for the helicopter to land. It could hover above the walls, lower the bas-ket into the courtyard, pick up the escapees, and fly off.

Initially, I thought of escape by sea. If the helicopter could drop us off on a foreign ship, preferably a warship, outside the three-mile limit over which South Africa had jurisdiction, then we could appeal to the captain of the ship for political asylum. I abandoned this idea because I was sure the SA government would show scant respect for the niceties of international law. Its planes and destroyers would very soon intercept the ship, from which we would be removed bodily by the South African armed forces. After weighing up all the possibilities, I came to the con-clusion that the course offering the greatest chance of success was for the helicopter to fly directly from the Island to the embassy of a government sympathetic to the ANC. We could seek asylum there and then, perhaps a year or two later, plan an escape to somewhere outside South Africa.

Once I had determined the best route to success I dreamt of the plan night and day. It became an obsession with me. I kept

watch on the helicopters, noting that occasionally one would lazi-
ly criss-cross the Island as if it were on a sightseeing tour, and
gradually refined the plan.

I gauged the height of the prison walls by taking a stick, which
I had previously measured, and propping it as upright as possible against a wall. I sauntered some distance away and mentally
counted the number of sticks it would take to reach the top. I
estimated the wall was five metres high, meaning the basket had
to be attached to a steel cable at least that much in length.

The basket, which had to be large enough to hold and conceal
two persons lying down in it, would be lowered down to the
yard. As soon as the subjects had clambered in, the helicopter
would fly off, winching in the basket as it went. The subjects
would remain lying down in the basket until the planned destination was reached.

I figured that the basket should be covered with a big South
African flag, and have bunting and trimmings. This would give it
a festive air, and hopefully cause prison guards to think twice
before shooting at it.

The more I thought about the plan, however, the more I
realised it could only be planned and executed from outside the
prison. The day of my release was drawing nearer, which meant
I would be in a position to co-ordinate the escape, but that raised
the question of who the escapees would be. I immediately
thought of rescuing Nelson Mandela and Walter Sisulu, men for
whom, as I have said before, I had great admiration and respect.

Many members of the ANC in our section had, on their release
from the Island, smuggled out letters written by Nelson to the
ANC in exile. I thought to myself how much more effective
Nelson's contribution to the Struggle would be if he was in a
position to write any number of letters, telephone whomever he
wished and broadcast to the world. In my mind's eye I already
began visualising the next stage of the 'Two steps to Freedom'
plan, which would be to get Nelson out of the embassy and outside the country.

I approached Nelson after having thought the plan through as
best as I could. I knew I could not approach him with any frivo-

lous plan, it had to be well thought out, because he would never be part of any reckless scheme. I outlined the plan and we discussed it over time.

One of the questions Nelson posed to me was: 'Danny, what do we do with the helicopter after we have landed in the grounds of the embassy?'

'Dalibhunga (Nelson's circumcision name),' I replied, 'We just abandon the helicopter in the grounds, run straight to the embassy buildings; bang on the door if it is closed, or run straight in if the door is open, and ask for political asylum.'

Nelson showed keen interest in the plan. As he so succinctly put it, 'We are revolutionaries. It is our duty to try and escape the clutches of the enemy.' He expressed in words something for which I had only had a gut feeling.

I told Nelson I gave the plan an 80 percent possibility of working, and he said he would put it to the ANC's High Command in prison. They approved the plan, on condition that it be submitted to ANC High Command in exile for final approval and execution.

In the meantime, Walter Sisulu approached me to tell me that Nelson and he could not both go. One would have to stay behind on the Island. This stand exemplified the magnanimity of these men, who gave their all to the great cause they believed in.

The success of the venture hinged heavily on the elements of surprise and speed. The escape was planned for New Year's morning, 1981, at 9:15 a.m. As I was being released on 16 November 1979, this would give me time to report to the High Command in exile. Also we had heard rumours that Nelson, and possibly others, were to be removed from the Island in the not-too-distant future. We therefore could not tarry.

The morning of New Year's Day was chosen for a couple of important reasons: usually on this morning we would be shown a film in the hall, and the warders on duty in our section would join us. In earlier years the warders would lock themselves and us in the hall, but over time they had begun to leave the gate open, allowing those who were bored with the film or who wanted to read, walk in the yard, or study to leave the hall.

New Year's Day was a visiting day and warders would have to be on duty at the visiting booth from before 9:00am, so the prison force would be at full stretch. We also hoped the warders' reactions would be a bit dulled as a result of their New Year's eve celebrations.

There were other factors we thought might assist us: the lookout towers surrounding the prison were no longer manned during the day, unlike previous years when they were manned around the clock. Also, security on the Island was geared to preventing escapes by sea. Therefore, when the siren shrieked out its message that an escape was in progress, the warders' first reaction, I figured, would be to look to the coast. Their miscalculation would gain us valuable time.

The responsibility for choosing the embassy in which we were to land and seek political asylum, the recruiting of a pilot and the hiring of the helicopter itself would be the ANC's. We felt a good pretext for the hire of a helicopter would be that we were a commercial firm wanting to take some of our international directors on a sightseeing trip. We would need the helicopter for a few days beforehand, in order to prepare the winch, cable and basket.

I felt my presence on the trip was essential, as I would be able to point out the courtyard from which Nelson would be picked up.

Early on New Year's Day I would meet up with the pilot, and we would set off at a time which enabled us to be directly over the yard at exactly 9:15 a.m. I worked on the premise that we would be picked up on radar as we approached the Island and the prison authorities informed of our presence, but they would have little idea what our intentions were. If they radioed us we could either pretend that our radio was broken, or inform them that we were bringing gifts from well-wishers, 'for our brave boys in khaki who are guarding those terrible terrorists such as Mandela and others'. This message and the gaily-decorated basket would hopefully disarm the authorities until such time as we were directly above the Isolation Section and out of sight of officials on the ground.

The roar of our approaching helicopter would inform Nelson of our arrival. He would already have wandered out into the courtyard. Other prisoners in the hall who were in the know would also hear the noise and they would rush out of the hall, seemingly out of curiosity, and block the narrow corridor, preventing the warders in the hall from leaving.

The warders in the hall would be unarmed (for security reasons they did not carry arms in our section), but they were furnished with two-way radios. The most they could do, if they guessed what was going on, would be to radio the office.

In the meantime we would be hovering above the yard, and would have lowered the basket. As soon as Nelson had scrambled into the basket, where he would lie down flat, we would fly off and start winching up the basket. Having the basket against the underbelly of the helicopter would prevent SA Air Force pilots from seeing into it, if we were pursued by SAAF planes.

We would head for our destination about 9 km away. We felt there would still be confusion on the Island, and that few people would have worked out what was going on. Even if some suspected it was an escape, the flag and the bunting would make them hesitant to open fire on the helicopter. The fact that we were heading for the mainland and not out to sea would ease their minds: they would think if it were an escape, and not some hare-brained lark, it would be easy to pick up the escapees on the mainland.

By the time any airforce planes reached us we would be above built-up residential areas, which would make them reluctant to shoot at us. We would pretend that we did not understand what they were indicating, wave to them and wish them a happy New Year. They, like the warders, would know it was a matter of time before we were forced to land, and they could then radio our position to ground forces.

Once we were over our destination we would quickly lower the basket and land next to it. We would abandon the helicopter in the grounds, run flat out to the embassy building, and ask for political asylum.

On the Island I had discussed this plan thoroughly with

Nelson. It had been approved on condition that the High Command of the ANC in exile approved and executed it, and secret arrangements had been made for me to meet ANC president Oliver 'O.R.' Tambo in Botswana.

On my release from prison, however, I was immediately served with three banning orders, which included house arrest. If I left the country for Botswana I would be breaking my banning orders, and would find it difficult to return to South Africa to take part in the escape venture. I had to be there. I felt I could play a useful role as navigator, given that I was familiar with Cape Town and the Island. But a more important reason for me, perhaps, was that I really wanted to be part of the venture: I had a great admiration for Nelson and I really wanted to help him and the Struggle where I could.

So I had to work out an alternative plan to get the letter to O.R. I heard from a trusted friend, Moira Henderson of the Black Sash and founder of Cowley House-a place where families of political prisoners could stay when visiting the Island-that she was going to England soon. I asked her if she would be kind enough to take something, which was very confidential, to Randolph Vigne in London. She agreed.

I set out the plan, in tiny writing, on very thin tracing paper. I then found a postcard with a scenic view of Table Mountain on it, and mounted it on fairly thick cardboard, which overlapped the sides of the postcard. I hollowed out the mounting and placed the plan, folded and flattened, in the hollow. Then I stuck another piece of cardboard on the back. However, when I held it up to the light, I could still see the hollowed out section. I added yet another mount, and this effectively hid the plan from any prying eyes.

I addressed the card to Randolph's wife, Gillian, and gave it to Moira to deliver to him. In the meantime I wrote to Randolph, asking him to pass on the postcard to Nelson's 'brother-in-law' — Nelson and O.R. had been partners in their own law firm-with instructions that he must treat the postcard in the same way he had treated the photo album. (One of the methods we had used to smuggle messages out in the past was to pack pages of closely-written script in the covers of a photograph album. I knew O.R would understand the reference.)

Randolph figured out who Nelson's 'brother-in-law' was, and after receiving the card from Moira he delivered it to O.R. at the home in London where Oliver's wife, Adelaide, and their children were based. Randolph informed me later that what I had requested had been done. I was very grateful to both Moira and Randolph for their invaluable assistance.

That was the last I heard of the plan for 13 years. After the time for putting the plan into effect had passed, I assumed that either the High Command had turned it down, for whatever reason, or that O.R. had misunderstood the reference to the photo album and treated the postcard as just that, a message from an admirer.

In my mind's eye I could see my postcard propped up, quite innocently, on Oliver's mantelpiece. And there the matter rested, to my great disappointment.

On 19 June 1993, I received a telephone call out of the blue. It was from Dr Odendaal of the University of the Western Cape (UWC), to inform me that my plan had resurfaced. I was thrilled beyond measure. After Oliver's return from exile I had tried a couple of times, through Ahmed Kathrada, to find out what happened to the postcard. I was hoping to get it back for sentimental reasons. However, because of Oliver's poor health and busy schedule I did not receive a response. When O.R. died I accepted that the postcard, if it had been around, was now gone. Then came this unexpected call.

It turned out that the ANC High Command in Lusaka, Zambia, had received the escape plan after all. While they were studying it, however, they got wind of an impending South African Defence Force raid. All important documentation, including the escape plan, was to be destroyed to prevent it falling into enemy hands. Connie Braam, a member of the Dutch Anti-Apartheid Movement, was present at this gathering in Lusaka, and she rescued my plan from destruction and took it home with her to Holland.

When Connie heard that a Robben Island Museum was being set up she graciously sent the plan to South Africa to be included as an exhibit. I am grateful to her for having preserved this plan over the many long years. The plan was displayed in the Cape Town Museum in a Robben Island exhibition in 1993 and created a great deal of interest in the media.

PART

4

Chapter 20

Discharged and banned: 1979 - 1983

I was transferred from Robben Island to Pollsmoor Prison on the eve of my release. I was put in the punishment block, given a felt mat, three threadbare blankets, and a quarter loaf of bread with a layer of jam to keep me company. I slept in my prison clothes on the floor. I complained to the captain the next day about the conditions under which I had been held, but I did not make an issue of it.

I was released that morning, Friday 16 November 1979. I was hurried by both the warders and the security police, who were waiting for me at the prison. I told them I first wanted to wash, shave and change my clothing before leaving prison. Reluctantly, they allowed me half-an-hour for my ablutions.

The sergeant who accompanied me had the task of finding a tolerably clean bathroom. The place was filthy, and I had to walk gingerly over the muck to get to the shower, which was in the same condition. This brought to mind a remark made by Nelson Mandela on the Island, when I commented on how beautiful the gardens surrounding Pollsmoor prison looked. He replied that jails were like graves, beautiful on the outside with lovely flowers, but filled with decaying humanity.

At around 7.00am I was whisked away by three members of the security police led by Sergeant van Meulen. It was a beautiful morning and I enjoyed the drive through the suburb of Constantia.

I was taken straight to Caledon Square police station, where I was served with three banning orders. One placed me under house-arrest, another stipulated that I had to report to the police every Wednesday, and the third, among other things, listed a wide range of gatherings I could not attend and places I could not enter.

I thought back to the time when my first banning orders had been served on me. Those confined me to the Wynberg

Magisterial Area, making it illegal for me to visit my mother who lived in the adjacent Cape Town Magisterial Area. I would sneak into Cape Town on occasions and visit her. She was always over-joyed to see me but very apprehensive that I might be arrested for coming to visit her. I would give my special knock on her door, and she would hurry over and whisper through the door, 'Is that you Eddie?' 'Yes Mom,' I would reply. 'It is me.' She would usher me in and quickly close the door to prevent prying eyes from seeing who was visiting her. Our lingering farewells were always heart-breaking for her, as she never knew if it would be our last farewell.

Now I had an even more stringent set of banning orders served on me. The one consolation was that I was confined to the Cape Town Magisterial Area. I could now visit my mother legally, pro-vided she was alone and that the visits took place between 6:00 a.m. and 6:00 p.m. on a weekday.

Sergeant van Meulen remained behind at the police station, and the other two security policemen took me home. My family had been on a wild goose chase to Pollsmoor, having been told that I would be discharged from there, but they were back home by the time I arrived.

When I arrived at the house I shook hands with a young lad at the front door and went inside, where I received a wonderful welcome from my family and friends. After I had hugged my sis-ter-in-law, Linda, she asked me if I had seen my son Donovan. I said, 'No, where is he?'

She said, 'He was waiting for you at the front door.' I had not recognised my own son. When I went to the Island he was one year old, and we were not allowed visitors under the age of 16. I found Donovan quietly crying in the lounge. I hugged him and kissed him. Then he told me it was his 16th birthday. An extra bonus: I had been released on my son's birthday.

My brother Norman and his family, who have been tremen-dously loyal to me over the years, gave me a place to lay my head. On entering my brother's home I noticed a bright red car-pet on the floor in the passage. I assumed it was part of the usual furnishings of the house. It was only a few days later, when I saw

Linda rolling up the red carpet and replacing it with a more well-worn carpet of a different colour, that I realised the red carpet had been placed there in honour of my home-coming. I felt quite ashamed of myself for not appreciating such a lovely gesture, and apologised profusely to Linda.

I did not find it very difficult to adjust to normal life again. Perhaps my house-arrest was a blessing in disguise, in that I could not attend meetings or be swept off my feet by social engagements. This hiatus may have helped me adjust to my different social environment.

It was lovely seeing babies and small children again, as well as girls in their colourful summer frocks. Bright and fresh colours were intoxicating. To see the mountains, the sea and the horizon was magic. To enjoy lovely home-cooked meals as well as plenty of fresh fruit was thrilling.

Another thing that fascinated me was the sight of indicators on motorcars. In the evening, when I was travelling on a busy thoroughfare and the motorcars ahead had their indicators flashing to indicate that they were turning off the road or changing lanes, it looked like a Christmas Tree, with all of those coloured lights flashing away merrily.

Before I went to prison the buses had carried both a conductor and a driver. One would enter the bus, take a seat and wait for the conductor to come along and collect one's fare. On the first occasion that I caught a bus after having been released from prison, I sat down in the single-decker bus and looked around for the conductor. Other passengers looked at me rather strangely. I then saw the bus driver gesturing towards me. I went over to see what he wanted. He told me that I had not paid my fare. I realised there was no conductor, apologised and paid my fare. The driver's parting remark was, 'You must always greet me when you enter my bus.' The next time I entered a bus I again walked past the driver, but on sitting down I realised my error and quickly got up to pay before I was chastised for 'not greeting him'.

My banning orders prohibited me from attending any kind of gathering, a gathering being defined as three persons or more, and confined me to my home between 6:00pm to 6:00am on weekdays and from 6:00 p.m. on Friday to 6:00 a.m. on Monday. (A relaxation in this order allowed me to attend church on a Sunday between 9:00 a.m. and noon.) I was also confined to home for the duration of any public holidays.

Except for a medical doctor, I was not allowed any visitors. Not being a socialite, and just having been released from prison where the restrictive conditions were far more arduous, I did not find the banning orders very irksome and managed to survive from day to day. I also broke my banning orders if I felt it to be necessary. I had to be careful though, because if I were caught I would face a minimum sentence of 12-months imprisonment.

Shortly after my release Ann Tomlinson phoned to make an appointment on behalf of Nelson Mandela's daughter, Zinzi, who wished to see me. I did not realise my telephone was bugged, and we arranged to meet on a Saturday morning at my house. When Zinzi, Ann and two other friends arrived, we settled down to chat in my bedroom at the back of the house. After about 15 minutes Linda knocked very loudly on my bedroom door and shouted in an agitated voice that the security police were coming to the house. She had seen them approaching from the kitchen window, which faced onto the street.

My visitors immediately left my bedroom and went and sat in the lounge with Norman, who pretended they were his visitors. I remained in my bedroom reading. A few minutes later my door was pushed open and the security police walked in. I looked at them inquiringly. Sergeant van Meulen said I must come with them. In the passage he indicated that I should enter the lounge. I told him I could not enter the lounge, as there were visitors there and I was not allowed to be in their company.

'Don't worry,' Van Meulen said. 'We saw you leave the lounge before we came into the house.' This was a blatant lie. The security police could lie without batting an eyelid. It seemed they saw it as their duty to make life as difficult as possible, using any means, for anyone who dared to challenge them.

I felt sick to the core. I had just served 15 years in prison and now, a few weeks after being released, I was being framed by the security police on a charge that carried a minimum sentence of 12 months.

I spent a good part of Christmas Eve in the Kensington police station, where I was charged with contravening my banning orders. My lawyer, Sam Kawalsky of Frank, Bernadt and Joffe, was present while Sergeant van Meulen questioned me. After a number of questions, which I answered, Van Meulen asked what my educational qualifications were. I told him that had nothing to do with him or the matter in hand. Van Meulen began huffing and puffing, and Sam urged me to answer the question. I did so reluctantly, telling Van Meulen that I had a BA and a B. Comm. He wrote down the information in an exaggerated manner.

While the sergeant was taking my fingerprints Sam asked if he intended detaining me. He replied, magnanimously, that they did not detain people over Christmas. I chipped in and said, 'You have already detained me for 14 Christmases.'

As we were leaving the police station Van Meulen said sarcastically that if he had my educational qualifications he would write them down on a piece of paper, paste the paper on his forehead, and walk around with this paper stuck there.

I told him that, in actual fact, I had three degrees, and that my first degree was 'the third degree I received from you people'. My lawyer hastily ushered me out of the police station.

Norman, who was waiting hopefully outside the police station, was greatly relieved to see me. A family thanksgiving dinner had been planned for the next day, and if I had again been locked up the dinner would have been a sad one indeed. But it was not to be. We had a tremendous family dinner, with good food and loving company, my first in 15 years.

Chapter 21

Romance: 1980

I had first met Eleanor in 1955, at Consolidated Diamond Mines in Namibia. I left CDM in 1959 and had no further contact with her, except for a moment in the early '60s when she, her husband Jock Buchanan, and her family came to Cape Town on holiday. When they were leaving I met them at the airport for a brief hello and goodbye. Jock died of a heart attack several years before my release from prison.

Eleanor read in the papers about my release and tried to get in touch with me. She put messages in the personal columns of newspapers asking me to contact her. Unfortunately, I never read the personal columns. She also spent many hours, and much money, phoning the large number of people with the surname Daniels who were listed in the telephone directory, hoping to find someone who knew how I could be contacted.

Then, through a happy coincidence, she made contact at last. One morning she arrived at the building where she worked a bit earlier than was usual. She was on her way to her office when a telephone rang in another office. As there was no one else on duty at that time, and wanting to be helpful, she answered. The caller was a mutual friend, George Gerard, wanting to speak to his grandson who also worked at CDM. After an exchange of pleasantries George told Eleanor that he had been in contact with me, and Eleanor asked him for my telephone number.

That evening Eleanor was anxious to phone, but she was having a close mutual friend for supper. As she did not want to share her call to me, she waited till our friend left then phoned me, at 11:OO that evening. The following evening she again phoned, but this time she shared the call with our friend.

Eleanor wrote to me saying she was going to take early retirement (she was a chief buyer in Oranjemund) and move to Cape Town to be close to me. I wrote back telling her she must not resign from her job, that coming to Cape Town to be near me would cause her only heartbreak and bring about all kinds of complications. She ignored my advice, took early retirement, and moved to Wynberg, Cape Town.

Unfortunately, Wynberg was outside the area to which I was restricted. Every time I visited her I broke my banning orders. Eleanor would also come and visit me at home but as a friend of the family. When she realised I was risking imprisonment every time I visited her she moved to Maitland, which was inside the Cape Town Magisterial Area.

There was a clause in my restrictions that allowed me to be away from my home on a Sunday morning from 9:00am to noon to enable me to attend church. I attended the Methodist Church in Buitenkant Street. Eleanor also began attending the services regularly and subsequently became a member of the church. We were therefore able to meet for an extra half-hour after church on a Sunday morning.

I then arranged to play squash every second Sunday with a friend, Alan Baldwin, at the Green Point squash courts, where it was unlikely I would meet anyone who knew who I was. Eleanor accompanied me to the squash courts. Slowly but surely we were finding more and more time to be together.

I also made an arrangement with my then employer at the Urban Foundation, Judge Jan Steyn, whereby I worked an extra 30 minutes every day, and took every second Wednesday off. Both Eleanor and I used to look forward to our fortnightly Wednesday, but my manager, Mr Silvey, was always taken aback when I informed him the day before that I would be off the following day. He would ask, 'But wasn't it last week that you took the day off?'

As I racked my brains for more ways of spending 'legal' time with Eleanor, I suddenly realised that I did not use the time between 6:00 a.m. and 7:00 a.m. on weekday mornings. I wrote to the Minister of Justice, Louis le Grange, pointing out that my banning orders allowed me, on a Sunday morning, 45 minutes to travel from my home in Kensington to my church in Cape Town on quiet roads, but that I had only 30 minutes to get from my home to work each weekday, along congested roads.

In addition I had to report to the Kensington Police Station every Wednesday before 6:00 p.m. as well as be home before 6:00 p.m. I pointed out to the minister that there was a strong possibility I might transgress my banning orders through no fault of my own.

I suggested to him that he could solve my problem by changing the terms of my banning order to state that I had to be at home between the hours of 7:00 a.m. and 7:00 p.m. My request was granted. Eleanor and I now had an extra hour each evening to spend in each other's company.

There was still a risk involved in our relationship, however, as Eleanor was white and I was black. We faced the very real possibility of being charged under the Immorality Act, which prohibited interracial relationships.

In July 1983 my banning orders were lifted and not reimposed. I was now as free as any black person could be in South Africa at that time.

Eleanor and I decided to get married and live in her flat, as it was not known to the security police. We got married on 29 July 1983 in the Buitenkant Street Methodist Church, a church that had catered for the spiritual needs of its members in District Six before District Six was declared a white Group Area. Our marriage transgressed the Mixed Marriages Act, which was still in force, and Eleanor and I both faced imprisonment if discovered. However we felt that instead of just living together we had to make a stand and show that, if we were forced to choose between the laws of God and those of man, we would choose the laws of God and accept whatever consequences might follow.

We bought each other wedding rings from a pawnshop in Long Street, for about R45 each. Before the service we had our initials and the date of our marriage engraved inside the rings.

The wedding itself was a quiet affair. We had invited only two guests as witnesses, my brother Norman and Eleanor's son, Sandy, who had shown great loyalty to his mother. But the news of our impending marriage had spread and we had quite a number of guests in church for the ceremony. Because the marriage was illegal our minister, Reverend Jollife, could not issue a marriage certificate. He did, however, give us a note stating he had performed the ceremony and that our marriage, though it transgressed the law of the land, was recognised by the Church.

(We were still outlaws, though, and we lived in a perpetual state of apprehension. In the early hours of one morning Eleanor heard a commotion out in the street. She peeped through the curtains of our second-floor flat and saw two police vans in front of the building, with policemen moving around. She immediately assumed the worst. We waited apprehensively for the dreaded knock on our door, but no knock came. Later in the morning we discovered there had been trouble in a downstairs flat, and the police had come to investigate after a complaint from a neighbour.)

Seven years later to the day, on 29 July 1990, after the portion of the Mixed Marriage Act that applied to us was repealed, Eleanor and I got married again. We married in the same church, on the same date, with the same two witnesses. Only the minister, Reverend Taylor, was different; Reverend Jollif had been transferred. Our marriage was now recognised by both the Church and the State.

While I was in prison I had dreamt of climbing Table Mountain once again. I was born at the foot of the mountain, in District Six, and I had climbed it many times as I grew older. Shortly after our marriage I told Eleanor I would take her on my favourite climb, Woody Buttress. I had previously taken her for one or two easy walks on the mountain, but this route required some 'rock work'.

I did not realise the climb would be so difficult for Eleanor. I told her she should use her feet at all times, but being short, and desperate, she often found it more convenient to use her knees. I could see she was battling but it was more difficult going down than up, so we had to continue going up. Eleanor's knees became bruised from her using them to support herself on the hard rock. She also got stuck in the chimneys a few times.

After much effort and anxiety, we finally reached the top of Woody Buttress. I was hugely relieved that nothing had befallen (emphasis on fallen) Eleanor. Just a week previously we had met with our lawyer, Sam Kawalsky, and drawn up wills naming each other as sole beneficiaries. I told Eleanor I would have had a tough time, if something had happened to her on the climb, trying to explain to the world that it was a pure accident. We hugged each other and laughed with relief that nothing more serious had occurred than Eleanor's bruised knees.

Eleanor may have retired from her job, but when she married me she undertook another, although it is one she refers to as a labour of love: she became a 'Home Executive'. She would get up every weekday morning at 5.30 a.m. to get me off to work by 7:00 a.m. She has added years to my life by feeding me good, healthy and tasty food (also for the dog and cat), the correct vitamins (also for the dog and cat) and by providing me with lovely company. She wears many hats at home, among which are cook, baker, competition addict, food-coupon collector, secretary (to me), researcher and librarian.

Chapter 22

Support and opposition: 1955 onwards

The British-based International Defence and Aid Fund (IDAF) was an organisation which made an invaluable contribution to the Struggle against apartheid. The full story of IDAF has yet to be told, and the considerable role it played in contributing to the downfall of apartheid is not well known because of the 'cloak and dagger' methods it was forced to adopt.

IDAF evolved from the Christian Action organisation. Under the dedicated leadership of Canon Collins (now deceased), ably supported by his wife Diana, it raised millions of pounds to assist the oppressed in South Africa. It helped finance the cost of the Treason Trial (1956), the Rivonia Treason Trial (1963), the ARM trials (1964) around the country, and countless other political cases over the four decades it was involved in assisting the victims of apartheid in South Africa.

Because IDAF had become a painful thorn in the rotten flesh of apartheid, the government in 1966 passed a law making it a criminal offence to receive money from the organisation. A short while later IDAF was banned in South Africa.

The organisation adopted a strategy of channelling its funds through a firm of London lawyers, thereby making the source of funds untraceable. The funds were sent to lawyers in South Africa, to pay for the legal defence of those charged with acts perpetrated against the government, and to assist families whose breadwinners had lost their jobs, were in detention, in exile, in jail or who had been executed. IDAF also recruited individuals who were tasked with forwarding funds to selected victims of apartheid, and, through the World Council of Churches (WCC) and the South African Council of Churches (SACC), funded the establishment of the Dependants' Conference and Cowley House.

On behalf of the millions who benefited from the valiant efforts of all of those who made up this organisation internationally, and all those private citizens, organisations and governments, who donated funds to this tremendous organisation, I say, 'Thank you.' Your contribution to the new South Africa was enormous.

The Dependants' Conference came into being following the banning of IDAF. Funded through the SACC, it played the same role as IDAF, making financial grants available to families whose breadwinners were in exile, jail or dead because of political activities. But the Dependants' Conference went one step further: it founded Cowley House.

Moira Henderson, a brave and committed lady if ever there was one, was put in charge of the Cowley House project. She died while continuing with the Struggle. I was on the Island when the project was launched. I remember Nelson telling me about it, saying what a boon it would be to our visitors who came from as far afield as Namibia. On reaching Cape Town they were strangers in the city. Because they knew no one in Cape Town and could not afford the expensive lodgings available, many of them spent the evenings on the railway station. They would wash and prepare their food in the toilet. They would be afraid to ask the police for assistance or directions because the response from the police was usually crude and rude.

Eleanor was a voluntary worker for the Dependants' Conference. She told me how they would contact the families of those who were in prison for political offences and (in conjunction with the International Committee of the Red Cross who paid the transport fares) arrange for them to travel to Cape Town. They would meet the visitors at the railway station and take them to Cowley House, where they would be fed and securely housed without cost. Permits to the Island were arranged on the visitors' behalf and they would be taken to the docks and fetched again in transport supplied by Cowley House. If the visitors had a few days to spare then they stay on at Cowley House free of charge.

Prisoners released from the Island who had no immediate place of abode could stay at Cowley House until arrangements for alternative accommodation were made on their behalf. On release each prisoner would also receive a sum of money to help them over the immediate future. In my case I received R100.

One marvels at the goodness of people both in and outside South Africa. The majority of people on the receiving end of apartheid were both poor and uneducated, and if it were not for the kindness and thoughtfulness of many, epitomised by people such as Moira Henderson, they would have been lost in the evil maelstrom of apartheid. Therefore on behalf of the millions who have benefited over the years from the good offices of the Dependants' Conference and the ICRC, I thank all those brave and good people who risked their own welfare in the interest of helping others. Thank you.

Two days after I was released from prison Judge Jan Steyn came to see me at home. We shook hands and he sat down on my bed. He said he had applied for a permit from the security police for permission to see me (no one was allowed to visit me without permission, other than a doctor) and wanted to know if I had any objection to this. I told him that I had no objection and, as a matter of fact, we could now have a relaxed discussion instead of being alarmed every time we heard an unfamiliar sound.

But I did point out that I was not asking him to apply for a permit every time he visited me, nor was I asking him not to do so. The choice was his. I also pointed out that he, as a judge of the Supreme Court, had great respect for the law, whereas I had none and would comply with or break the law as it suited me.

The following day I had an interview for a job as storeman in a paint factory, offered to me by a person whose family had suffered under Hitler. On my way to the interview I stopped in at my lawyers' offices, where I received a call from home saying Judge Steyn was trying to contact me.

I decided that I would first go and see Judge Steyn before continuing on to the interview. I met the judge who offered me a job with the Urban Foundation, which he headed. I accepted his offer. I then contacted the gentleman who had offered me a job in his paint factory, thanked him for the offer and informed him I had accepted another offer. I also explained to him that I had been apprehensive about working in a paint factory, because I suffered slightly from both emphysema and asthma, and he accepted this.

Judge Steyn was good to me in many ways. When the security police tried to frame me for breaking my banning orders, as mentioned earlier, he intervened on my behalf. After the third adjournment of my case he asked me what was happening. I told him and shortly after that the case was withdrawn.

He also managed to get my banning orders changed insofar as they applied to my place of work, enabling me to communicate freely with my fellow employees.

Judge Steyn put together an application for the lifting of my banning orders, which he set out as if it was coming from me, and submitted it to me for my approval. I rejected it. I told him if he wished to apply to the minister he was free to do so, but he must do it in his own name. I told him I appreciated his kindness towards me, but I had not asked him to apply for the lifting of my banning orders. Whatever he did on my behalf he must do because he wanted to, not because I asked him

Shortly before my banning orders were lifted, an action which neither the judge nor I had known was going to happen, the foundation's accounts section in which I worked was transferred to Johannesburg. I knew I could not go to Johannesburg and believed myself to be effectively out of a job. However the judge came to me and said I should not worry; I still had a job in Cape Town with the Urban Foundation.

Various people asked how I, a person who was so heavily committed to fighting apartheid, could work for a semi-government organisation like the Urban Foundation. I replied that I thought the Urban Foundation was doing a necessary job in trying to provide houses, among other things, to the many who were deprived and destitute. But my stock answer to my critics was: 'Offer me another job.' None of them could.

There was one incident in this regard that hurt me quite deeply. A high school teacher, whose wife was a secretary at the Urban Foundation, criticised me rather severely on one occasion for working there. I asked him why he did not object to his wife working for the Foundation. He dismissed the question by saying she was apolitical. About two months later his wife told me, very excitedly, that her husband had applied for a lucrative job that the Foundation had been advertising in the newspapers. When she saw the expression on my face she realised she had made an error in telling me. I felt sick. I said to her, 'Your husband criticised me so severely for working for the Urban Foundation. He has a job, he has no banning orders imposed on him, yet here he is applying for a job with the Urban Foundation.' I walked away in disgust.

After my banning orders were lifted I kept a relatively low profile, although I spoke at several public meetings and supported the Struggle in different ways. In about 1985 I started to receive death threats by telephone. The threats continued for about a year, until I laid a charge with the police.

About 18 months later the threatening calls started again, and carried on for about two years or more.

I applied for a licence to own a gun but my application was turned down by the police. No reason was given. Eleanor in turn applied for a licence. Her application was being favourably considered when the policeman taking down the details asked Eleanor for her address. When she gave it to him he looked up at her and said, 'You can't live there!' (It was not a white Group Area). Eleanor replied, 'Well I do,' and walked out of the police station. I suggested she drop her application to avoid unnecessary complications, and she agreed.

A friend of mine rigged up a tape recorder to my telephone that enabled me to record both my own voice and the voice of the caller. I would get calls at all times of the day and night. Eleanor was good. Several times in the early hours of the morning when the phone rang, she would tumble out of bed and have the recorder connected before I answered the call.

At times I anticipated that the caller was the person making threats, and as I lifted the phone I would shout: 'Voetsek, you filthy scum!' Twice I miscalculated, once when my son, Donovan, phoned me and another occasion when it was my cousin May. On both occasions I had to apologise profusely and explain to them why I had been so rude on the phone.

As I had done before, I laid a charge of harassment against a person or persons unknown. The post office put a trace on my line that I could activate myself by depressing the cradle of my telephone. We discovered from a printout generated at the telephone exchange that the calls were being made from different public call boxes.

Eleanor (who was also a victim of some of the calls) and I were asked by the police to identify different voices over the telephone, but this was an exercise in futility. All the voices sounded the same. It may even have been a conspiracy.

Then one day the post office managed to trace the call to a private home.

A Sergeant Bleakey from the Sea Point police station was charged with crimen injuria. He appeared in the Wynberg Magistrate's court on 26 March 1991 and admitted that he had phoned me once, anonymously, but had not threatened me over the telephone. He was found not guilty, but the magistrate scolded him for being so childish as to make anonymous calls.

Since that court case we have received no further threatening phone calls.

Chapter 23

Teaching; the Schools' Uprising: 1976 - 1985

With the lifting of my banning orders my horizons widened considerably. Although my employment at the Urban Foundation still held good, despite the transfer of the accounts department to Johannesburg, I was now in a position to look further afield for employment. A friend of mine, Stephen Dietrich, suggested I take up teaching, and I embraced the idea.

I thanked Judge Steyn for the kindness and goodwill he had shown me, and bade both him and the Urban Foundation farewell.

For the next nine months I worked for Reliance Printing Works, selling paper for photocopiers and typing.

In 1984 I enrolled at the University of Cape Town (UCT) to do a teacher training course, which I completed in a year. During that year student teachers were farmed out to various high schools to do a teaching practical. The policy of the university was that student teachers would usually be allocated to a school near their place of residence. I was allocated to Milnerton High, a 'white' school. A week before starting my practical I went to see the principal, Mr Visser, and gave him my background. I explained that I had gone to jail for opposing the government's policy of apartheid, and that if he should object to my presence at his school I would understand and apply to do my practical at another school. His reaction was calm. He welcomed me, then told me that they did not teach politics to the children at his school. I replied that I had not come to his school to teach politics but to learn how to teach academic subjects.

The first thing that struck me when I entered the school grounds was the acres of green grass that made up the sports complex. They also had tennis courts and I saw Mr Visser teaching some schoolgirls golf. It was quite pleasant teaching there.

A few weeks after that stint I was again allocated to Milnerton High to complete my second and final practical teaching session.

On the first day Mr Visser sent for me. He informed me that the principal of Fairburn High urgently needed a business economics teacher for his matriculation classes, and had appealed to him for help.

'Well, Mr Daniels,' said Mr Visser. 'Are you prepared to accept this challenge?'

I was, although secretly I thought Mr Visser was glad to get rid of me.

I started at Fairburn High the following day. Again I was struck by the acres of green fields which greeted me on my arrival.

The principal insisted on paying me for 'helping him out.' I felt I was not entitled to payment because I was on a practical, and told him so, but he insisted. I was possibly the only black teacher ever paid by the white department of education for teaching in a whites-only school. I made a photocopy of the cheque for posterity.

During breaks in my teaching I would tell the children about the Pass Laws, the Group Areas Act, and the terrible suffering of blacks, particularly Africans, because of apartheid. They seemed quite interested in what I had to say. A teacher who sat in on one of my lessons was quite taken aback at what I told the children after I had finished my lesson, but as I was never reprimanded I assumed I had not been reported.

One of the questions I put to the children was, 'If a stranger should come and visit and you told him this is a white school he would be quite bewildered. Why?'

There was a puzzled silence. I said, 'Because this is not a white school it is a green school; the walls are painted green. And that school in the black area is not a black school; it is a white school because the walls are painted white.' The children seemed to appreciate this.

At the end of the final term, after a pleasant year at UCT, I received my Higher Education Diploma, which qualified me to be a teacher.

When I looked for a teaching post in 1985 I decided I would not apply through the relevant education department but instead approach the principals directly. I telephoned a number of principals, appeared for an interview, and explained my background. They all turned me down. Some of them referred, rather lamely, to the odd anti-apartheid meeting they had attended sometime or another. (In their reckless youth?)

Eventually I wound up at Garlandale High. After the usual interview I once again explained my background. Instead of the expected weak smile and limp handshake, I received a firm handshake and a broad smile from the principal, A.J. Snyders, who said, 'Welcome aboard.'

At least one other ex-Robben Islander, who was a teacher before his arrest, had applied for a teaching post. He was initially accepted but, after a few months, received a slip in his pay envelope stating that his services were no longer required. I do not know how I managed to survive in an education department that was so conservative. Not to mention a department in which many blacks were playing ball with the government, not only to survive, but in pursuit of promotions and higher salaries.

I believe there must have been somebody high up in the department who was shuffling my papers around, keeping them away from the eyes that would have had me fired. All I can say is 'Thank you' to that unknown Samaritan.

In 1985, my first year of teaching, black schools were in turmoil. The United Democratic Front, under the able leadership of Dr Alan Boesak, Albertina Sisulu, 'Terror' Lekota, Trevor Manuel, Cheryl Carolus and other brave people, had whipped up tremendous opposition to the government. The schools were also caught up in this feverish political activity. In the past politics had been the terrain of adults only but, since the Soweto uprising of 16 June 1976, the picture had rapidly changed. By 1985, schoolchildren from standard six upward were actively involved in opposition to the government and its apartheid policies.

The children were well organised and extremely brave in spite of the State of Emergency, declared on 21 July 1985, which gave the police sweeping powers of arrest and detention, and enabled them to torture and kill with impunity.

The children would secretly organise a rally to take place at a particular school, and the word would go out. On the day thousands of schoolchildren would converge on that particular school. The principal and staff would just have to accept the situation. Anti-government speeches would be made, a small band would play, freedom songs would be sung with gusto, energetic dancing would take place and for every cry of 'AMANDLA!' or 'VIVA!' a thousand fists would shoot skywards with vigour. At times there were rallies at two or three different schools on the same day.

Then the police helicopter would appear; 'the eye in the sky'. Everyone would brace themselves for the coming onslaught. Little girls would adjust the handkerchiefs on their faces in preparation for the teargas shells which would soon be landing in their midst.

The police would arrive in Saracens and Casspirs, huge landmine-proof armoured vehicles with ports for automatic rifles. These terrible machines, designed for full-scale war, were completely out of place in a situation where unarmed school children were the enemy.

Policemen would pour out of the armoured vehicles and immediately block all entrances to the school. Teargas canisters would be fired into the schoolyard. If the gates were locked, the Casspirs would crash through them. The police would rush among the children, clubbing, kicking and whipping them furiously. There would be pandemonium. Children would be desperately trying to escape. They would climb fences, scale walls, or hide in classrooms to escape the vicious beatings. When the police were satisfied they had broken up the rally they would move off. But tomorrow and the day after and the day after that the children would continue to organise. They were transforming the schools into places of political learning.

Children were beaten, imprisoned and killed. One of the most notorious incidents was the 'Trojan Horse Killings', when a group of policemen hid inside crates on the back of a government railway truck. The truck drove up and down Belgravia Road in Athlone, a volatile area, until schoolchildren began stoning it. The policemen popped up from the crates and opened fire indiscriminately with automatic rifles. Three children died, one inside a nearby house.

When marches took place under the banner of the UDF, the children, in their school uniforms and with their school cases on their backs, would join the adults facing the police with their dogs, sjamboks (whips), teargas and war machines. The police were in their element. Except for a few stones thrown occasionally, no one hit back at them. It was usually an unarmed, disciplined crowd that marched and defied the police. Because of the State of Emergency every march that took place was illegal, even before it started.

One of the schools in the forefront in the 1985 uprising was Alexander Sinton Secondary, headed by Mr Desai and Mr Swartz, the principal and vice-principal. Both these gentlemen had been arrested in the process of defending their pupils from the police, and many rallies were held at the school. The school's contribution to the Struggle was later acknowledged by the ANC with a personal visit by Nelson Mandela, who thanked the students and staff for their commitment. Nelson also praised the bravery of all the pupils from all the schools who had contributed positively to the fight against injustice and discrimination. A large mural on the school wall was dedicated to Nelson who, in turn, planted a tree in the school's indigenous garden.

The student uprising continued for years, resulting in many of the students losing out on their schoolwork and failing their examinations. This gave rise to the term 'the lost generation'. This term is often used in a dismissive and contemptuous manner, which is extremely unfair to the children. This so-called 'lost generation' helped to bring the apartheid government to its knees that much sooner. They joined their parents in the Struggle and suffered the consequences. Many of them, because of their bravery and commitment to the cause of freedom, became casualties of the Struggle against oppression.

The irony of the situation is that many who risked everything for justice, dignity and democracy are today battling to make ends meet in the new South Africa, while others who kept out of the Struggle are living in upmarket areas and enjoying the pleasant lifestyle previously denied them by apartheid laws. Many who criticised the liberation movements are today enjoying the fruits of the victory attained by those that fought, suffered and died for liberation.

Chapter 24:

Nelson Mandela's release;
the Sisulus' visit: 1990

In January 1990 I received a call from Victor Verster Prison, where Nelson Mandela was being held after having been transferred first from Robben Island and then to Pollsmoor, saying he wished to see Eleanor and me on the following Wednesday.

I was extremely excited. I told my school principal, Mr Snyders, about the invitation and asked for the day off from school, which he readily granted. The whole school was agog with the news. At a special assembly the school asked me to convey their best wishes and 'Long Live' to Nelson.

The Tuesday before the visit was to take place I received another call from the prison, saying it had been cancelled. No reasons were given. When I reported this a pall of disappointment fell over the school. I shrugged off the disappointment as 'one of those things'.

A few days later Victor Verster informed me that the invitation had again been extended. The reason for the previous cancellation was that Nelson had received an urgent request for discussions with the then state president, F.W. de Klerk.

It was a lovely day when Eleanor and I went to visit Nelson. The last time I had seen him was when I was released from prison 10 years earlier. I now once again saw the man for whom I have the greatest admiration and respect. He was as upright and dignified as ever. He was a bit greyer than when I had last seen him, and had a slightly strained look on his face, as was to be expected from one living in isolation under prison conditions and carrying tremendous responsibilities. We hugged each other. He then hugged Eleanor, whom he was meeting for the first time.

Nelson told me about the negotiations between him and government ministers for his release and the unbanning of the African National Congress. Once again, he was being extremely courteous towards me. But Eleanor and I had not gone to visit him to discuss such weighty topics. There were many others far more competent than I with whom he could discuss these issues. I had come to cheer him up and give him one day free from his heavy responsibilities.

On the Island we had been allowed to organise concerts over Christmas and New Year, and at one of these concerts Nelson had sung 'Bonnie Mary of Argyle'. On another occasion Nelson and I were in his cell when he suddenly recited a poem, 'Invictus', by W.E.Henley. I had told Eleanor about both these incidents and she immediately undertook the task of unearthing the poem and song. For Nelson's visit Eleanor and I learned both the poem and song off by heart. After lunch I got up and recited 'Invictus'. We then stood up, with Nelson in the middle, and with our arms around each other sang 'Bonnie Mary of Argyle'. That was a very happy day for me. I just hope it was such a day for perhaps the greatest son that this country has ever produced.

The next day at school the principal called a special assembly for a report on my visit.

Nelson had written a short note to Mr Snyders thanking him for the good wishes he had received from the school. I told the assembly what had transpired on my visit and then again recited the poem and sang 'Mary of Argyle'. Loud and prolonged applause followed my report.

Incidentally, since 1985 when I first started teaching at Garlandale High, I had been discussing 'Invictus' with the pupils. I had always emphasised the last two lines of the poem, substituting 'You' for 'I'.

You are the Master of your Fate:
You are the Captain of your Soul.

I would tell them that they could use themselves for good or evil. They could be responsible or irresponsible. The choice was theirs. They were the captains of their souls, they were the masters of their fate.

On 2 February 1990 there was wild jubilation when F.W. de Klerk, in his address to the opening of parliament, announced the unbanning of all organisations and the impending release of Nelson Mandela.

The following Saturday, 11 February 1990, Nelson was

released from Victor Verster Prison. There were huge celebrations in Cape Town, throughout South Africa and many parts of the world.

It was thrilling to see this great man, who had spent the past 27 years in jail, walking hand-in-hand with his lovely wife, Winnie Mandela, who had proved such a tower of strength. Upright and noble, and with a natural dignity, he acknowledged the tumultuous applause and waves of adoration with a brave, soft smile and a gentle wave of his hand. The whole beautiful, unbelievable scene just gripped my heart.

Few people, I feel, can realise or appreciate the tremendous pressures Nelson was under both politically and psychologically when he was released from prison. After living for more than a decade in a universe made up of about 30 adult males in drab prison clothing, he was moved to Pollsmoor prison, where his universe shrunk to six other prisoners, and then to Victor Verster, where he was on his own.

After 27 years in places where sound was muted and the environment barren, he was suddenly, without any counselling to prepare him, catapulted into a bedlam of noise and light and colour. He was confronted with a barrage of TV cameras and the screaming, shouting and clamouring of thousands of people, expressing their joy on seeing this great man in the flesh for the first time in decades and desperately trying to get near enough to touch him.

But, in addition to this violent and sudden change in environment, he now faced, and he knew that he faced, the perpetual threat of assassination from anyone who wanted to further destabilise an already unstable South Africa.

In spite of all this, he rose to the challenge as magnificently as he had always risen to the many challenges with which he had been confronted throughout his life.

I was on Cape Town's Grand Parade that afternoon, with Eleanor and 100 000 others. In earlier years I had attended numerous public meetings on the Grand Parade, but none could compare with that enormous crowd. They had all gathered to welcome this great man whose 'head was bloody but unbowed';

who was so magnanimous in his lack of bitterness towards those who had denied him, throughout his life, the dignity to which all human beings are entitled. Not only the Parade but also the surrounding streets were filled with people. Neighbouring buildings were festooned with people jammed into crevices in the walls and clinging precariously to invisible handholds and footholds. The organisers had the tremendous job of trying to control the crowd, keeping them good-humoured and preventing them from being crushed in the mass of humanity.

At about 4:00 p.m. there was a sudden burst of heavy gunfire. A wave of panic rippled through the crowd. Calm was returning when there was another burst of gunfire, and the crowd surged away from the sound, forcing Eleanor and me back as well.

We later heard that criminals were taking advantage of the situation by breaking into shops, and the police, so we were told, were forced to open fire on them.

In other areas in the vicinity of the Parade some plate-glass windows were cracked and others broken because of the tremendous crush.

At about 5:00 p.m. a motorcade appeared and tried to make its way to the City Hall through the throng. The drivers gave up and the motorcade roared off in the opposite direction. We later learned that security guards, fearing the crowd would engulf Nelson, had decided to get him out of the area and return later, by another route.

The enormous crowd, still in good humour, waited patiently for their hero to appear. At last Nelson appeared on the balcony of the City Hall. The cheers and applause were deafening. Eventually the noise abated. The crowd stood in awe as they listened to the first of the many speeches that Nelson would deliver as a free man in the land of his birth.

Our wedding anniversary was on 29 July but, when we heard that Walter and Albertina 'Mama' Sisulu were coming to spend the weekend with us, at our home in Hout Bay, we postponed our celebration so that we could share it with them. Walter had come to Cape Town to participate in a documentary the BBC was filming of Robben Island, and we put up Walter and Mama and the two bodyguards who had accompanied them from Johannesburg. The ANC in the Western Cape supplied six additional bodyguards.

It was wonderful having the Sisulus with us. In spite of the very wet and cold weather we experienced that weekend I am sure they had a relaxing time.

The weekend was marred by one incident, however. On Sunday afternoon, while Walter and Mama were having discussing with representatives of different organisations who had come to see them at my home, loud gunshots rang out. I expected to see the bullets come crashing through the windows.

Just a few weeks earlier one of Walter's bodyguards had been killed in what the ANC considered to be an attempt on Walter's life, and a few months before that he had been involved in an altercation at a police roadblock.

I immediately lowered the window blinds of the lounge in which Walter and Mama were sitting. Outside all the bodyguards were on the alert, trying to place where the shots had come from. As they trained their binoculars on the nearby mountain, the Sentinel, two possible suspects came into view.

Three bodyguards and I sped in that direction by car, as I knew the most direct route to that spot, while the rest of the bodyguards stayed at the house.

We left the car at the foot of the Sentinel and scrambled up the mountain, which was wet and slippery. We eventually reached the people whom we had viewed through the binoculars. Initially they denied that they were responsible for the shooting, but, after we pointed out that they were the only people in the vicinity, they confessed. They apologised profusely, saying they had just been practising shooting. I told them that the area in which they were practising was a popular hiking area, and they were a danger to other people. One of the bodyguards suggested that if they wanted to practise shooting they should go to a shooting range.

On returning to the house we found all parties still engrossed in deep discussion.

The peculiarity of that incident was that I had been living in that area for the last ten years, and this was the first time anybody had practised shooting on the mountain. That the shooting took place on the very weekend that Walter and Mama Sisulu were visiting me, and shortly after two other frightening incidents, was quite nerve-racking.

Chapter 25:

From violence to peace - the new South Africa: 1990 - 1994

Writing about the shots fired during the Sisulus' visit, recalled, painfully, the times which we lived through in the last three years of the regime. As the memories of the vicious days of apartheid are fast fading, so too are the events of even those few years before the election of 27 April 1994, which ushered in a new era for South Africa. At the beginning of 1994 I wrote down my feelings and hopes, which I reproduce now as a reminder of those times:

The present state of violence in South Africa is horrific. Massacres occur almost daily. One dreads listening to the news on a Monday because it usually reports the total number of killings over the weekend. The violence is absolutely brutal. The victims are shown no mercy. They are callously shot, burnt, hacked, stoned and beaten to death.

Criminals are cold-blooded in their execution of their crimes. Robbery, rape and murder are the order of the day. John Citizen and his family are afraid to leave the security of their home because of the senseless and brutal killings that are taking place and, at times, even the security of their homes is not adequate protection against the perpetrators of violence, who have easy access to guns which they do not hesitate to use.

An added tragedy about the criminal violence is that as the crimes increase in scale and the brutality of the crimes escalates, the court sentences and bail applications and conditions seem too moderate, instead of being more severe on these criminals. This moderate approach by the law courts towards the criminals gives them the green light to go ahead and commit crimes and destroy families in the process.

Political violence is taking place between the ANC on the one hand and the IFP and the rightwing on the other, with agents provocateur fanning the violence, especially between the ANC and the IFP. Then there is the 'third force' which is believed to originate from aspects of Military Intelligence, the armed forces and the police. There have been numerous eyewitness reports of the army and police escorting large groups of armed hostel dwellers to and from attacks on residential areas; of merciless and indiscriminate killings on trains by quiet killers; and of indiscriminate massacres of taxi passengers over and over again without any possible motive other than to spread terror.

What then is the real motive behind these senseless massacres? The motive, I feel, is to destabilise the country so that the elections of 27 April 1994 cannot take place in an atmosphere that could be described as 'free and fair'. Increasing political violence from those who do not want the elections to take place can be expected. Political violence also contributes to criminal violence because an atmosphere of lawlessness is created which pervades the country, thus encouraging the criminals to commit crimes. But it is imperative that the elections do take place, otherwise the perpetrators of violence and sowers of death and chaos would have won the day.

I wish my country, South Africa, peace and prosperity for the New Year as well as for ever. May we, after 27 April 1994, be blessed with a just and democratic government which will not only rule in the interest of all the citizens of the country, but that the government will be accepted by all the citizens of South Africa.

I write on 1 January 1994. Mr Mandela and Mr de Klerk have been presented with the Nobel Peace Prize, a good omen for South Africa. The Transitional Executive Council (TEC) has come into being bolstered by the entry of General Constance Viljoen, a general of the far right, whose entry into the TEC has partially neutralised the threat of violence from the far-right, thereby setting South Africa firmly on the road to a democratic government. At the request of the ANC, international sanctions against South Africa have been lifted. The future looks hopeful.

The opinion polls give one cheer, with their indication that the ANC will have a substantial lead over its political opponents, with the National Party coming in second place in the April 27 election. We will at last have a democratic government. My personal knowledge of the 'Old Guard', as well as of some of the 'rising stars', is of people who have both integrity and drive. This knowledge instils me with confidence in the future.

I am confident of the future of my country, South Africa. The country is rich in physical assets, especially in its mineral wealth, and great beauty. Above all, its people want to see South Africa succeed. South Africa has tremendous political and economical potential as the catalyst and economic engine of southern Africa and beyond.

Finally, the New South Africa will uphold an inviolable Bill of Rights, will demand the accountability of people who hold public office, and guarantee the independence of the judiciary and many other constitutional safeguards. All this must ensure that democracy will prevail and that violence and corruption will be at a minimum. We have won the war; we have yet to win the peace.

Thus ended my thoughts as 1994 began. As I look back on the election, the great day of the inauguration of President Mandela at the Union Buildings in Pretoria, the opening of our first parliament of all the people, and recently, the glorious return to Robben Island, where I met so many of my old friends and comrades, I begin to see the fulfilment of the hope I had expressed, that South Africa would win the peace. So many suffered and died for it, paying a high price for it, but it was a price that was not paid in vain.

*　　*　　*

I pick up the thread where I have dropped it in 1994. Crime and corruption were rife, problems of illiteracy, poverty, homelessness, and unemployment inherited from the apartheid regime are still with us. They are an albatross around the neck of our fragile democracy. Mandela the Great with his courage, charisma and insight had nursed our fragile, infant democracy through its five years of social and political turbulence.

When the ANC won the June 1999 General Election the Great Madiba with charm and grace handed over his presidency of the RSA to his deputy president, Thabo Mbeki, whom he had groomed for the position of President of the Republic of South Africa over the previous three years. Madiba, unlike other international leaders, did not yearn for life presidency and the material wealth that goes with it, but, instead, graciously relinquished his leadership of both his organisation and his country. He now is an elder statesman who travels the world striving to bring peace where there is war, compassion where there is pain and love where there is hate. What a role model for humanity!

President Mbeki, a modest and sincere man, on becoming the President of the Republic of South Africa was seen as a 'hands on' president. He, unlike Mr Mandela who, when released from prison, was embraced by the whole world, has had to work and prove his worth which he has done successfully. In doing so he has won the respect and acceptance of the whole world. We, in democratic South Africa, have indeed been blessed with two leaders of great integrity, calibre and humility.

One of the sad and unexpected factors which has undermined the government's valiant efforts to alleviate the continual suffering of the masses is the fact that a number of the members of the Liberation Struggle, who occupy important and lucrative positions both in the government and the private sector, who once swore by the Freedom Charter today swear at the Freedom Charter in their efforts to enrich themselves through corrupt methods at the expense of the suffering of the masses, whose cause they had initially championed.

South Africa's image as the economic engine of southern Africa and Africa has been enhanced by our political and economic stability. We are still in the position to spearhead the African Renaissance which, hopefully, will eventually bring peace and prosperity to the African Continent.

LETTERS

A letter written to the author, shortly after his release from prison, by Adrian Leftwich who was a state witness in the author's trial.

Nottingham,
England.
10/1/80

Dear Eddie,

I have wanted to write to you for a long time, but have not really known what to say or how to say it. But I heard from Dot that she had seen you on your release and I was overjoyed to learn from her that you looked well after all that you have been through. I hope you are well and stay well.

All that I can really say can be boiled down to two words – shame and respect. Shame at my own weakness for having collapsed so totally under pressure and respect for you for what you have been through, done and achieved. Of all the people involved, you alone carried the heaviest load with the greatest of courage. I don't suppose that anyone can know what you feel and think after 15 years on the Island. All I can say is that I will always wish that I could change the past, but know that I cannot. Would you change the past if you could?

So you will always live with a profound sense of self-respect and pride; and I with a sense of guilt and inadequacy, for I failed my friends terribly. Nothing can ever change that.

Whether you will ever be able to forgive that I do not know. However, I salute you and yours, and wish you all the best in everything you do. And while I cannot change the past we can still hope for a better future in S.A.

With deep respect,

Adrian.

Author's reply to Adrian's letter.

Kensington,
Cape Town,
9/2/80.

Dear Adrian,

I hope that my release from prison will alleviate the terrible mental pressures that you have been suffering all these many years. You ask me if I would like to change the past. Both you and I know that we cannot change the past – but to indulge in some wishful thinking I'll say, yes. I would like to change your role from the time you were arrested, for example, you may have escaped or joined others in the dock. Why I wish this is because of the brave role you played in the organisation prior to your arrest. You were an outstanding organiser, leader and a person held in high respect by all.

But you slipped, unfortunately, very badly. Your giving evidence against me was unfortunate – but I can understand your reasoning. As far as you were concerned you were fighting for your life. In any case you did not recruit me, and to my knowledge, I was in the NCL before you were. What disappointed me greatly was your giving state-evidence against those whom you recruited into the organisation. I felt that there your responsibility and duty were clear – you had to protect them and, if possible, cover up for them where possible.

A further disappointment to me was that while you were under detention you volunteered information to the S.B. which was never asked for. This point I must point out is unconfirmed. At that time I was still being interrogated about 'Jacob' (Neville Hillman). The S.B. approached me at different times saying that you saw Neville and myself on the mountain. On another occasion, that we met outside the Tafelberg Hotel. Then again that that Jacob's first name is Neville and then finally, that Neville is a friend of my family. I was told by the S.B. that you were actually sending for them and volunteering these bits of information as you recalled them. I denied all knowledge of what you said and told the S.B. that you are mistaken. But it did mean that I was under additional pressure. I refer to the above points not to raise unpleasant memories but to show you how I viewed the situation.

You've had an agonising time. You were an international figure. You were placed on a pedestal by many and then you slipped and your world crumbled. It was the first time you found yourself in this situation and the penalty you faced for transgressing the law was severe. You had the choice of one of two evils – standing trial or co-operating with the state. You chose the latter.

This choice resulted in all those whom you loved and who loved you withdrawing from you. This attitude on their part is quite correct. People who let the side down must be treated harshly so as to discourage others from taking this 'easy road' out.

What has made things very difficult for you are 1) the people with whom you associated are people of calibre and principle who can take a hard and painful stand if necessary and 2) you did not cross over to the enemy – something which you could not do because your values were different to theirs. Your lapse was a momentary one. One, which unfortunately, has caused you much mental torture and heartbreak.

I've recently read Alan Paton's book 'Kontakion'. I was told that his forgiving you on behalf of others has given rise to much resentment. I, personally, feel no resentment towards Mr Paton for this kindly gesture. In fact it means nothing if others do not support it. This book also indicates that you gave evidence in other trials as well. I'm sorry about that but I suppose that was part of the conditions imposed on you.

Your lapse, unfortunately, is not the same as a man who had stolen R100.00 and who can replace it with R1 000.00 in three years' time. But I do not consider you a complete write-off from the struggle against injustice and oppression. In your, perhaps, isolated way I'm sure you are still trying to push the ideas and ideals which you have always stood for.

I personally have no personal grudge against you. I hope that this letter will help you to find mental peace. I also wish you happiness for the future.

Yours sincerely,

Eddie.

* NCL: National Committee of Liberation. Later renamed African Resistance Movement (ARM).
* S.B.: Security Branch.

A Tribute to the Women in the Struggle
1960-1994

Many a glowing tribute has been paid to the men who fought so bravely in the struggle against apartheid. But there has been few tributes paid to the women in the struggle against apartheid. They too risked their all in the struggle for freedom and democracy and suffered in the process. Suffering included being banned, detained, tortured, exiled, imprisoned and killed.

In paying tribute to the women in the struggle I focus on the mothers, the black mothers. Those humble, unsung, unknown and long-suffering women who contributed so mightily to the struggle and suffered so deeply in the process. Their untold sacrifices have been lost in the great ocean of suffering brought about by decades of bondage.

The greatest sufferers in any conflict are the women. They see their husbands, sons and fathers go off to war. They bravely wave goodbye to them, knowing in their hearts that their personal struggle is about to begin, that of keeping their families together. It is the mothers, especially, who experience the greatest hardship. They do not only have to raise their families but also show loyalty to their menfolk, wherever they may be.

Under apartheid we saw the contrast of the white mother who had a husband and son in the South African armed forces and the black mother whose husband and son were actively opposed to the apartheid government.

The white mother sees the men she loves answer to their patriotic duty as they join the South African army. How smart they look in their army uniform. Her heart fills with pride. The neighbours' behaviour towards her has become much warmer. Inquiries are regularly made as to the welfare of her loved ones. When they come home on leave she proudly stands with the many others welcoming our boys home.

In the distance she can hear the strains of the military band. People strain their necks just to get an early glimpse, knowing their loved ones are somewhere in that smart marching throng. Here they come! The music is loud and stirring. The drum major, striding smartly in front, skilfully twirls his long baton sending silver flashes leaping off the glittering silver head of the shining baton. The marching throng, with large colourful flags waving, draws abreast. Her heart misses a beat, because they look so smart in their well-ironed uniforms, the sun sparkling off their brass buttons and shiny boots, which are lifted in unison. The marchers with their shoulders thrown back and chests pushed out, show their medals and coloured ribbons on their broad chests. The applause and cheers of the crowd are exhilarating.

Speeches follow, presented by impressive looking generals. Medals are awarded, salutes and handshakes are exchanged, then it is all over. Wives embrace husbands, mothers embrace sons, sweethearts embrace sweethearts. The world is such a lovely place. Their loved ones have survived the killing fields and returned, each one a hero.

The black mother is apprehensive when her son goes to anti-apartheid meetings. Her husband has been arrested and imprisoned for activities against the government. There is a State of Emergency. These meetings are illegal from the word go. The mother lies awake, her ears attuned to the creaking of the gate which will tell her that her son is home. She worries. What will happen to her and her children if he is arrested and loses his job? What will happen to them if he should be shot and killed? She clutches the mattress in fear and anxiety.

The family is now on its own. The family has withdrawn one child from school because there is not enough money to pay the bus fares of the three children. The political organisation to which her husband and son belong to is unable financially to assist all the families whose breadwinners have been killed, whose husbands, sons, daughters, mothers and wives are in detention, banned, imprisoned or in exile.

The creak of the gate. He is home. He is safe. This strain and anxiety have been going on for years. How much longer will this have to carry on? When will she be in a position to await her husband's and son's homecoming with love and joy instead of perpetual fear and apprehension? She pretends to be asleep as he quietly slips into the bed, that he shares with his two younger brothers, on the floor. His younger sister shares a bed with his mother. He only has a few hours sleep before having to go off to work. He has survived that meeting. What about the next? They are having a protest march on Friday. The march is illegal. He has to take off from work. He may lose his job. His boss has warned him about taking off from work for his politics. He will lose at least a day's pay.

Friday evening arrives. It is late. Her son is not home yet. The later he stays out the easier prey he will be for the gangsters. The Boers are turning a blind eye to the activities of the gangsters because their brutal activities keep people indoors and away from political meetings.

There is activity in the street. She goes to her front gate. "What's happening?" she asks her neighbour, who is just opening the gate of his small, one-roomed house. "There's been shooting at the march today" says her neighbour, breathlessly. "They were waiting for us. They beat us and shot us. There were people killed and lots arrested. I managed to get away." "What's happened to Johnny, my son?" "I don't know Mama. I'd better go inside before the vans come looking for us."

No Johnny throughout the night. The next few days she spends enquiring from her neighbours and Johnny's friends. No one knows of his whereabouts. What now? She is afraid to go and make enquiries at the police station. But where else to go? She plucks up courage and goes to the police station. "Ja, kaffir meid wat wil jy hê?" ("Yes, kaffir woman what do you want?") "Ek soek my seun, Johnny". ("I'm looking for my son, Johnny".) "Jy moet baas vir my sê wanneer jy saam met my praat. Jou Johnny is 'n terroris. Hy moet vrek. Net soos sy pa gaan vrek op die Eiland. Ek weet nie waar hy is nie. Stap! Voor ek jou opsluit." ("You must call me master when you speak to me. Your Johnny is a terrorist. He must die [the word 'vrek' is only applied to blacks and animals] just like his father is going to die on the Island. I do not know where he is. Go! Before I lock you up.")

She leaves the police station humiliated and defeated. The next stop is the hospital. She has no telephone. Travelling by train and bus is so difficult and expensive. At the hospital no one can help her. "Have you tried the morgue?" "The morgue! Where is that?"

Weeks have passed since that fateful Friday's march. No money is coming into the house.

The neighbours have helped, but they too are poor and have their own problems. Nine months later a neighbour brings a message that he had received via the grapevine. "Mama, your Johnny is dead. He was shot by the Boers while trying to blow up a pylon. He had left the country after the march to join the Liberation Army. I'm sorry."

Johnny had slipped out of the country. He could not inform his mother of his whereabouts for security reasons. He went to join the Liberation Army to fight for his country because he too was a patriot. He returned to his country, an outlaw, to continue the struggle, and died trying. There was no public acclaim when he left his country to join the Liberation Army. There was no loud music, waving of flags, bright brass buttons and medals when he returned. All that awaited him, as a guerilla, was torture, imprisonment and death and perhaps an unknown grave. There was no monthly income, no pension, no gratuity, only anguish and despair.

This was the experience of countless black mothers, over decades, whose families had dared to challenge the cruel and powerful apartheid regime.

I salute all the women who suffered so intensely in the struggle against apartheid. They are heroines one and all.